W9-AET-956

PRAISE FOR *CROSSING THE DESERT*

"*Crossing the Desert* is a page-turning, big-hearted memoir that is both harrowing and full of hope. Payam's story is jaw-dropping and thought-provoking. Well done!"
—Rainn Wilson, actor, philanthropist, and *New York Times* bestselling author of *Soul Boom*

"Payam's story is a profound testament to the strength of the human spirit and the transformative power of faith. From a childhood fraught with persecution to building one of the most successful IPOs in US history, this beautiful narrative shines a guiding light on the hope and optimism needed to forge any path ahead."
—Zhang Xin, cofounder and former CEO of SOHO China, and founder and CEO of Closer Media

"Payam Zamani's story embodies the American Dream. His drive is to succeed, not just for himself, but for the world at large. Payam is an inspiration to anyone looking to make the world a better place, which I hope is all of us!"
—Lauren Bush Lauren, founder and CEO of FEED

"Payam's story is one of great strength, intelligence, and integrity. His escape from religious persecution in Iran to an extremely successful tech entrepreneur would be enough for most people. But he is on a mission to change the way we think about business with bold, thought-provoking ideas about capitalism and spirituality."
—Julie Wainwright, founder and former CEO of The RealReal and founder and CEO of Ahara

"Payam has given us a precious guide through some of the prickliest brambles we share as a society—and points to the most essential and inspiring reasons for hope. Along the way he invites us to dialogue with him, ourselves, and each other. *Crossing the Desert* is essential reading."
—Stephen DeBerry, managing partner at BRONZE

CROSSING THE DESERT

CROSSING THE DESERT

THE POWER OF EMBRACING
LIFE'S DIFFICULT JOURNEYS

PAYAM ZAMANI

BenBella Books, Inc.
Dallas, TX

BenBella Books, Inc.
10440 N. Central Expressway
Suite 800
Dallas, TX 75231
benbellabooks.com
Send feedback to feedback@benbellabooks.com

BenBella is a federally registered trademark.

Printed in the United States of America
10 9 8 7 6 5 4 3 2 1

Library of Congress Control Number: 2023049201
ISBN 9781637744604 (hardcover)
ISBN 9781637744611 (electronic)

Editing by Leah Wilson and Joe Rhatigan
Copyediting by Michael Fedison
Proofreading by Denise Pangia and Jenny Bridges
Text design and composition by Aaron Edmiston
Cover design by Brandy Cole
Printed by Lake Book Manufacturing

To my parents, Abdul and Mahboobeh,
for the lives you led

To my dear wife, Gouya, and our precious daughters, Sophia and Ella,
for being the lights of my life

CONTENTS

PART III—THE WAY FORWARD

INTRODUCTION

Optimism.

Holding out hope for the possibility of what's to come, no matter what our lives might look like right now.

Sadly, we live in a world that often embraces the opposite, the doom and gloom, as if all hope is lost. But I'm here to tell you that it's not. No matter how bad things look—politically, economically, personally—there is hope. And the amazing thing I've learned over the course of my life and career is that the simple act of bringing optimism to every challenge we face often serves as the lifeboat that carries us through to the other side.

I have lived what most people would describe as a challenging life. Born in the Middle East to a family that was persecuted simply because of our peaceful Baha'i beliefs, I endured numerous traumas before I was sixteen years old. Twice I found myself in circumstances that I did not think I would come out of alive. And while the difficulties I faced in my early life likely left psychological imprints that I may not be cognizant of, they did not define me. Rather, they paved the path forward. They emboldened me, made me stronger, and ultimately led me on this journey that I'm about to share with you—and for which I am nothing but grateful.

From an arduous trek out of Iran to arriving as a refugee on U.S. soil, to launching a billion-dollar initial public offering (IPO) on Wall Street just ten years later, my story (in part) follows the arc of the immigrant's all-American Dream. But I'm also grateful for what happened next:

1

living through losses, financial and otherwise, which might have stopped many people in their tracks—losses that for the most part were caused by outdated flaws built into our capitalist system. And then? Finding the strength, support, and love that was needed in order to rise up again, emotionally as well as economically.

None of that would have happened, nor would it have been possible, without my Faith. And yet, the surprising lesson I learned along the way is that faith and spirituality are almost entirely missing from the capitalist system to which we've all become accustomed. Which left me asking myself, "Why?" Why would we leave our highest callings by the wayside in the business world when, in the rest of life, they often serve as the difference between what works for us and what works against us?

The entirety of my life's journey led me to where I am today: to a belief that capitalism needs to change. Together, we can learn from the triumphs and woes of our past and present in order to create a system that will allow our economic life to be an inseparable part of our service life. One that lifts our spirits rather than leaving us empty and unfulfilled.

And no, I'm not talking about socialism. What I'm talking about is something called "spiritual capitalism." I'm talking about a collective realignment of values that can transform the business world into a system that focuses less on greed and more on the betterment of the world and each other.

Is that a lofty goal? Sure. But that's where the optimism comes in.

Today I run a successful business called One Planet Group, one that's grown on a model that I hope will one day serve as an example that might lift us all toward a brighter future. And with this book, I hope to show how every one of us can learn from the challenges we face, and then act—as individuals, as communities, as companies, as countries, as part of humanity itself—in order to help make life better for us all.

Throughout these pages, you will find questions meant to help you reflect on what you've read—not as it relates to me and my story, but as it relates to you and your story. Because no matter where we're from, what our background is, whether we're rich, or poor, or something in between, there is no way around the fact that challenges and difficulties

will mark each of our journeys in life. We will not reach great achieve-
ments or accomplishments without overcoming obstacles, many of which
we cannot anticipate or even imagine until we face them.

Our struggles and difficulties are inevitable.

There will be no highs without lows.

But perhaps more importantly (as my Faith has taught me): All lows
are followed by highs.

Which is why, right now, no matter what is happening—in our personal lives, our business lives, or in the world at large—we all have reason
to be optimistic about what will come next.

Perhaps after reading these words, you will see your life's journey so
far, as well as the difficult journeys that lie ahead, as less traumatic, less
daunting, and maybe just a little more joyful. After all, as almost every
faith on Earth reminds us, there is power to be found in embracing the
journey itself . . .

With love,

payam zamani

PART I
ESCAPING THE PAST

"Our past is not the thing that matters so much in this world as what we intend to do with our future."
—Shoghi Effendi

CHAPTER ONE

PASSING GO

My suite at the Four Seasons in Lower Manhattan felt like something straight out of a palace: a corner room, on a high floor, with big windows and a balcony.

I lay back on the bed, staring up at the ceiling, trying to imagine what the nightly cost of such a room must be.

Credit Suisse First Boston bank had arranged my reservation. The tab for my stay would be drawn from our proceeds once tomorrow was over. After the market closed. After our IPO had launched. When the price of a room even this luxurious might suddenly seem insignificant to me.

I noticed a button next to the bed that appeared to be something other than a light switch. I was curious what it did, so I pressed it—and the blinds came down. I had never seen remote-controlled blinds before. I had never even heard of them at the time. So I sat there raising and lowering the blinds, thinking, *This is crazy.*

The dream that my brother and I had set into motion just five years earlier was about to come true—a vision that would have been impossible for us to even think of achieving five years before that. Before we arrived in this country. Two refugees seeking to build a new life in a foreign land.

Neither one of us were refugees any longer, but it felt a bit like we were entering foreign territory by stepping into the Wall Street den.

We had just returned from an all-expense-paid dinner at Sparks Steak House. "Not just a steak house, but *the* steak house in Midtown Manhattan," as one of our hosts from Geocapital Partners explained. Sparks was a restaurant as famous for its steaks as it was notorious for being a mob hangout. It's the spot where the head of the Gambino crime family was gunned down by four of John Gotti's men in 1985. Why such a reputation would make a restaurant more popular rather than less popular was a mystery to me, but Sparks was definitely the place where the wolves of Wall Street wined and dined their best clients at that time, in March of 1999.

My brother and I had flown in from San Francisco. Business class. (Also arranged by the bank.) After five years spent driving to meetings to woo potential clients because flying was too expensive—then flying coach, sharing hotel rooms, taking red-eyes, sometimes storing a change of clothes in a locker at a connecting airport so I could avoid hotel expenses altogether while we built our startup from the ground up—we were now the ones being wined and dined (or at least the dined piece; neither of us drink).

In the morning, our company, AutoWeb, was set to go public—at the height of the late-1990s dot-com boom.

The bank was sending a car with a driver to pick us up, take us to Credit Suisse's trading floor, and then whisk us off to meet the president of the Nasdaq Stock Exchange. We had already spent the afternoon at Geocapital's headquarters across the Hudson River in Fort Lee, New Jersey, reviewing the books with the bankers and our board of directors, deciding where to set our initial share price. We had gone in planning to sell five million shares at $8 to $10 per share; but pre-IPO demand was now anticipated at somewhere around ninety-five million shares. So, sitting at a conference table on speakerphone with the gang from Credit Suisse, we set the IPO price at the very top of our dream range: $14 per share.

That's the same price Netscape had launched at two years earlier, when its stock price exploded into the stratosphere, making it one of the most successful IPOs in history.

The way things are going, I thought as the shades went up, *that could be us in less than twenty-four hours.*

My brother and I had retained 40 percent of our company going in, which meant that after the IPO, we would both be millionaires, many, many times over. All because of an idea and a business model that we had dreamed up and built from absolutely nothing. I didn't even know what the internet was when we first started. My brother was the tech guy. I was the sales guy. The get-it-done guy. The scrappy kid who was already in business for himself, employing college kids to paint houses after working my way through school by taking part-time jobs at a pizza joint, a cannery, a T-shirt printing shop, and more in Modesto, California.

There are movies and TV shows built around these sorts of only-in-America stories—of kids who start with nothing and reach the top through hard work and a little good fortune. But we weren't even from America. We had only been in this country a little over ten years, and I barely spoke any English when I arrived.

As I sat there, on the most comfortable bed I had ever encountered, pressing that button, opening and closing the blinds, I couldn't help but think back to where it all began.

So far from the U.S.

So far from the big-city lights that lit up my room when the blinds went up.

So far from the freedom and opportunities that exist in this country I now called home.

"Hey, you. You!" an older boy yelled. "Dog!"

At first, I didn't realize the boy was yelling at me. But he was. He was walking right toward me. He looked angry. So I stopped.

I was on my way to school. Minding my own business. It was cold, and my mom had dressed me in a warm winter hat she had hand-knitted for me to wear on the long walk to first grade.

I honestly don't remember what other insults came out of the boy's mouth before he reached me. I just remember that he pulled my hat from my head, spit in it, then put it back on my head, squishing his spit down into my hair.

This was my welcome to Aliabad, a small city not far from the Caspian Sea, in the northern part of Iran where my parents had just moved us.

To be honest, even at such a young age, I was pretty used to that sort of treatment. It was nothing, really. The same boy would do that to me again and again, all winter long. Other boys also occasionally beat me up after school. My older sister (who was in her early teens at the time) got beat up more often and far worse than I did. So I just did my best to steer clear of those who wanted to hurt me—to go about my days living peacefully and lovingly, as best I could. "Living my Faith," as they say. Leading by example, as my parents taught me I should.

As a young Baha'i in Iran, it was the only choice I had. The only life I knew.

I was too young to understand why the Faith my parents chose to embrace was hated by so many people. My older brother and sister and I had never been taught to hate anyone. I had been taught only to love and to be loving in my interactions with others. No matter how inhospitable other kids and their parents acted toward us, my parents insisted we live up to Baha'i principles, which include respecting all religions and praying for the unity of all people.

Why would anyone find fault in that? I wondered.

The house my parents rented in Aliabad was located in an orchard, surrounded by fig trees, which sounds pleasant enough. But with no real walls surrounding the property and a bathroom that was located outside of the main house, it was scary to me. People often climbed in the trees in the yard, and at times, especially at night, I was terrified to go to the bathroom. I would choose not to go rather than risk a confrontation in the dark.

My first-grade year wasn't all bad. In fact, most of my memories of that time are good ones. I was a happy kid. So much so that teachers, friends, and relatives sometimes asked, "Why do you always have a smile on your face?"

I remember the excitement of going to visit my mother's relatives in the capital city of Tehran on holidays—and making trips to see small villages, too, passing breathtakingly beautiful fields along the way. Plus, no matter what happened, I never saw myself as a victim. My parents insisted that living our Faith, especially in places where the Baha'i Faith was misunderstood or maligned, was a noble cause. We were showing the world what it meant to be Baha'i, just as the writings of our Faith tell us: "To be a Baha'i simply means to love all the world, to love humanity and try to serve it—to work for Universal Peace, and Universal Brotherhood."

From my parents, I witnessed acts of love, service, and kindness flowing in every direction.

That same year, one of my aunts in Tehran was diagnosed with terminal cancer, and my mother dedicated herself to traveling back and forth to see her as much as she could. Since we didn't own a car, she traveled by bus or by train, which meant that those trips were long. I didn't like it when she left because she was our pillar. In this inhospitable town, she literally kept our family safe—and at six and seven years old, I worried a lot more whenever she was away.

One day, I was visibly sad as I watched my mom get ready to leave. So she decided to do something special to try to make up for her absence.

"What do you want?" she asked. "I'll buy you a gift in Tehran."

It was extremely rare for my parents to offer to buy us gifts. We were not wealthy. I would say we were a lower-middle-class family, which meant we always had enough to eat, and a roof over our heads, but gifts were only given on special occasions. So I was surprised by her offer, and my mind went spinning at the opportunity: Tehran. The big city. The Iranian capital. A city more connected to the world than anything to be found in this little town.

What do I want? What do I really want?

"A Monopoly set!" I blurted out.

Surprised by my choice, my mother laughed and promised to look for one as she hugged me goodbye. Just the thought of it turned my mood around. Instead of feeling sad, I was excited for her to make the trip, and especially to make her return.

I don't remember where or when I first heard about Monopoly, but the concept of the game fascinated me: an American game where you could amass real estate, collect rents, and receive $200 just for passing "Go."

Of course that's what I want!

My mother did not disappoint. She brought me back my first Monopoly set, and I was thrilled. It brings me to tears as I write this. She had so many problems, from keeping her kids safe while living in danger herself to worrying about losing her sister, yet she remembered what she had promised. For me.

The game she brought home wasn't a knockoff, either, like so much of the Western merchandise one could buy in the markets of Tehran. It was in its original box, made by the American game maker Parker Brothers. It was an Iranian version of Monopoly, so the streets were named after streets in Tehran instead of Park Place or Baltic Avenue, but it was real. I valued that set so much. I didn't want anything to happen to it. I didn't even want the fake money to get wrinkled, so I took all those colorful paper bills and glued them, piece by piece, onto hand-cut rectangles of cardboard so they wouldn't get messed up.

Playing that game was an escape for me. I would lose myself in the excitement of it, the strategy of it, the dream of it. I'm sure I drove my parents and siblings crazy, and my Baha'i neighbors, too, asking to play as often as I did.

Life in town wouldn't get any easier. It actually grew far worse for my sister before the school year was over, prompting my parents to move us to another town that wasn't quite so inhospitable to Baha'is. And I was thankful for that move. Especially since my love of Monopoly grew into a real-life love of all things business and would spill into my early life as a budding entrepreneur.

Fast-forwarding a bit here, I was eight years old when I first tried to figure out my financial net worth. I didn't know the term "net worth," and I'm not sure that anyone taught me the concept at all. I was just curious to see what I had accumulated in terms of stuff during my child-hood years, and what it might be worth. So I went around our house and put value tags on everything that was mine, from an eraser, to a pen, to my books, to my clothing. It didn't add up to very much, but I enjoyed knowing that I had assets, and I wanted to keep track of them.

Maybe a year later, my mother bought me a new cap. A baseball cap. And I loved it.

I wasn't the only one.

On the street one day, I walked by a random man who said, "Oh, nice baseball cap."

Without even thinking about it, I said, "You want it?"

To my surprise, he said, "Yes."

"Well, how much?" I asked, and he gave me a price that I knew was higher than what my mom had paid for it.

"Okay, here, you have it," I said. I handed him the cap, and he handed me the money. My first-ever sale for profit! I was so excited I ran all the way home, and the first thing my mom said when I walked through the door was, "Where's your cap?"

"I sold it!" I said proudly, but before I could tell her the story (or show her the money), she got really upset.

"The clothing we buy you is not for sale," she told me.

"But I sold it for more than you—"

"What did I say?"

"The clothing you buy me is not for sale."

"Will you sell the clothing we buy for you ever again?"

"No," I replied, lowering my head. "I'm sorry, Mom. I didn't have that information before. I won't do it again."

The value of the hat, to her, was much more than just monetary. As a family, we would only shop for clothing twice a year: once for the Persian New Year, the other for back to school. It would take something extraor-dinary to prompt my parents to buy anything at any other time.

My parents taught us to value and take good care of the things we owned, so I should have known better than to part with it so easily.

A couple of years later, in the early 1980s, I desperately wanted a pair of Adidas shoes. I was maybe ten by then, and they were more than just shoes to me. They represented the freedom found in America. They represented the kids of my generation and a whole new brand of music and culture that was sweeping the world.

They didn't sell Adidas at the local shoe stores. Only certain fashionable boutiques in Tehran sold them, and I knew where one of those boutiques was located. So, after saving up enough to buy them, all on my own, I pestered my dad (who was working in the city at the time) to take me with him so I could buy the shoes.

I'm sure he thought it was frivolous of me to spend my money on an overpriced pair of shoes, but he also believed that anyone who saves their own money has a right to choose how they spend it. So, a few weeks later, he took me to Tehran. We bought the Adidas. I'll never forget what it felt like, carrying that Adidas box back to his place of work in the unmarked offices of Tehran's Baha'i Local Spiritual Assembly, sitting down, gently removing the shoes from their box, lifting them to my nose and smelling that new-shoe smell, then returning them to the box ever so carefully.

I kept and wore those Adidas until there was nothing left of them. That's how I was raised: When we had a pair of shoes, we would only buy another pair after the first pair was no longer wearable—not because it was old, out of fashion, or simply not good enough anymore, but because it was literally falling apart.

That's just how it was.

When my dad got his paycheck at the beginning of the month, my mom and dad sat down together to divide it up. Together they decided how much we could spend as a family that month (after the bills were paid), and that money went to my mom. My brother, sister, and I would each get a small allowance, and they would always set some savings aside, but my mom was the one responsible for managing the monthly expenses and making sure we would not run out. My father was the breadwinner, and she was the one in charge of budgeting. There was equality in that relationship that never wavered. And they always set aside enough money to assure that we wouldn't get into trouble. They managed it well, which allowed us to live a dignified life.

I really believe that my parents and their unique paths led me to become the budding entrepreneur and business-minded kid I was—but also a kid who would understand from an early age that living a life of service was important, even when it required some pretty extreme sacrifices. Like having my hat spit in. Or being picked on and beat up so often that I considered it normal.

The values of service and sacrifice were rooted deeply in my parents' lives, in every decision they made, because those values ran so deep in our Faith.

Honestly, there is no way for me to go on trying to explain who I am or how I got here without telling you more about the story of my parents and the sacrifices they made on a daily basis for the betterment of the world around them. So that's where I'll take you next.

REFLECTIONS ON CHAPTER ONE

What was your first business experience as a child? When did you first learn the value of money? Do you remember how finances were handled in your home? How much of an influence did those early financial lessons have on the way you handle your finances now? And is that a good thing, or something that you feel could use some improvement?

Thinking back on your own childhood, what were some of the first joys—and hardships—that influenced who you became? If you went through difficult times, facing adversity or prejudice from others, how did you handle it? Looking back, would you have handled things differently knowing all that you know now? Are there ways in which you'd like to improve how you handle adversity or prejudice going forward?

Did you feel welcomed in your own community when you were younger?

On the flip side, were you and your family welcoming to others?

"Be generous in prosperity, and thankful in adversity. Be worthy of the trust of thy neighbor, and look upon him with a bright and friendly face."
—Baha'u'llah

CHAPTER TWO

ON FAITH AND FAMILY

M y father was born in 1935, during an era of great change in Iran. It was the very same year that Reza Shah—the king of the country between 1925 and 1941—first asked officials from around the world to refer to the country as Iran rather than Persia. This meant that Iran's citizens would come to be called Iranians, as they are still called today, rather than Persians, as they had been referred to for thousands of years.

Reza Shah did this after making several other sweeping—some might say progressive—reforms aimed at modernizing Iran and better aligning the country with certain Western nations starting in the 1920s. For instance, he insisted that women uncover their hair in public, and that men wear Western-style suits instead of the long, traditional Muslim garb. His reforms also included establishing the University of Tehran (the country's first modern university), along with a nationwide system of contemporary, Western-style schools for Iran's children.

My father wasn't allowed to attend those schools.

Abdul was born on the outskirts of Isfahan, in the small village of Sedeh in central Iran, a town known for its population's very traditional, even fanatical, Islamic views. Those views included the idea that the only education a child needs in life is to learn the Quran—the central religious text of Islam, which Muslims believe was dictated by God directly to the Prophet Muhammad.

My dad's father (my grandfather) believed there was another reason to keep him far from any modern classroom as well: "If you go to school, you'll become a Babi!"

As a child, my father had little idea what the term Babi referred to. He only knew that it was considered to be something shameful, distasteful, and against tradition.*

My grandfather came from a wealthy family. Apparently, he inherited a good deal of money and land, but over the years he lost all of it to an opioid addiction, which caused him to become harsh, even violent. There were stories of him killing a man, a farmer, during an argument over water rights to his land. Worse? He killed one of his own sons, my dad's older brother, while disciplining him—and when my dad was just an infant, my grandfather threw him into a garden, where a stick went into his eye. My dad has been blind in that eye ever since.

Even as a young child, my father knew that he wanted nothing to do with such violence.

He also wanted nothing to do with fanatical beliefs. So he decided to do something about it.

His uncle from his mother's side was a well-known clergyman who owned a small store in town. Once every month he gave my young dad an important errand to run: He would hand him some money to go make a payment against a loan he had received from a local wealthy individual.

On one of these occasions, my dad took the money, went to the bus station, bought a ticket to a far-off city, and never returned.

He was eleven years old.

For the next two years, my father took whatever odd job he could find to keep going. He found work in stores, as a sort of servant in somebody's home, doing hard labor on the Iranian railroad projects—hitching

---

* "Babi" means a follower of the Bab, who was the forerunner to Baha'u'llah, the prophet and founder of the Baha'i Faith. Many people who couldn't tell the difference called Baha'is "Babis," and the term was far from a term of endearment.

rides or walking from town to town. He ultimately journeyed all the way to the southern part of Iran, to an oil-rich province where a lot of people from his area would migrate in the hope of finding better-paying jobs. By my estimate, according to the list of towns he visited, he traversed more than 1,500 miles as a child, mostly on foot, by the time he settled on the streets of Ahvaz.

That part of Iran, near the Persian Gulf and the Iraqi border, gets hot. It's not unusual for the thermometer to reach 120 degrees Fahrenheit. But he didn't find work there. He became a street kid, living in the shadows. And that's where he found his younger brother, who had also fled home in the hopes of uniting with my dad. Together, they lived as street children, doing whatever it took to survive, as the world began to pick up the pieces from the ravages of World War II.

By that time, Reza Shah had been forced by the Allied powers to abdicate the throne, replaced by his son Mohammad Reza—the man whom most Westerners today remember simply as "the Shah," as he held the throne from 1941 until February of 1979. He was a young king, still in his twenties when the war ended, and in one of many efforts to continue to modernize and westernize the country, his government developed a pilot program to get kids like my dad and my uncle off the streets.

In 1950, the Shah's agents swept through Ahvaz, taking my dad, his brother, and other street children to a "foster home," which was more like a detention center in southern Tehran—about five hundred miles away by bus. Whether they liked it or not, they were locked up in that facility until they turned eighteen.

"That's the best thing that could have ever happened to me," my dad has told me on several occasions. "I had food. I had a place to sleep. They were educating me . . ."

My dad had never been taught how to read and write. He was frustrated by not being able to read street signs as he walked across the country. But in that facility, at the age of fifteen, he finally started learning how to read and write. He was so hungry for an education that he studied constantly, skipping his way through two grades in one year, and three years the next. He could hardly wait until he turned eighteen, when he would be free to go back into the world as an educated young man.

Unfortunately, before that day came, his brother got sick with measles. He was taken from the foster home to a hospital, where he died.

Upon learning the news, my father's mother and uncle showed up at the facility.

"It's time to come back home," his mother told him.

After all those years, and remembering the life he and his brother had left behind, he replied, "No, thank you. I'm happy here. I'm getting everything I need."

He refused to go with them.

After his eighteenth birthday, when my dad was finally free to go his own way, the administrators at the facility set him up with a job at a public hospital in Tehran. He started doing bookkeeping while continuing to take classes, incentivized by a government program that allowed him to earn more once he completed his high school education. It wasn't long before he earned his diploma and started earning a government paycheck that would serve him for the next twenty years and beyond.

My dad is living proof that no matter how old (or young) we may be, and no matter how misplaced we feel in the circumstances of the family or even the country in which we were born, real change and growth are possible. Anything is possible.

> "Regard man as a mine rich in gems of inestimable value.
> Education can, alone, cause it to reveal its treasures,
> and enable mankind to benefit therefrom."
> —Baha'u'llah

My mother was born Mahboobeh Ibrahimi in 1933, in a small town called Osku, just outside the city of Tabriz in East Azerbaijan Province in northwest Iran. Her family, like the majority of families in that part of the country, was of Turkish descent, which meant that she was raised speaking Azeri Turkish as her primary language.

She was raised Baha'i.

While her mother only became Baha'i after getting married, her father was a longtime Baha'i so devoted to the Faith that he once made a pilgrimage, walking on foot to the Holy Land, Israel, to personally meet Abdu'l-Baha—the son of the founder of the Faith.* That is how young the Baha'i Faith is, that my grandfather was able to meet one of the Faith's most important figures in person.

Indeed, compared with all major religions, the Baha'i Faith is very young. It was founded in the nineteenth century by Baha'u'llah, a modern-day prophet regarded by Baha'is much in the same way other religions regard Muhammad, Moses, Zoroaster, Krishna, the Buddha, or Jesus Christ. (For a deeper explanation of this aspect of the Baha'i Faith, see Appendix A.)

Baha'u'llah designated his son Abdu'l-Baha as his successor and he continued to spread the message of the Faith into the twentieth century, which ultimately took him on an epic trip to Europe and North America in 1912.

It's hard to imagine that my mother's father met this man himself—that the son of the founder of the Faith that shaped my parents' lives, my life, and the lives of millions of Baha'is around the world was alive so recently that he traveled to the West to spread the message of the Faith. There are photographs we can see of Abdu'l-Baha, along with first-edition copies of the many books he and Baha'u'llah wrote, not just paintings, writings, or oral histories from hundreds or thousands of years ago as it is with many key figures in the world's largest religions. This offers Baha'is (and frankly humanity) a treasure trove of original and authenticated teachings that go beyond one single book. There are thousands of primary sources—books, letters, and documents written by the Bab; Baha'u'llah; Abdu'l-Baha; the Guardian of the Baha'i Faith, Shoghi Effendi—as well as guidance from the Universal House of Justice, a democratically elected body that serves

---

* Baha'u'llah and his family had been sent in exile to that part of the Middle East, which at the time was under the rule of the Ottoman Empire and was called Palestine (today, it's Israel).

as the supreme governing body of the Faith, which according to the sacred writings of the Baha'i Faith and as ordained by Baha'u'llah was established in 1963.

Of course, speaking of Baha'u'llah and his forerunner, the Bab, as "prophets" strikes some followers of other religions as objectionable, if not blasphemous. This is what makes being Baha'i so dangerous in certain parts of the world—especially in the Middle East, where extremists believe that Muhammad was God's final prophet and that believing otherwise is an insult worthy of death.

It is a subject that hits very close to home, and which affected my mother's home when she was still very young.

My mom's father was an importer of fabric who regularly traveled on foot to Ashgabat, Turkmenistan, to buy textiles to bring back to Iran. When my mother was six years old, her father left on one of these trips—and never came home. His family was told that on his way back, not far from their town, a group of Muslims discovered he was Baha'i and drowned him in a river.

My mom is one of four siblings who survived to adulthood, and their mother, who was in her thirties at that point, was left to raise them as a single mom. As if that weren't challenging enough, the northwest part of Iran was taken over by the Soviet Union during World War II, and living conditions became unbearable for years. There were times when my mother (who was two years older than my dad) recalls having no food to eat. She recalls that it was not uncommon for her and her siblings to see dead people on the streets.

When the war ended, their mom got sick and was taken to an American hospital in Tabriz. Worried she was going to die, she and her siblings traveled to the hospital together, but my mom wasn't allowed inside. "You're too young," a nurse told her.

As the rest of her siblings went inside, she cried outside alone—until she looked up and saw her mom standing in a window, mouthing the words, "Don't cry." Standing next to her was the nurse, also gesturing to my mom to keep quiet.

Decades later she would retell the story, saying, "I saw this nurse in a beautiful white hat, looking so professional, and I thought to myself, 'I'm gonna become a nurse, and I'm gonna let all the kids in the hospital.'"

Her mother recovered, and when my mom was fifteen, she moved the family to Tehran—about four hundred miles to the east.

My mother did not speak a word of Persian, which is the dominant language in Tehran. Yet, at that young age, she was able to get a job as a cleaner at a nonprofit hospital that was funded and run by Baha'is. She let everyone know that she wanted to be a nurse someday. She grew close to some of the doctors and learned from them how to read the English alphabet, so she could fetch the right medicine boxes when they asked for them. Without being allowed to continue her formal education, she kept on learning, rising through the ranks at that hospital—not only to become a nurse, but eventually to become the head nurse for the surgery room.

My mom is not alive anymore. She passed away in 2017. But you could not talk to my mom without her talking about being a nurse. That was her pride and joy. She loved the profession and loved what it meant to be of service to others in a way that so aligned with the tenets of her Faith, as described by Abdu'l-Baha: "This is worship: to serve mankind and to minister to the needs of the people. Service is prayer. A physician ministering to the sick, gently, tenderly, free from prejudice and believing in the solidarity of the human race, he is giving praise."

Perhaps the best example of her dedication came when she was in her early twenties. A child was born to a Muslim mom in the nonprofit hospital where my mom worked, and during the birth, the mother died. The dad was beside himself. "What am I going to do with this baby?" he cried. The man was blind, but his primary concern was that the baby was a girl. "I don't want her," he declared, and he walked away, never to be heard from again.

My mom decided then and there to adopt the baby girl. That's how loving she was.

As a single young woman in Iran, it became clear that there was no way that her family would ever approve of such a thing, nor was it possible to make such an adoption legal, so instead, she did the best she could.

The hospital allowed her to take the child home and care for her until she found a couple who were willing to adopt her. Thanks to that couple, the girl was educated, got married, and lived a life that otherwise could have ended before it had a chance to truly begin. I know all of this not only because I heard the story from my parents, but because I happened to meet the girl's husband, many decades later, while on a pilgrimage myself to the holiest place for Baha'is: the Mansion of Bahji, the Shrine of Baha'u'llah, near Haifa, Israel. He said, "You'll never believe this, but you're my wife's brother." I was confused for a moment, thinking, *I don't have another sister*, but all those years later, this man had come to think of my mom as this girl's mom. Even though she had moved to Australia, and we had never met, she always remembered what my mother had done for her.

So, before my mom and dad ever met, my mother already had a reputation as a Baha'i who valued service. She was the young woman at the nonprofit hospital who stepped up to save a little Muslim girl from abandonment—and that was just one of many selfless acts she performed while working at that hospital.

In 1955, at the age of twenty, my dad heard a voice on the radio that caught his attention. It was the country's most widely known and admired Mullah (that's the word for any Muslim clergy or mosque leader), and this man was railing against the Baha'is.

At the time, my father didn't know much about the Baha'i Faith. All he knew was that this Mullah was trying to incite people to violence against Baha'is, to beat them up, to do bad things to them.

Why? he wondered.

Nothing the Mullah said made it clear why these people were so bad, or why they deserved to be the target of such harm.

The radio campaign continued for weeks, backed by propaganda schemes painting Baha'is as heretics and enemies of God, spurring horrific acts of violence against them, men, women, and children alike, all over the country, until finally the Mullah incited a mob to occupy and demolish the Baha'i Center in Tehran.

My father was riveted by the news—not because he wanted to follow the Mullah's lead in any way, but because he wanted to understand. He had been raised Muslim, gone to mosque, and prayed to Allah five times a day, every day, for as long as he remembered—and he vividly remembered the disdain in his father's voice when he told him that a modern education would turn him into a "Babi."

"But why?" he wondered. "Why should anyone rise to violence against these people?"

He decided it was time to seek answers.

He wasn't sure where to begin, but as fate would have it, that very same week, while talking to a woman at his work, he said, "I noticed you were not here yesterday." And she said, "Yeah, I was not here because it was my holy day. I'm a Baha'i."

"Oh!" he said.

He thought it was brave of her to admit this to him considering current events. He also knew this was his chance. "Can you introduce me to somebody who can tell me more about the Baha'i Faith?" he asked.

She kindly introduced my dad to two people: Mr. Bakhtaver and Dr. Majzub. They were both around his age, and they ended up taking him under their wings. I mention their names here because they are important to me. They became two of my dad's best friends, and were it not for them, life might have taken a very different path for my dad and his future family.

Mr. Bakhtaver and Dr. Majzub, these two kind individuals, answered my father's questions and took him to Baha'i gatherings. Ultimately my dad became a Baha'i—but not before truly and deeply studying the Faith. "The independent investigation of truth" is a tenet of the Baha'i Faith, even for those who are born into a Baha'i family. So he took his time and drove his new friends nuts with all the questions he asked. He also read the writings of Baha'u'llah and other central figures of the Faith with the same voraciousness he had applied to learning to read and write. He probably absorbed more history and understanding of the Baha'i Faith in a year than the average person might in a decade. But the most important things he learned were found in the fundamentals of the Faith—a fountain of ideas and beliefs that aligned with much of what his gut had told him was right, even when he was a young boy.

First of all, it was a Faith committed to a world without violence.

A Faith based on love.

Baha'is believe in peace, harmony, and unity; the independent investigation of truth; the equality of women and men; and finding agreement between science and religion. They also believe that no religion should be inherited, including the Baha'i Faith itself. At the age of fifteen or older, children raised in a Baha'i family are considered to be spiritually mature enough to determine for themselves whether or not they want to continue, and they're free to put off that choosing until they are older if that's what they feel is the right thing to do—the polar opposite of how my dad was raised.

He loved that idea, and so much more. The Baha'i Faith's central purpose is the unity of humanity. Its followers join no political parties. There are no secret alliances, motives, or interests. Major Baha'i principles include the eradication of all forms of prejudice, the abolition of the extremes of wealth and poverty, and the protection of the human rights of all people.

As a result, Baha'is don't have clergy. There are no clerics who dictate thought or participate in political agendas. The affairs of the community and its administration are seen to by volunteers, democratically elected in free elections (without nomination or campaigning) to serve on Spiritual Assemblies at the local and national levels—and those elected to the Baha'i supreme governing body, the Universal House of Justice, who are elected during gatherings of the National Spiritual Assemblies in Haifa, Israel, every five years. In fact, that election serves as the only fully democratized international election in the world, and Baha'i elected officials serve with no agenda other than to serve the Baha'i community and to serve humanity.

My dad could hardly believe such a faith existed.

He decided to devote his life to the Faith and to share its teachings with anyone who was interested in listening.

He never expected that this would also lead to finding the love of his life.

Just after he turned twenty-six, my father was speaking with a doctor who worked in the same hospital he did, and this doctor said, "There's a woman I want to introduce you to. She's a nurse at the other hospital I work at. You're a Baha'i, she's a Baha'i," as if that simple fact alone would make them a perfect fit. My dad laughed at first. In Tehran, there were approximately one hundred thousand Baha'is. So what were the odds that this one Baha'i woman would become his wife?

Apparently, the odds were in his favor. He was interested in her from the moment they met, and my mom was just as interested in him. She was taken by his enthusiasm and dedication to wanting to lead a life of service himself.

Traditionally, when an Iranian boy wants to marry an Iranian girl, he takes his parents to meet her parents, to ask for their permission. In my dad's case, that wasn't about to happen, so instead, he took Mr. Bakhtaver—who, if you remember, was about the same age as my dad.

My grandmother's initial reaction to the sight of the two of them asking for her daughter's hand was, "No! Absolutely not!"

First of all, my dad wasn't Turkish. He wasn't from Azerbaijan. Second, he was brand new to the Baha'i Faith. So her reaction was something along the lines of, "Go read a little bit more. Bye!"

Parental consent for marriage is part of Baha'i law, too. My dad was worried. But on the way down the stairs from the second floor, Mr. Bakhtaver looked back at my mom, and my mom mouthed the words, "Make it work."

Mr. Bakhtaver was Turkish, and my mom's family loved him. And so, he made it work.

My parents ended up getting married, and it didn't take long before everyone realized just how much the two of them saw eye to eye.

My dad was on fire for his newfound faith. He wanted to spread the message everywhere. And in Iran, that was dangerous. Yet he did not care.

He would say, "The worst thing is they kill me. It's okay." And my mom, her father's daughter, the girl who went from cleaning floors to running the surgery room, was right there beside him.

Together, they decided to spend their lives living in some of the most inhospitable places for Baha'is in Iran, just for the sake of spreading the message. They would find places where no other Baha'i lived, so they could be the first Baha'i there. They would share the example of what it meant to live the Baha'i Faith, and that is where they would find their joy. Not by preaching on street corners or handing out flyers, but by teaching through their presence and their deeds. They would live according to what Baha'u'llah wrote in *The Hidden Words*: "Guidance hath ever been given by words, and now it is given by deeds. Everyone must show forth deeds that are pure and holy, for words are the property of all alike, whereas such deeds as these belong only to Our loved ones. Strive then with heart and soul to distinguish yourselves by your deeds."

Did that create a lot of challenges and suffering? Yes. Yet they felt that any suffering was worth the effort, and they would not let threats of harm stand in the way of living their lives to the fullest—which included starting a family of their own.

My sister, Ahdieh, came into their lives and joined their journey in 1962.

My brother, Farhang, came along a couple of years after that.

And it was shortly before my birth on February 12, 1971, when I was still in my mother's womb, that my parents left the relative comfort and tolerance found in the diverse population of Tehran to move our family to the small village of Kalak—fifteen miles to the west, and a million miles from ease.

REFLECTIONS ON CHAPTER TWO

Have you ever thought about how much of your fate, especially early in life, was determined by where you were born? Or where you lived? Or whether or not there was a dominant religion in your country or region, and whether or not your parents were a part of it?

How much do you know about your own parents' life journeys, and how their experiences shaped the way they raised you or the values they taught you—whether consciously or unconsciously?

What other major circumstances of your parents' lives, values, or decisions framed your view of the world as a child? Did you embrace their views, consciously? Or at any point have you rebelled against them (as some teenagers, young adults, and occasionally children—as was the case with my father—tend to do)? Are there views you hold on to today that were established by your parents which perhaps no longer suit you? Have you thought about what it would take to change those views, to act on your own new ideas and understanding of the world around you—or the impact you would like to have upon it?

What is the source of your core beliefs and principles?

Are you actively living and working in alignment with those beliefs and principles today? If not, how much are you willing to change to try to live up to those principles tomorrow? How far are you willing to go?

CHAPTER THREE

WATERING THE DIRT

The violent turn against the Baha'i Faith that my parents experienced in Iran in 1955 wasn't simply incited by the rogue preaching of a populist mullah. It was built on a history of hatred incited by powerful and influential clergy that stemmed back to the mid-1800s—propaganda so strong that it is not uncommon for Iranians in the U.S. to still lower their voices and almost whisper the word "Baha'i" to this day. The word itself was made taboo.

And yet, thankfully, by the 1970s, conditions had turned to being mostly peaceful for Baha'is in the city of Tehran. The population there was more connected to the outside world and generally better educated than the population in more rural areas where fundamentalist and extremist ideas often take hold and refuse to let go.

Outside of Tehran, Baha'is were still openly harassed, sometimes hurt, and in a few cases murdered in cold blood.

It was in those areas where my parents chose to live and serve, with the hope of changing hearts and minds through their presence.

As soon as they moved to Kalak, they faced rejection from the local population. When people found out they were Baha'is, they refused to do business with them. They refused to sell them goods from their stores.

Soon, parents in Kalak were telling their children of the infidels who lived in their midst and attended their schools, and my older brother and sister found themselves harassed and occasionally beaten up by their classmates.

Prejudice and disdain weren't the only hardships my family faced. My father still worked for the public health department in Iran, where he had worked for more than fifteen years by then. That meant he had to wake up early and make a fifteen-mile commute every day, which doesn't sound too bad until you consider that he didn't own a car. He had to walk to a bus stop and rely on an unreliable bus service to take him to Tehran, where he then had to walk a long distance to the hospital—no matter what the weather. And the weather in that part of Iran at that time often included major amounts of snow all winter long. There were times when the buses simply didn't show up, and he'd be forced to stand on the side of the road, hoping a car would stop and some generous soul would offer to take him the rest of the way.

My mother had left her job at the nonprofit hospital to raise her kids full-time in Kalak, but that did not mean she planned to give birth to me in a small town, away from a modern hospital, or away from the doctors and medical services in Tehran. So, on February 12, 1971, after my father had gone to work and she realized I was suddenly ready to come into the world, she had no choice but to make that long commute herself. Alone. (There were no cell phones at the time, and no easy access to any phone line to make contacting my dad possible.)

Somehow, through the wind and snow, she made it. I was born on Abraham Lincoln's birthday, which was perfect since I would come to love Lincoln and what he stood for when I grew up. And my mom got to spend two days recovering at my aunt's home in Tehran before making her way back to Kalak and introducing me to Ahdieh (or Addy) and Farhang.

Although my siblings still have many memories of the drastic changes they faced when they moved to that tiny town, I don't have any personal memories of our time in Kalak at all. Just a year later, my parents had the opportunity to buy a piece of land and build us a home in the town of Hashtgerd—a larger, quickly growing town even farther away from

Tehran—a good thirty-five miles or so farther west. And my time there would deeply influence my life.

One of the many interesting things about Hashtgerd is it's divided in two (or at least it used to be). There was a two-lane highway that ran straight across the middle of it. To the south was the older part of town; to the north, the newer part. The southern part was visually distinctive because most of its architecture looks similar to the adobe-style buildings found in the American Southwest, especially those in Santa Fe, New Mexico. Hundreds of years ago, that style of building (constructed out of mud) was created by Muslims in the Middle East. At one point, those Muslims took over Spain and brought that architecture to Southern Europe. The Spaniards later brought it to Mexico, and eventually that part of Mexico became part of the U.S.

But the architecture wasn't the only distinguishing feature of southern Hashtgerd. It was also populated by a particular sect of Shia Islam* called Ali Allahi, or as they prefer to be called, Ahleh Hagh. They are a different sect of Shia Islam, known broadly as a very peaceful people, and their physical appearance is different from the Shia Muslims that make up most of Iran: The men all wear thick and nicely groomed mustaches rather than beards.

The thing is, speaking in broad terms, during that period, other Shia Muslims did not like the Ahleh Hagh. It's not outrageous to come right out and say it: They hated them. Given the chance, they would beat them up. They would do whatever they could to make their lives miserable. They're all Muslim, and in this case all Shia Muslims, but for some reason that didn't matter.

In the northern part of Hashtgerd, homes were generally built out of brick and mortar or other modern materials, and that's where the majority of Shia Muslims lived; the Shia Muslims who—again, speaking broadly here—were far more challenging to deal with.

---

* While approximately 85 percent of the world's Muslim population is Sunni, approximately 15 percent is Shia. The two groups formed over a dispute about who should carry on as leader of the faith after the Prophet Muhammad died in AD 632. While there are many differences in the sects, Shia Muslims believe that their leaders, called Imams, are appointed by God, and therefore their interpretations of the Quran are infallible. These Imams are not recognized by Sunnis.

You can guess in which part of town my parents chose to build us a home.

I was too young to remember all of the events in this early period in Hashtgerd, which occurred between 1972 and 1976, when I was between the ages of one and five. But my parents and siblings have many stories of this time when more than a few of the northern-Hashtgerd residents did everything they could to make our lives miserable.

Our house was built on a small piece of land my parents had purchased. The front yard had a wall around it with a front gate, creating a large courtyard in front of the home. That's a pretty common style of building in Iran. Inside, we had one room in the back corner, opposite from where the kitchen and bathroom/shower were located (with a small storage space in between), and two large symmetrical rooms, one on either side of the hallway that ran front to back. In between the two symmetrical rooms was the biggest open area, which is kind of like a great room, where we would be most likely to greet guests. Each of the symmetrical rooms was divided by a half wall between the front and back portion, which in a way created two separate spaces in each room. Again, a common style for homes in Iran. And while many families assigned one of the rooms in the front as their family room and dining room, we were forced to eat farther back, behind the half wall—so we wouldn't get hit in the head by rocks or have glass shattered into our food.

Our windows frequently had rocks thrown through them.

Iran, not unlike most countries, was a country with laws. A country with a constitution. It was illegal to destroy someone else's property. It was illegal to harass, harm, or even threaten to harm another human being. When my parents moved to Hashtgerd, they didn't expect to be welcomed with open arms, but they did believe that our most basic human rights would be protected by local law enforcement: The police station (or "gendarmerie" as we called it, taken from the French) was located barely a hundred yards from our front door, facing our house. It should have been a safe location for us to live. But when my parents went to them and said, "They just broke our windows; you know who they are," the gendarmes refused to enforce the law. Instead, they said things like, "Well, tell them you're Muslim; they'll stop." Or, "Why don't you leave town? Go live in Tehran. Why are you here?"

For Baha'is in Iran, the laws and protections that other citizens enjoyed were often only a façade.

And so, the sound of breaking windows and the vision of my parents and siblings picking up pieces of shattered glass from the floor mark some of my earliest memories in life.

My brother and sister got beat up at school, and there were never any consequences for the bullies. My father had rocks thrown at him on his way to the bus stop while trying to make his now much-longer commute to Tehran, and there were never any consequences for his bullies either. But the physical attacks were just the beginning. The owners of the small, Iranian-style grocery stores on our side of town refused to sell us meat and milk and other necessities, which meant we had to walk long distances just to access our basic needs. And my parents would later tell me that, at one point, there were flyers distributed all over the northern part of town, proclaiming, "On such and such day, we're going to kill the Baha'i family."

Even though everyone knew who printed those flyers, and even though my parents asked for help, the gendarmes did nothing.

The morning of the expected attack, my mother dressed the three of us in our nicest clothes—so if the mob came, we would be well dressed when they arrived.

It would not be the only time we went through this drill.

Coincidentally, the man who was leading that effort had a heart attack and died on the very day they were supposed to invade our home. So the mob never came. The attack never happened.

In the coming years, there would be other times when such a threat to our family hung in the air, when mobs actually gathered at our gate, and my mother would always say, "Go change your clothes so you look presentable when they come inside to kill us."

I know it's difficult for some people to understand. I realize that some people may misinterpret my parents' choices as almost fanatical—as if they were willing to die and sacrifice their children to please God. But that is not the case. There is no gain to be made through such martyrdom in the Baha'i Faith. The choice they made to live in areas that were less than hospitable to Baha'is was a choice made in service, and sacrifice, to the cause of peace.

Everything is relative, of course, and this was rural Iran in the 1970s. So, while some areas were more hospitable to Baha'is than others, the chances of children from any minority group witnessing or being subjected to some form of harassment or violence were high. The belief that my parents held was that by going to these particular areas and living in a way that showed they were part of a peaceful and progressive religion, one focused on uniting people through love and service, some of the violence and harassment might stop—not only for the Baha'is, but for everyone. The hope was to bring a more joyful life to the inhabitants of these towns, including those who were at first the instigators of the harassment.

By comparison, during the early days of the Baha'i Faith, in the mid-1800s, nearly twenty thousand Baha'is were killed in Iran—just for believing as they believed. Just for existing and living amongst people who believed differently than they did. If it weren't for those who sacrificed their lives for the Faith, there is no telling how the progress of the Faith may have been affected.

No religion has come about without sacrifice. Jesus was crucified. I don't have to be Christian to believe that humanity is better off because there was a Jesus, and that he sacrificed himself, and that his followers have sacrificed in his name. Even outside of religion, sacrifice of some sort is usually necessary for good things to happen, and that's okay. But parents also have an obligation to protect their kids as best they can, which my parents did.

Moving just down the street from the police station was purposeful, even though it didn't help in the end. But my parents also made friends with those willing to speak to them. They attended to the needs of the neighborhood, spoke to school officials, and sheltered us from harm in every way they could think of without giving up their mission.

It was not an easy life. I was constantly afraid that one of us, or all of us, would be harmed. And yet, looking back, I'm not sure I would have changed it. Why? Because I feel strengthened by my upbringing and have always felt that the circumstances of my life helped me build a strong foundation that would carry me forward, wherever life took me.

Facing the particular challenges I faced as a child made me less afraid to face other challenges later in life. And in that sense, it was an incredibly important part of my personal journey.

I also know that what I'm about to say might be difficult to believe given the context, but my early memories from Hashtgerd—just like the memories I would make later on, in first grade, in Aliabad—were filled with far more happy moments than terrible ones.

For instance, we often rented rooms in our home to other Baha'is, which meant we had young Baha'is living with us. Those people became a part of our family, and to me, they were always interesting. I learned so much from them. On weekends, we would all get up—my family of five and typically two Baha'i guys in their twenties—and we would walk to villages to offer service, to take care of people in need, and to talk to people about the Baha'i Faith (if they asked). I remember one of the renters was very tall, and he put me up on his shoulders as we made the walk. I loved those days traveling across the prairie, in springtime, with colorful fields of tulips stretching out as far as the eye could see.

Hashtgerd is located on a major route across Iran, leading from Turkey in the west through the city of Tehran and on to Turkmenistan in the east, so people visited us from all over the place. Knowing we would welcome them, fellow Baha'is and others just stopped in. In that way, our home became kind of like a Baha'i Center—a gathering place that was open to all, and at which all were welcome.

I remember my mother's homemade tomato paste bubbling in a giant pot on the stove, and the scent of fresh-cut herbs from our garden, flavoring whatever was bought from the market that day for our dinner. In the evenings in summertime, my dad and I would go to the stream in front of our home and carry back bucket after bucket full of water to spread all over the dirt road that surrounded our property, so dust from cars and passersby wouldn't float up into our backyard as we sat on our patio, enjoying our dinner as a family and often sleeping outdoors during the hot summer nights. This practice of pouring water over dust to prevent it from floating was also viewed as a service to the community. To this day, the smell of freshly watered dirt is one of my favorite smells. It always reminds me of our home long ago.

Our home was also filled with friends from all over during Baha'i Holy Days and other occasions, be it the Baha'i New Year (which is also the Persian New Year) on March 21—or every nineteen days throughout the year, when Feast night is celebrated in Baha'i communities all over the world.

On those days, Baha'is from other towns often joined us in our home. But in my parents' home, truly anyone was welcome at any time.

There were some Muslims from the northern side of town who were nice to us, and they would come and want to see my parents because my parents were there to talk to everybody. They wanted to make friends. Even some of those who didn't like us (i.e., were opposed to the Baha'i Faith) but had some sense of reason came just to debate my dad. I witnessed discussions as a young boy, listening to the rising voices, at times shouting at my dad, and the thoughtful silences when one or the other made a point worth considering.

There was always a lot going on in our home.

One day, there was a commotion in the street. We went out to see what was happening and saw a young, white, blonde couple, stuck with a flat tire in their strange-looking car. They were surrounded by a group of the very same people who liked to throw rocks at our house. The couple looked scared, and rightfully so. The gathering quickly turned into a mob. People were shouting and some were throwing rocks at them, breaking the car's windows as my parents ran to them and shielded them and brought them into our home.

I would later recognize that the car they drove was a Citroën. (My love of cars started early.) This couple was from France. My parents didn't speak French, and the couple didn't speak Farsi or Turkish (even though they had come on a road trip through Turkey, as they pointed out on one of our maps). But somehow my parents were able to communicate with them just enough to make them comfortable. They stayed at our home for a couple of nights, until their car was fixed, and then went on their way.

Most of Iran wasn't that inhospitable or dangerous to foreigners. Not in the mid-1970s, anyway. They just happened to break down at the wrong time, in the wrong part of Hashtgerd, where the locals considered it a holy crime to not believe exactly as they believed, which included wearing the clothing and head coverings they believed God wanted all women to wear.

They were attacked for looking like infidels.

A year later, there was a knock on our door. We opened it, and it was them—this same tall, blonde couple on another road trip. Only this time they showed up with gifts to thank us for our earlier kindness. I vividly remember they brought a doll for my sister, and she loved that doll. Funny enough, I don't remember what my gift was. I think I was too overwhelmed by what was happening. As a young kid, it was an amazing experience to see these people show up from France, with gifts from their country. It was my first real contact or interaction with anyone from Europe, which was so exciting to me.

There is so much I love about Iran, and when I talk about the people who did bad things, I want to make it clear that they did not represent the whole country. The country is filled with all sorts of wonderful people, and it's so sad to think of the impact of the fanatics—how those few caused so much hurt and devastation to so many. My parents had friends and made new friends all over, including right there in Hashtgerd—especially on the southern side of town.

All we had to do was cross the highway that divided north from south, and people were instantly nice to us. We passed people on the street, and they would say to my dad, "Hey, Mr. Zamani, how are you? Good to see you."

We could walk, shop, play—all without a problem.

The Baha'is and Ahleh Hagh coexisted peacefully, perhaps because we were both persecuted by the same group. But our connection to the people of southern Hashtgerd ran deeper than that.

There was an American lady, Miss Davis, who came to our home every now and then. She lived in the southern part of town and I remember that she had a cattle farm. How and why an American lady ended up in southern Hashtgerd running a cattle farm, I do not know. But she and my mom partnered to open a free clinic in the southern part of town for women who had no access to medical attention. They opened the clinic to provide advice and feminine hygiene products (which weren't readily available, either), and on certain days they had doctors come in from Tehran and other places to provide basic medical care and make referrals to specialists. Women in our community were able to get care they might never have had access to or even known about if it weren't for what my mom and Miss Davis created.

I sometimes wonder how many women's lives were changed and even saved in Hashtgerd because of the selfless acts of those two women, who acted in the best interest of others despite so much discrimination and persecution. Two women who did not let the prevailing winds of oppression against them and all women stop them from changing the way things were done in the past to make things better for everyone in the present.

So, no—my earliest memories aren't flooded with the terrible things that went on in that town.

My memories are filled with the beauty, friendship, acts of kindness, and inspiration my parents brought to that town.

My dad still worked for the public health department in Tehran when we first made the move to Hashtgerd. After a couple of years he managed to transfer to a position in Karaj, which reduced his commute by about half the distance. And in the latter part of his time there, the department of health appointed him to serve on a small team tasked with eradicating malaria in Iran.

His team accomplished that mission, saving countless lives through the work they did. And once he was forty years old, in 1976, he retired from the health department.

An amazing part of Iran's social system back then was that anyone who worked for the government was eligible for retirement after twenty years. Since he started working for the department of health full-time before his twentieth birthday, he was able to retire and start collecting a pension around the time I turned five years old.

While the pension wasn't enough to raise a family on, it was enough to give my parents a new sense of freedom. And with that freedom, my parents decided to make a drastic change.

My father had always been fascinated with India. He stayed on top of every headline that came out of Bombay and New Delhi, and he especially loved Indian films. He was a huge fan of "the Greatest Showman of Indian Cinema," actor and filmmaker Raj Kapoor, and he always wanted to travel to that country, to see the beautiful landscapes that served as the backdrop to Kapoor's films.

He also thought it would be a wonderful place to go and spread the message of the Baha'i Faith. My mom agreed. So, once his pension came through, my parents said, "You know what? Let's rent our house out and move to India."

My parents knew one person who worked in Bombay (which is now called Mumbai), and no one else in that country. Yet, in what seemed like no time at all, in 1976, the five of us got up, sold everything, and with nothing but five suitcases between us, we went to the airport and boarded a shiny new Boeing 727. (I remember the plane distinctly because that flight marked the start of my lifelong fascination with planes and flight. But more on that later.)

When the plane took off from Tehran, my dad leaned over and told me with so much excitement, joy, and pride in his voice: "I'm forty, flying for the first time. You're five, and you're flying for the first time."

That's a lot of progress in one generation.

We stayed in Bombay for just a few days before traveling to a small town called Panchgani, in a lush, green, rainforest region where my parents knew there was a Baha'i school. There, my parents met with the local Baha'i institution, and together they decided that we should settle in Kolhapur—a city known for its Hindu temples, where the dominant language was Marathi. That is the first place I ever enrolled in school. Not a Baha'i school. There wasn't one. Instead, I went to kindergarten at a Catholic school, St. Xavier's School, which was considered the best school in town. The school taught kids in a British system, from grades K through 13 (which is a little different from American schools), so my brother and sister went to the same school as me; but because our days started at different times, I took a different school bus. I had to walk a good distance to get to the bus stop, and I did that by myself—in a place where no one spoke my language, and where my kindergarten class was taught in English, which I also did not speak. It's kind of mind-blowing that my parents trusted that I would be able to handle so much change at such a young age, but I did. I didn't learn much English. I never learned much Marathi or Hindi, either. I just sort of watched and listened and got by as best I could.

Despite all of the very obvious differences between us and the local population in India, our Faith did not bring us harm. People were tolerant of other beliefs, and to me they seemed much more peaceful than what I was used to.

We were better off financially than some of our neighbors, not only because my dad got his pension as well as collected rent on our home back in Hashtgerd, but because there was such an amazing exchange rate for the Iranian currency in those days. It was all exciting, and new, and interesting, and it seemed like the start of a whole new journey—but in the end, we were there for less than a year. India would not give us residency. Not because of any particular discrimination or law, but because, as my dad explained it, we wouldn't pay the government officials a bribe.

"We're here to teach the Baha'i Faith and the values it enshrines," my dad told us. "One of the most important tenets of our Faith is to be truthful. We're supposed to be honest in all dealings. So we're not going to pay a bribe. We cannot negotiate over this."

Holding onto his convictions and beliefs left us no choice but to pack up and go home.

So the adventure was short-lived. But how many kids get a chance to live in another country while they're so young and impressionable? How many parents have the courage and conviction to move their family to a far-off land, without hesitation, to live out a dream? It's the kind of bold move that changes hearts and broadens minds, and I'll forever be thankful to my parents for giving me that experience.

Without it, I'm not so sure I would have been so prepared to leave my country for a new start in America years later—where I would live a free life that I could not begin to imagine back in 1977, when the five of us returned from India to our homeland, to the capital city of Tehran.

REFLECTIONS ON CHAPTER THREE

What were you most scared of as a young child? Was it something tangible, real, happening on a regular basis? Or was it something perceived, imaginary, or taught to you? How did those fears shape your view of the world outside your front door? How did those fears shape your view of other people, and especially other groups of people (as distinguished by race, religion, ethnicity, gender, or anything else)?

How did your parents handle conflict, either within your community or in your home? Do you deal with conflict similarly or differently in your life today?

What are some of the things your parents accomplished—at work, at home, or even at school—that excited you or surprised you as a child? Did they perform acts of service in your community or for your family? What did they do with their lives that makes you proud?

What kind of legacy are you creating in your own life? What have you accomplished that you're proud to talk about? Are these the sorts of things that your children or other people in your life will remember and be proud of even after you're gone? Or do you have more work to do in order to make that happen?

CHAPTER FOUR

UNWANTED LESSONS

O n the morning of the IPO, a black car picked me and my brother
up at the Four Seasons and took us to Credit Suisse's trading
floor. The trading day had already opened by the time we got
there, and our IPO was set to launch at 10:30 AM. The pre-market trading
was intense. I had never seen anything like it before. The traders were so
busy; they never hung up the phones. They just left them hanging by their
cords from the edge of the table, and then this guy from the other side of
the table would grab one of them, and whoever was on the other end of
the line would still be there, and he'd listen for a second, and yell, "Fidel-
ity is asking for so many shares." I couldn't even tell who he was yelling
at. And the language they used—they were so vulgar. Not just yelling but
screaming, taking orders, throwing paper at each other. It was wild.

Finally, trading on AutoWeb officially opened. We had priced our
stock at $14 a share—and it opened at $27.

It just kept going up from there.

There were screens and televisions everywhere, and every business
program on cable was talking about AutoWeb. After spending the last
few years watching other Silicon Valley–based companies explode on
Wall Street as part of the tech boom, I knew this would be a big day.

I knew that my brother and I, and our employees (to whom we had awarded shares from the start), were all likely to become very rich from this IPO. Yet even though I was standing in the center of where it was all unfolding, it was difficult to believe it was finally happening—that our vision, our hopes, and our dreams for this company had reached this once-in-a-lifetime milestone.

At some point, we were led outside to a black limousine to go meet the president of the Nasdaq. A reporter from *SmartMoney* magazine who had been following us around for the better part of a week climbed in with us. He was working on a feature story about what it was like to launch an IPO in the middle of the dot-com boom.

Our new CEO climbed in, too.

This man had been hired just a few weeks earlier, after the venture capitalists (VCs) decided that I wasn't experienced enough, old enough, or American enough to run my own company once it went public. While the VCs were all minority shareholders, as investors they held what are referred to as "preferred shares," and board seats, and ultimately my brother and I did not have enough votes to counter what we thought was a mistake. As nice as this guy was, and as experienced as he was running other, much smaller, companies, we simply did not think he had the passion, the vision, or the experience it took to run a company designed to massively impact the automotive industry—which is what AutoWeb had set out to do.

On paper, by the end of the day, this CEO's shares of AutoWeb would be worth about $70 million.

That seemed unfathomable to me, too, but in a different way: This company that we took public wasn't built by him in any way. It was built by the founders (my brother and I) and our employees, not by a newly appointed CEO who had so recently been forced on us by the VCs.

I was learning the hard way that this is one of the ways riches are made in a system that exists for one purpose and one purpose only: making money for those at the top, and specifically for those who are welcomed as part of the club.

Our new CEO was all excited in the back of that limo, just feeling good and acting crazy. And in front of the reporter, as we rolled down

the street, he lowered his window, leaned his head out, and shouted, "F---
you, New York!"

F--- you? I thought. *Why is he cursing the city where he just made
millions?*

I tried to ignore his odd vulgarity and instead tried to take in the
excitement of the day.

We had so much to celebrate. We had done this. My brother and I had
accomplished this.

I was twenty-eight years old. My tax filings from just a few years
earlier showed an income of less than $20,000. I still had student loans
that needed to be paid off. By the end of that first trading day, AutoWeb's
stock closed at $40 per share.

My personal stake in the company was 20 percent.

Which meant that my personal net worth had skyrocketed to more
than $200 million. And that's in 1999 dollars. Adjusted for inflation, it
would be a lot more valuable today.

Maybe I should have been the one leaning my head out of the window
and yelling at passersby, too.

As far as I'd come from my life in Iran, as much as I'd embraced, and
some might say conquered, the American system of capitalism in a very
short period of time, I still had much to learn.

And I was about to learn. Fast.

I had visited Tehran quite often during my early childhood days, mostly
to visit my grandmother (my mom's mom), my mom's sisters, and my
cousins. Most of my cousins were much older than me, but the youngest
male cousin, Shahram, was only five years older, and he and I grew close.

In 1977, Shahram's dad worked for the U.S. Embassy in Tehran, so
he had access to a lot of cool stuff, which I loved. He was an artist who
would draw caricature-type pieces for pamphlets and so on, and he had
a studio at the embassy, which was almost like a city compound in the

middle of town. A couple of times I went with Shahram and his dad to his work. He gave me things, like Scotch tape or a No. 2 pencil—things that seem so trivial today but were so special back then, just because of the novelty of them.

I tried French fries for the first time at the embassy—my first real taste of America—when Shahram's dad took us to the employee café for lunch. And I enjoyed Tehran and its hustle and bustle: The shops and boutiques, the energy, and maybe the fact that no one knew who I was as I walked the streets. No one automatically knew I was Baha'i as they did in the small towns and villages, so although it was a big city, I felt safer.

The home my parents rented in Tehran upon our return from India was located right behind the Pepsi-Cola factory. That's where I learned that "good Muslims don't drink Pepsi." Why? Because in Iran, Pepsi-Cola was owned by a very successful Baha'i entrepreneur, which meant "good Muslims" would not drink it.

They only drank Coke.

It seems like no big deal, but it's one more example of how deeply the prejudice and hatred toward the Baha'is ran. Good Muslims would not shake our hands or eat in our homes, and "Pepsi is unclean," people said. "Coke is clean."

It made no sense to me. Coca-Cola was owned by Christians.

"Aren't they considered infidels, too?" I asked my dad.

"Yes!" he said, laughing.

How could one infidel be worse than another? Why were some infidels stoned and killed and others not harmed at all? (I later learned that Christians are not generally considered "infidels" to Muslims. Judaism and Christianity are revered in the Quran, and both faith communities are recognized and supposedly protected under the Iranian Constitution.) Why was anyone killed or harmed at all for having differing beliefs? In many ways, it's far too much to ask any child to understand such things, especially since adults can't make sense of these things either. But I was about to start learning. And fast.

My parents' mission in life was not to stay in the relatively comfortable setting of Tehran. It was to serve. So, after living un-harassed in India for a short period, and then three months living in the capital, my parents decided to move us to a small town by the Caspian Sea. To a rented house in an orchard in Aliabad—where I was soon welcomed to first grade with the warmth of a boy's spit in my winter hat.

My sister, Addy, was eight-and-a-half years older than me. She was nearly fifteen when my parents explained why we were making that move, and she was not happy about it. She didn't want to risk being harassed anymore. Addy just wanted to live her life, as most teenagers do. And unlike me, who was still too young and inexperienced to understand it all, she understood just how risky it could be for her to move to that town.

She was scared for her life, and rightfully so.

Life for a Baha'i girl in rural Iran was much more difficult than it was for a boy. To the fundamentalist Muslims who believed that women should be hidden from view and kept in their place, the fact that my parents were raising Addy to be an equal to men was an affront to everything the fundamentalists believed. Getting spit on, made fun of, and occasionally beat up during my first-grade year in Aliabad was nothing compared to what happened to my sister. Her harassment was daily. Her beatings came from older kids. Bigger kids.

And toward the end of the school year, she and one of her Baha'i friends were run down by a car outside the school.

They were targeted.

The police called it a hit-and-run and never found the driver. (Of course.) But the attack left Addy badly injured. So much so that another Baha'i family brought me to their home after school that day and wouldn't let me see her at the hospital. Addy's friend, the other girl who was hit, was their daughter. She was there. I remember the blood still dripping from her forehead when they told me my sister was in a coma.

My parents never thought things would get this bad. Harassment is one thing. A few broken windows, they could justify. They believed the presence of their Faith offered answers to help these people come out of the dark ages. After all, these sorts of extreme behaviors and attacks are simply not experienced in places where people are more educated and taught to care about virtues. They were acting in support of an important cause, and they were willing to sacrifice to make the world a better place. It was service, which in itself is the highest form of worship. But this?

Fortunately, Addy came out of the coma and recovered quickly. But I remember the sound of my parents' voices through the walls, talking late into the night, wrestling so much with what had happened—and what they should do next.

In the end, they decided it was time for us to move.

They decided to move our family back to Tehran, where my brother and sister and I could go to school and live our lives without the daily threat of violence. They would continue to share their Faith with others. My father would go back to work, this time working directly for the Local Spiritual Assembly of the Baha'is of Tehran. Their lives would still be dedicated to service, but without so much risk to themselves or their children. (At least for the time being.)

My sister was officially old enough to decide for herself whether to remain part of the Baha'i Faith.* She was old enough to have studied other religions. She had every reason to rebel against my parents and the Faith they had raised her in if she wanted to. Yet, even after the hit-and-run, even after being so directly targeted, she decided to stick with it. She realized that the Faith itself, with its peaceful goals for humanity, provided the hope, love, and support she needed in order to move on from the trauma, and to move forward in life.

She was also very glad to be moving back to Tehran, away from the daily abuse.

Me? I was happy, too. I was happy to be going back to the excitement of the city.

There was a slight delay as my parents searched for an apartment. We wound up spending the summer of 1978 in Ooshan, a truly beautiful town with a river running through it, just outside of Tehran—the sort of place where you'd want to spend a summer. We lived in a modern house

---

* Baha'is believe that religion should not be inherited. We believe in the concept of independent investigation of truth. Even Baha'i kids are not automatically considered Baha'is until, at age fifteen or older, they choose to declare their Faith and accept Baha'u'llah as the messenger of God for this day and age.

while my father worked in the city, and my mother took me back and forth to Aliabad a few times to take exams at my old school. Together, my parents and teachers determined that I was ready to skip second grade and move directly to third when I started school in Tehran. I truly didn't care what grade I was in. I was just excited to go to a school where I was less likely to be targeted and harassed.

We moved to an apartment in a neighborhood called Beautiful City in Tehran, which wasn't as beautiful as Ooshan but was beautiful in its own way. It was a purposefully designed neighborhood, organized with schools and parks that were meant to give citizens a peaceful setting to share.

The part that wasn't so beautiful were the apartment buildings themselves, which were built out of concrete, with up to forty units per building in the style of Eastern Bloc buildings—just massive cubes of concrete. They were big and some might say ugly, with small windows, and they were filled with cockroaches.

There was a juvenile rehabilitation facility across the street from our building, and I remember that building was much prettier than ours. But none of that really mattered to us. What mattered is we would be safe.

Going to school in the fall of 1978 was like breathing a sigh of relief. My brother and sister were both much happier. I was much happier.

I was shocked to find out on my first day of third grade that my classes were coed. There were girls in class for the first time in my life! I liked that.

We also started learning about the world, which I loved so much. Especially learning about America. I kept a map of the U.S. on my wall, and I memorized every state and most state capitals. I still loved to play Monopoly, and it was around this time when I did my first assessment of my net worth; shortly afterwards, I sold my baseball cap to a man on the street and started thinking about other ways to make money on my own. Just living without daily harassment and fear made everything feel better, as if we had come so far in such a short period of time, just by moving into the city.

But my parents were uneasy about other things that were happening in Tehran and elsewhere in the country. There was a tension in the air. My father bought the paper every single day and clipped certain headlines and articles, collecting them in a scrapbook.

"History will remember these days, and these headlines," he would tell me.

The tension this time wasn't about the Baha'is. It was about the Shah, the modernity of Iran, and the Westernization of the country that the Shah and his father had been pushing, even forcing, on the population since the end of World War I. Their approach, which flew in the face of many Islamic traditions and ran afoul of the teachings of some powerful Mullahs and Imams, was now facing pushback from those very clerics.

I don't have room to write a long history lesson for those who weren't alive then or didn't follow the news at the time, but protesters against the Shah began taking to the streets during the summer of 1978. The protests remained mostly peaceful, until August. That's when a horrible attack occurred at a movie theater called Cinema Rex, which many say was the impetus for what would become the Iranian Revolution. To this day, there is a lot of debate about who caused the fire—Shia extremists, anti-government protesters, or possibly the Shah's agents looking to create a propaganda backlash against the clerics who were calling for his overthrow. But this very large movie theater in a working-class neighborhood was targeted, just as a number of smaller movie theaters had been targeted for decades by Islamic extremists for showing films filled with Western ideas and what they believed to be immoral content (i.e., sex scenes). In this case, the terrorists locked the doors from the outside and set the theater ablaze with gasoline, killing around four hundred people.*

The horror of that one incident, which at the time marked the largest-ever death toll from a single terrorist attack in history, led to protesters clashing in the streets, calling for an overthrow of the monarchy and the establishment of a democratic system. (Of course, we know that's not what happened. The uprising ultimately resulted in the establishment of a fundamentalist Islamic theocracy with a supreme leader who is in

---

* Officials and historians have never agreed on an accurate number. Some reports put the Cinema Rex death toll around 370, some closer to 500 in total.

charge for life and has a final say on everything—which sounds a lot like a king to me.)

To quell the protests, the Shah declared martial law. But the protests didn't stop.

On September 8, 1978, my father came home from work looking shaken. My mother asked him what was wrong.

"As I was coming home through Jaleh Square, I saw tanks coming in," he said. "There were a lot of people in the square. I got away as quickly as I could, but tanks were coming in and I could feel something bad was about to happen."

Not long after my father walked through our door, military forces opened fire on the gathered crowds. Gunfire and explosions echoed through the city streets. As many as one hundred people were killed. Hundreds more were injured.

What my dad witnessed and was nearly caught up in would come to be known as Iran's Black Friday: the massacre that one can conclude marked the beginning of the end of the Shah's reign.

The use of military force did the opposite of what the Shah had hoped to accomplish. Instead of quelling the protests, his violent actions—which seem moderate compared to the oppression forced by the Islamic regime that would replace him—caused a backlash, uniting protesters from all sides against his regime. It was chaos.

Over the next few months, I remember hearing gunshots and tear gas being fired in the middle of the night. Through the windows of our apartment in Beautiful City, more than once, I heard a man's voice yelling, "Stop!"—like someone in the military yelling "Stop" or "Freeze"—and then a bang.

One day, a mob opened the doors of the juvenile house across the street. All of the kids inside were set free. That wasn't a nice sight. These kids that were supposed to be in jail were suddenly all over town.

Schools all over Iran were closed for months.

I remember my dad reading the paper one night, cutting out another headline to add to his scrapbook. "These people don't know what's going to happen," he told me. "This country's gonna go backward fast."

And, of course, it did.

In a matter of months, the Shah was forced out of power. He fled the country in January of 1979, opening the door for the return of an exiled cleric named Ayatollah Khomeini, who would take over the government and change everything.

A new Islamic government was established in February 1979; then later that year, the hostage crisis started, which turned into a direct, intense clash with the U.S. that put the whole world on edge.

The new leadership of what was suddenly renamed "the Islamic Republic of Iran," along with a broad section of the Muslim-majority population, felt empowered and emboldened like never before to impose their beliefs on everyone, everywhere.

When we were finally allowed to go back to school in 1979, our teachers had everyone open up their history books. They then told us which pages to rip out and throw in the trash.

This new regime would dictate the very history we would be allowed to learn.

The more peaceful, modern, educated, tolerant, diverse life we had sought in Tehran, a life we briefly lived and loved, disappeared in a flash. Just like that.

It wouldn't be long before those in power would come for the Baha'is.

It was only a matter of time before a mob would come for me.

REFLECTIONS ON CHAPTER FOUR

What has been your biggest accomplishment in life so far? Do you remember how it felt in the moment? Were you surprised by your own feelings or the feelings that other people around you expressed when it happened?

At your highest peak so far, did you ever feel that something was a little off? That something didn't make sense? As you think back on it, can you put into words what it was that might have been missing?

What terrorist attacks, mass protest events, or sudden, sweeping changes in government or politics have occurred during your lifetime? How did you become aware of them? How did they affect your life or change your life? Did you feel well prepared to navigate those changes when they came?

Knowing that life has a long-established pattern of presenting us with unexpected events and sometimes massive changes that occur overnight, what are you doing now to prepare yourself, your family, and/or your business for the "unexpected" changes that are sure to happen in the future? Have you built a foundation upon which to stand, including a savings plan and a spiritual/emotional base you'll be able to rely on? Are your foundations strong enough to hold up to the winds of change?

CHAPTER FIVE

THE BLEEDING MILE

Whether I was fully aware of it or not, I was busy learning a very important lesson: Tests and difficulties are simply a matter of life. When one goes away, another one shows up. Ups are followed by downs, and vice versa. Change is constant. We all have to adapt to the changes the world throws at us, and we really only have two choices: to give up or to move forward—with optimism.

If we're not giving up, then isn't it up to each one of us to strive to live the best life we can, no matter what the circumstances may be?

As our country moved backwards over the course of 1979, a group of Indian doctors who were renting our old house in Hashtgerd moved out. From what my parents understood, there was far less violence and harassment of Baha'is in Hashtgerd now than there was when we first lived there. So, during the summer of 1980, my parents decided to move back to our old house.

Addy had recently gotten married. She didn't want to leave Tehran, so she and her new husband took over the apartment my parents had been renting, and my brother decided to stay with them, to finish high school in the city.

It was the first time our family ever lived apart.

Thankfully, what my parents had heard about Hashtgerd was correct. When we settled into our old house, no one threw rocks at us. No one broke our windows. Things had changed. I was happy about that, but I missed being with my siblings, and I missed the city.

I also missed my cousin Shahram and our occasional trips to the U.S. Embassy with his dad. He and his family had moved to the U.S. just after the Revolution, eventually settling in Modesto, California, which seemed so far away. We didn't have a phone in our home, so the only way for us to keep in touch was by writing letters.

It was strange to me to think that he was living in a place with so much freedom, while so many of our freedoms in Iran were being taken away.

The government began cracking down on every Western influence they could, forcing women to cover their hair in public, closing Tehran University, and then all universities (until they could redesign curriculums and add their own influence). They even shut down all the publishing houses in the capital, a thriving industry that had published original books in Persian and provided translations of books from around the world.

All my life, I had been expected to read, and I enjoyed reading. We had many books at home before the Revolution, including a few volumes of the Encyclopedia Britannica, which I had started to read cover to cover just to learn about the world. I enjoyed learning about the cosmos and the world beyond, too, and one of the books I read more than once was *One Two Three . . . Infinity: Facts and Speculations of Science*, a popular book by theoretical physicist George Gamow. The exploration and understanding of scientific principles were encouraged in our home, not only as a part of a broad education, but as a part of my Faith.

Under the Ayatollah, the reading of many of these types of books was no longer allowed.

I could not understand how anyone could think that censoring books would make a country stronger. But from that point forward, the government insisted on approving every book that Iranians would be allowed to read.

Those changes quickly trickled down to the school system. A new staff member was installed in every school, in every town. The Ershad teacher: a man with a gun who would lead the students in mass prayers every day and ensure that Islamic values were observed.

The government started taking away all freedoms. Banning music. Banning instruments. Banning card games. Banning backgammon and chess. Banning Western movies. Banning men and women from conversing with each other one-on-one (unless they were married or immediate family members). Banning women from attending soccer matches, even though soccer had always been a national pastime and passion in Iran, much like baseball or football is in America. They even prohibited women from using their voices, their own God-given instruments, to sing. (Also, fun fact: They banned the eating of shrimp. Apparently, eating shrimp was not acceptable to God. However, after a few years, they decided that shrimp was no longer unholy and removed the ban. I guess God changed his mind. The absurdity of the religious leaders' decisions was evident to me even then as a ten-year-old boy.)

It felt to me like they wanted to ban all joy.

People quickly found ways to get around some of the bans, of course. People always do. For example, there were certain underground places you could go where they would rent out VCRs and bootlegged VHS tapes, twenty-four hours at a time. We would stay up for twenty-four hours straight and binge-watch movie after movie to get our money's worth, trying to make sense of the blurry, scratchy images of such big American hits as *Rambo* and *A Nightmare on Elm Street*, since we couldn't understand the language and there weren't any captions.

We did our best to find joy, make joy, and share joy, day after day and night after night.

And then, just as my father predicted, the Islamic government turned on the Baha'is. Those at the top denied they had ordered such a thing, but the UN would later uncover documents, written by Khomeini himself, basically ordering the Revolutionary Guard* to cleanse the country of Baha'is.

---

* The Revolutionary Guard is a branch of the Iranian armed forces created by Khomeini to protect the ideology of the Islamic Republic. Known for using brute strength and harsh measures to quell "deviance" within Iran, the Guard has been designated as a terrorist organization by the U.S. and many other countries.

He also ordered the killing of anyone whom they believed was still loyal to the past regime. A mullah named Khalkhali was put in charge of that effort. He put together a squad of ten or fifteen cars. He made a list. Those cars filled with Revolutionary Guards then drove from town to town, city to city, where they would knock on doors. They would ask the people on their list to step outside, and they would shoot them, right there, and move on. Without any free media or internet to learn from, word of this political cleansing squad spread from household to household—along with the fear that, at any point, they could show up and knock on our door.

After all, as a young boy it made no sense to me how they could determine the difference between who was a political foe and who was a religious foe—since anyone who didn't believe the way they did was determined to be a foe, period.

While all of this was unfolding, a whole new danger showed up on our doorstep.

In September 1980, my mother and I were shopping for new school clothes a little closer to Tehran, in the town of Karaj, when we heard that the Tehran airport had been bombed. We rushed home, where we would soon learn that it was one of ten airports across Iran to be bombed that day as Saddam Hussein led his Iraqi Army on a full-scale invasion across our country's oil-rich southern border, with the Iraqi Air Force completing more than two hundred sorties in Iran that one day.

It was the start of a war that would last for eight long years. A war that doesn't seem to get talked about a whole lot but would become the longest, and some believe the bloodiest, war since World War II, resulting in the deaths of over a million people.

During a one-day visit to my sister's apartment a few weeks after the airport bombings, all the lights went out, and the skies filled with red dots that looked like they were dropping on the city. I ran into the bedroom, lay face down on the mattress, and pressed the blankets and my hands over my eyes and ears, thinking this was it. We were all about to die. But the red dots were anti-aircraft fire, and the whole thing was just a military exercise. A practice run.

Back in Hashtgerd, we would have to learn to live with no lights on in our houses after dark—a rule enforced by the government as cover against Iraqi Air Force bombing strikes, which would hit deep in the heart of our country with no warning. Hussein knew that our new government was in a weak position, with an army in disarray and the loss of the Western protection that the Shah had courted for decades. So he took advantage.

What he didn't expect is that his violent attacks would galvanize Iranians of all stripes to bind together and fight back against his aggression.

As a family, we adapted quickly, finding sheets of thick black plastic to hang in the windows so we could turn on a light or two after dark without worry. And thankfully, Hashtgerd remained untouched by the bombings. But there was hardly a family in all of Iran that wasn't touched directly by that war.

So many soldiers died that there were mass funerals held every Thursday, in every town, for all eight years of the war. The death toll was more than ten times the death toll of Americans during the Vietnam War—and the population of Iran is a fraction of the size of the U.S. The impact cannot be overstated. With that much loss to our forces, it wasn't long before the government started forcibly enlisting young men over the age of eighteen to join the fight whether they wanted to or not. And Baha'is, who don't believe in fighting or carrying weapons, were not exempt.

So the war remained in both the foreground and background of the other fears that pervaded our daily lives, including one night that same summer.

Because we had no air-conditioning, we slept outside in the backyard to beat the heat. Sleeping in the yard or up on the roof is a common practice in Iran. But on this night, sometime after midnight, we were awakened by the sound of multiple cars approaching, all in a bunch, followed by shouts from the surrounding streets.

The cleansing squad had come to Hashtgerd.

We heard the sound of those cars driving down our street and stopping near the orchard very close to our home. Then, the sound of a single gunshot.

We listened for the cars to drive away. And they did.

As my parents and our neighbors soon learned, the squad had dragged a man from his home and brought him to the orchard to execute him. He was not a Baha'i. He was most likely a political foe rather than an ideological foe.

Regardless, none of us fell back to sleep that night.

Sleep is never easy when the wolf is at your door.

I honestly wasn't afraid that they would do anything to me personally. Call it the innocence of youth, or maybe the imagined invincibility of youth. But I was afraid for my parents, and particularly my dad. He worked directly for the Baha'i institutions. And the elected members of those institutions were increasingly being arrested and killed.

Almost daily, my father came home from work in Tehran and told us that another well-known Baha'i had been executed. And with every passing month, the killings accelerated.

In 1981, two of my father's very best friends, the men responsible for my dad becoming a Baha'i—Mr. Bakhtaver and Dr. Majzub—were executed, separately, by the government of Iran.

Soon, a number of members of the National Spiritual Assembly of the Baha'is of Iran were kidnapped and killed. Innocent people. Elected volunteers, working for peace.

People that my dad worked for directly at the Local Spiritual Assembly of Tehran were kidnapped and killed as well. I had gone to their offices with him. I knew their faces. I saw them one day, and the next they were gone.

When those positions were filled through reelection, the new members of the Assembly were kidnapped and killed as well. This happened multiple times.

The government's noose of fear kept closing.

Soon, local Baha'i Spiritual Assemblies in towns across Iran (which existed in every town where there were at least nine adult Baha'is present) felt they had no choice but to hide their meetings.

Baha'is never hide their Faith. But as a community, given the circumstances, we no longer felt the need to proactively make our presence known—unless we were asked.

Finally, the government ordered that the institutions of Baha'i Faith be shut down in Iran. Since Baha'is, as a rule, are obedient to the government, the Universal House of Justice instructed the Baha'is of Iran to dismantle the institutions.

At that point, my father came home from work carrying boxes full of files for safekeeping. There was nowhere else to keep them. I couldn't help but worry whether his being the keeper of those files might put a bigger target on my father's back.

In the meantime, in the northern part of Hashtgerd, our neighbors and classmates started openly turning on Baha'is again.

I started getting picked on at school.

The rock throwing returned.

And every time the government called for the Iranian people to take to the streets in a nationwide protest against Israel, the people of Hashtgerd would choose to gather their mob in front of our home. Why? Because there wasn't an Israeli Embassy or presence in Hashtgerd, or anywhere else in Iran, but government propaganda had told the public that all Baha'is in Iran were spies of Israel—based on the fact that the Baha'i holy places are in Israel, on land that was formerly known as Palestine, where Baha'u'llah passed away and was buried in 1892. That is why the government (as operated by the clerics and fundamentalists) made sure the public came to consider us as representatives of Israel—simply because our holy places were there. They also lumped us in with Israelis because neither of us believed as they believed, so therefore, we were both equal foes. Politically, that was a convenient thing to do.

The mob was angry, and loud. Banging on our walls and banging on our front gate.

My mother insisted I put on my nicest clothes as we sat inside and waited for the doors to break open, or the mob to climb over the wall.

They didn't. After a while, the crowd dispersed.

It would happen again and again, as the government began calling for protests multiple times per year.

Why did those mobs keep to the outside of our walls? Was it luck? Fate?

All I know is that in the fall of 1981, I made it to sixth grade, my first year at the middle school in Hashtgerd, where my days were increasingly marked by harassment. Not just from other students, but from the adults. Especially the Ershad teacher at our school: the man with a gun who would not leave me be, and who made sure the good Muslim children wouldn't leave me be either.

Ershad teachers were also known as the Morality Police inside schools.

In private, I thought of this man as our school's Chief Hate Officer.

I did well in school, partly because I wanted to, partly because my parents forced me to get good grades, and maybe because focusing on my education was one way to avoid the trauma of constant confrontation. But in the spring of 1982, as my sixth-grade year was coming to an end, the school held a competition to see who could memorize the most verses of the Quran.

I won.

This upset the powers that be. I heard them speaking: "Oh, that's the last thing we need, a Baha'i winning this!"

There were three classrooms full of sixth graders in that school, over-populated with about fifty students each. And after I won that competition, the Chief Hate Officer went to my classroom and spoke so fervently against the Baha'is that my classmates wouldn't let me through the door. They forced me to leave, to walk down the hall, to join a classroom full of students I didn't know.

The tide was turning against me by the force and influence of hatred, which was taught to those children by adults.

A day or two later, the principal asked me to come to his office. I obeyed, and the Ershad teacher was there. Together, they started questioning me:

"Do you like Khomeini or the United States?"

That's an odd question, I thought. *One is a country; the other is a person.*

"I have no comment," I said.

"Well, why not?" they asked.

"I've never been to the United States," I responded.

Now, mind you, I knew all the states. I knew many of the cities. I had a map of the U.S., and I loved the U.S. It was my beacon of hope.

"I haven't been to the U.S. and I don't know Khomeini," I said. "You're asking me a question that I can't answer."

"Sit down, sit down," they said, and we all sat down, as if this were supposed to be a casual conversation. "What if we tell you that Khomeini is the one killing the Baha'is and Ronald Reagan is trying to save you guys?"

I felt trapped.

"Well," I said, trying to remain calm, "I don't know. I don't know if he's the one who's giving the orders or not."

"Let's hypothetically, for a moment, say we believe—no, we know for a fact—Khomeini's ordering the killing of the Baha'is, and the United States is trying to offer protection. Who do you like more?"

"Well," I said, "if you put it that way, I like the one who says, 'Don't kill the Baha'is.'"

The Chief Hate Officer stood up and yelled, "So you like the United States more than this country and our sacred Imam?"

What could I say?

The principal stood up and said, "Get out of my office."

"Okay," I said, and I left.

The next day, another Baha'i student, a neighbor who was one year older than me, and I stayed behind in one of the empty classrooms overlooking the school courtyard during mass prayer.

In the past, the Ershad teacher had regularly asked us to join in the mass prayers. We'd say, "We're Baha'is and we have our own prayers. There's just no point for us to say some other—" and he would say, "Okay, okay." He was actually very cordial about it. But during his sermon on that particular day, we heard him say over the loudspeakers, "Today, we're gonna cleanse our school of these Baha'i infidels," and he referred to us as *najes*, a word that means "unclean." A foul word that is only used to describe pigs, dogs, blood, dead animals, ejaculate—and infidels. "Today, we're gonna get rid of the Baha'is!"

This other student and I looked at each other. *Okay. Well, this is gonna be an interesting day.*

It wasn't like we could just get up and leave. The school gates were locked during the day, so no one could come in—and no one could get out.

When the school day ended, one could feel the tension. We went to the courtyard, where the two of us asked some of the teachers who had cars if they would please give us a ride home.

None of them would look at us or acknowledge us in any way.

I cannot blame them. Under the circumstances, even if they were nice people, they would have been putting themselves and their families at risk if they were seen helping us.

So the teachers all left, and the schoolyard fell eerily quiet.

Outside the gates, we could see them: a gathered mob of kids from our school.

All of a sudden, they started chanting: "Death to Israel! Death to Baha'is! Death to America!"

Some of them were holding sticks. Some bent down and picked up rocks.

These were kids we went to school with—somewhere between thirty and fifty of them, it seemed.

We sat on the three concrete steps at the school's entrance inside the courtyard, and we looked at each other, and we looked at the mob, and we realized there was no way to avoid what was about to happen.

"They're gonna come for us," I said. "We might as well look kinda brave and head out. What happens, happens."

My neighbor agreed.

So we stood. Side by side, we walked toward the gate, knowing we had to make it just over a mile down the main street in Hashtgerd to get to our houses, past all the shops on each side of the road, the busiest street in town.

It felt like we were walking into a death march.

As soon as we stepped through the gates, these kids started spitting and throwing rocks at us. We guarded our heads and tried to walk as fast as we could as some came closer and beat us with sticks and kicked us, spitting directly in our faces and all over our bodies. One of them picked up a half-broken brick to throw, but he missed and hit one of their own instead. That person fell, bleeding. I don't know what happened to him after that. I could see across the street that there were people watching. Adults who did nothing to help. And at some point, I stopped feeling pain. I don't know if I was hit in the head or if I was in shock, but I could not feel a thing. I was walking, but in a different state, almost outside of my own body, thinking, *Man, these people, these parents, these adults are watching this mob kill these two kids, and they don't care.*

I felt sorry for them. I felt that God had forgotten them.

It was a strange thought to have: "I'm gonna die, but I feel sorry for these people."

Somehow, we made it to our homes.

When I got inside, I realized I was wet from head to toe—from spit. When I say wet, I mean I could wring out my shirt and the spit would pour out. My hair was flat on my head.

I finally snapped out of my fog, and there was a moment when I went to grab a knife, to go outside and give those kids what they deserved. I didn't, but I knew that I had it in me.

My grandmother was there, my mother's mother. She didn't visit that often, but she was there with us that day. So she stayed with me while my dad and my mom and the other kid's parents marched over to the local school district office, where my dad went straight into the office of the person in charge and said, "How in the world can you allow this to happen to kids?"

His response? "Don't be a Baha'i. This will not happen."

"But your own constitution gives me the right to believe in something different," my dad responded. And the man started yelling at my dad: "You are questioning the constitution?"

My parents went to the Ershad teacher as well, a man who had previously acted cordially toward our family, who said he "loved everybody," and his response was, "Well, we tried to kill them today. On another day, we will. So I encourage you to leave town. Now."

That night, I didn't sleep in my home. My parents moved me to another Baha'i family's home under cover of darkness.

The school year was almost over, so my parents arranged for me to take my final exams at an all-girls' school in another town.

From there, they sent me to live with my sister in Beautiful City in Tehran.

I was eleven years old and forced to leave my parents.

I had no choice but to move. Again. To adjust again. To start all over. Again.

It was just the beginning.

In a world gone crazy, everyone in our family would soon have to learn new ways to adjust, to survive, and to try to make the most out of life. Any way we could.

REFLECTIONS ON CHAPTER FIVE

What is the biggest adversity you have had to overcome in your life?

Did you endure any sort of trauma in your childhood? If so, how did you get through it? Is it something you talk about, openly, or that you hold close to the vest? Either way, do you ever think about how much strength it took to overcome such a thing—to allow you to not only survive, but to grow and rise into the life you have now? Where does that strength come from?

When you think of your childhood, who did you look up to? Who guided you? Who impressed you?

Now, stop and think about the negative influences in your childhood: the adults who did not have your safety or best interests in mind. What did you learn from those particular adults? Have you purposefully tried to behave better than they did when it comes to the children (and others) over whom you have influence today?

What would you do if your government and the people all around you tried to force you to change your religion and/or personal belief system, through threats of violence and death? Would you denounce and let go of the faith in which you believed? Or would you stand tall and peacefully stand up for your beliefs?

CHAPTER SIX

OUT OF PLACE

I didn't want to be there.

I was too young to be on my own, but too old to be imposing on my sister and her husband like this.

I felt trapped. I just wished that I could somehow get up and go.

I spent a lot of my time outside, at least as much as I could, just out and about, wandering alone and exploring the city. I got to know Tehran really well. I went everywhere. I know that seems like a lot for a young boy to be wandering Tehran alone. It's not necessarily the safest city, but after growing up in truly rough places, being safe was a relative term to me. Walking for miles in a city full of people who could not tell whether I was Baha'i or not just by looking at me was so much safer than walking the single mile from school to my home in Hashtgerd.

Still, every weekend, I went home to see my parents, which wasn't an easy thing. For one, I didn't feel safe in Hashtgerd, particularly on the walk from the bus stop to our home. Second, it was forty-five miles away. Forty-five miles on three buses, in traffic, and in bad weather during winter, which could easily take me three hours each way. And once school started, we only had one day off per week, Friday. This meant I left on

Thursday after school and returned on Friday afternoon. So I didn't get to spend much time with my parents at all.

Whenever I was home, my parents gave me some allowance. For unknown reasons, my dad was still receiving his small pension from the government while most Baha'is were no longer receiving their pensions, and every now and then my mom gave me some extra money, too. One day, as she was giving it to me, she said, "Payam, I want you to do well financially and be wealthy."

"What do you mean?" I asked.

"Money will give you independence and flexibility in life," she replied.

She had watched my growing interest in America and my love of Monopoly, and she would always tell me, "When you grow up, invent something. Start your own business. Take charge of your life."

That summer, I decided: "Why wait?"

First, I tried selling Monopoly sets. This wasn't legal, of course. They were no longer being imported to Iran, but I figured people would still want to play the game. So I made them myself. I created a meticulous, hand-drawn board out of thin cardboard. I cut out rectangular pieces of colored paper and drew on them to make the fake money. I made everything myself and made them look as professional as I could, but they were still handmade. I then set up a table on a busy street to try to sell them. It worked! I sold every board I made. But it was far too labor intensive to make a profit worthy of the time it took to make them.

I needed to find something less labor-intensive to sell.

In wandering around the city one day, I discovered far from home that there were wholesalers selling children's clothing in downtown Tehran's historic grand bazaar. I had also noticed there were hardly any places to buy clothes in our neighborhood, which was full of families with children. So I went to one of the wholesalers and bought some of their clothes for resale.

"Do you have money?" the wholesaler asked, clearly thinking I was just a kid.

I pulled a handful of money out of my pocket, and the wholesaler looked surprised.

"Well," he said. "What would you like?"

I picked out a variety of kids' clothes that I thought people in my neighborhood would like, and I set up shop in front of the largest supermarket in Beautiful City.

I made a sizable profit on my very first day, but the management at the supermarket wouldn't let me continue selling from that spot in front of their store. So, after a few days, I had to stop. I didn't let that obstacle stop me from making money, though. One day I got a deal on balloons, so I sold balloons on the street. Another day, I sold popcorn.

I was just a kid with an interest in entrepreneurship and making money, but in a way, I was now one of many Iranian Baha'is who had developed a niche in small, entrepreneurial, almost-always-unlicensed businesses, running shops and offering services all across Iran. We had no choice: The government refused to issue business licenses to Baha'is. Under the new regime, Baha'is lost jobs, lost their right to buy and sell property; even Baha'i marriages were no longer being recognized, which meant that Baha'i children were considered "illegitimate." All of that meant that Baha'is were treated as second-class citizens, and also were forced to become entrepreneurs to survive.

Our family was no exception.

One day, my brother-in-law came up with an idea to reproduce and sell a product that used to come from the U.S.—a product that thousands of homes and businesses used daily, which was no longer available after the boycott of American-made products in our country: Scotch-Brite cleaning pads. I'm guessing you know what that is. You probably have some version of them either on or under your kitchen sink right now: a green pad that's scratchy enough to remove stuck-on food and grime, but soft enough not to damage your pans or dishes in the process. Often, they're attached to one side of a regular dish sponge, and those specialty items were one of the items that disappeared from the shelves of Iranian stores.

My brother-in-law had the idea to buy what was left of the available green pads and regular sponges separately, and then stick them together to make our own Scotch-Brite-like sponges to sell at the bazaar in Tehran. It was clearly a good idea, because the sponges were a big hit. He sold lots of them—so many that he invited our family to get in on the action. My parents started assembling more of these sponges at our home in Hashtgerd.

Oddly, despite the anti-Baha'i prejudice among a large portion of the population, the Baha'is had a reputation for honesty that often helped their small businesses thrive. And ours was thriving.

Under the worst of circumstances, we were all making money!

So, late in 1983, my parents moved to Shiraz in South Central Iran—a city that gave us hope.

Shiraz was known as one of the country's most progressive cities, which is distinctly different from what it means to be a "progressive city" in America. But it was what seemed like a step in the right direction after living in places like Aliabad and Hashtgerd. It's the city that gave the world great poets, including Saadi and Hafez, and with a population of one million people, it was also known for some of the best hospitals and universities in Iran.

To Baha'is, Shiraz is also a very special city: It is the birthplace of the Bab, the forerunner to Baha'u'llah, the prophet founder of the Baha'i Faith. The Bab's home, considered a holy site to the Baha'is, had been seized and demolished by the Islamic government after the Revolution, and a road now sat on top of it. Still, because of its history, my parents felt Shiraz was among the safest of all cities in Iran for us to live.

My brother joined them immediately, and I joined them there as soon as my eighth-grade school year ended, in the summer of 1984.

Up until then, my family had only assembled the cleaning pads. But it wasn't long before the green pads disappeared from our country altogether, so my brother-in-law decided to gather some chemicals and raw materials together to try to reproduce the formula that made Scotch-Brite pads work so well.

My brother had graduated from high school by then but was barred from attending university—because he was Baha'i. (The right to attend universities was one of many rights Baha'is were denied after the Revolution.) So both he and my dad got involved in the process. Together, they sourced materials and worked with others to try to make a green pad of their own that actually worked—and they did. Was the product perfect? No. But it was good enough. My brother and father rented a space to manufacture the cleaning pads from scratch, they started selling these knockoffs, and the demand for them was even larger than they anticipated.

We were able to buy giant rolls of material that resembled a combination of fiberglass and wool (I think), like something you might use as a pad under a carpet, but lighter and less dense. And then we had to make a mixture of paint thinner, polyester, and pigment to spray over the pad. We'd cut out big dining-room-table-sized pieces of the pad material, hang them on the walls, and spray the fabric with the mixture. We used gallons and gallons of paint thinner, which was not only toxic but could easily catch fire, and it did on more than one occasion. But we had to do what we had to do to make money. So we pushed through—even without the sort of protective gear that the job required.

Honestly it felt like some sort of chemical war zone in that warehouse. I would often do the spraying myself, covered from head to toe in a protective suit, and wearing a full face mask, but I would still get high from the fumes and start hallucinating. It's a wonder I don't have cancer or something!

After the spraying was done, we used giant rollers—like the rollers you see crushing pavement when building streets—to flatten the pads and sponges together before sending them through giant woodcutters to cut them down to size, and then placing them into packaging. That was our product.

I was young, but I was money-motivated, so I helped my brother a lot on the manufacturing side. I got paid per item produced, which motivated me to work long hours and be as efficient as I could.

Meanwhile, our dad took on the role of our main salesperson. If there's one thing my dad is not, it's a typical salesperson. He's not slick, and he is not capable of embellishing. He also had a difficult time asking for people's business, and especially closing deals. Strangely enough, that combination worked well for him. People trusted him at a time when it seemed as if no one in Iran could be trusted. So he sold contracts to sell lots of these pads, wholesale, to all sorts of different industries. Even to the army.

We would load up truckloads of these cleaning pads to deliver, and sometimes before we could get to our destination, we got stopped at checkpoints along the way.

"Where's your work permit?" a guard would say.

"We don't have one," my brother replied. "The government won't give us one."

"What's your religion?" the guard would ask.

"Baha'i."

We never lied. As I said, Baha'is don't hide their religion.

"Okay. Well, the truck stays right here."

We didn't let that stop us.

We found ways to move forward by selling to the public and to big distributors at bazaars all over Iran. We drove to the bazaar with truckloads of cleaning pads and sold them all—for cash. To this day, I can count money faster than anyone I know. We had to, in order to close those deals before anyone was caught.

Keep in mind, Iran's currency lost a lot of value after the Revolution, which meant that people would exchange boxes full of cash for big orders of these pads. Sometimes we simply counted stacks, assuming that each stack was made up of a hundred bills, and other times we counted those stacks ten at a time. To put things into perspective: In 1979, one American dollar was equal to 70 rials. Today it takes over 500,000 rials to exchange for one dollar.

The first time we made a huge sale, not long after we first started selling our product in Tehran, my father handed me a giant sack full of money. A sack the size of a fifty-pound rice bag. "Go! Get on the bus and take this home!" he said.

"Why me?" I asked, terrified.

"Because no one will suspect a twelve-year-old of carrying that much money."

He was right. Plus, he was paying me well to work for him. So I didn't question him the next time, or the next, and no one ever looked at me twice.

That's how many Iranians and particularly Baha'is did business then. There was no other way to survive. And it worked.

We soon became the largest manufacturer of cleaning pads in Iran. We sold millions of pads over the next few years. Did that effort make us rich? No. The profit margin was simply too low. But it was definitely an improvement over our previous financial situation, at least for a short period of time.

My mom had been telling me to invent something, and to start my own business. That wasn't something I ever really heard from my dad. But now? Our business was doing so well that one day, on the way home from bazaar, he said, "Payam, when you're old enough and ready to start your professional life, I think you should start your own business."

"Don't work for anyone," he said. "I'm making more money now in a year than in twenty years spent working for the government."

The neighborhood we lived in in Shiraz was close to the shrine of the poet Saadi. We moved there not knowing that a few months earlier, in the very same neighborhood, the residents had burned down the homes of many Baha'i families. (There was no Google then, and no free press. How could we have known?) And while Baha'is were being arrested for various "crimes" in all cities, including Shiraz, we had no idea that a few months before my parents arrived, the authorities had arrested many Baha'is, including arresting and executing ten young Baha'i girls and women for teaching Baha'i children's classes.

The youngest of the ten was named Mona Mahmudnizhad. She was seventeen years old.

On June 24, 1983—eight months after their arrest and torture, a few months before my parents moved there—the Islamic government executed all ten.

On the day of the execution, Mona, the seventeen-year-old with the beautiful smile, whom everyone described as being so full of light, requested to be the last one hanged. She made the request so she could say a prayer for each of the other women as they died.

The guards granted her wish—and Mona will forever be remembered by Baha'is for the bravery and faith she showed in that moment. At the end she kissed the noose and put it around her own neck and she was executed.

The government's officers buried all ten women in unmarked graves outside of Shiraz. They also executed Mona's father. In the months following, the Baha'is would come together to add a tombstone to Mona's grave, and the graves of the other young women, but the government destroyed those, too.

It was truly a sad period. And the news of Baha'is dying at the hands of our country's government kept coming. Hundreds of Baha'is were arrested and killed during those years, the youngest being Mona, the oldest being an eighty-five-year-old man—an elected member of a Local Baha'i Spiritual Assembly.

People often ask, "Why didn't your family just leave?"

It is a simple question that comes with a less-than-simple answer.

For one, this was our homeland. The country we loved. Home not only to our families and our history, but the Faith to which my parents had dedicated their lives. Unlike 99 percent of Iranians, Baha'is view Iran not just as a homeland and the country in which they were born, but as a sacred place that's home to our prophet founder (who was born in Tehran) and his forerunner (who was born in Shiraz). It's also important to note that, in general, Baha'is are unlikely to portray themselves as victims. We feel that we are simply paying a price to make the world a more peaceful place. Sacrifice is needed in order to accomplish that. The unification of humanity will not come easily. So Baha'is are always hopeful about the future, and we as a family remained hopeful, even while enduring the ongoing pain of watching so many Baha'is fall under the leadership of the Islamic regime in Tehran.

Also, our family simply didn't want to leave. Can you imagine being forced to leave your home, your state, your country? Because of a regime change? Those who have been through such a thing know how difficult such a decision truly is. It was not what we wanted, and even if we did, it was difficult to imagine how we could survive such a move. How would we pay for it? How would we escape without being arrested or killed? Even if we made it out, what would we do to survive in an unknown foreign place? It felt as if the only reasonable choice we had was to do our best to carry on and make the most of our lives under the worst of circumstances. What else could we do but try to live our lives to the fullest, and pray that all of this ended peacefully as soon as possible?

Lastly, the war with Iraq was still going on. It was not unusual for people to witness dogfights between military jets in the skies above Shiraz and other cities, sometimes right over our heads. So travel in and out of Iran was difficult for anyone in the 1980s. But that wasn't all. Under the Islamic government's new rules, Baha'is weren't allowed to use or apply for passports, which meant it was illegal for us to travel beyond Iran's border. The government had taken away our very right to leave Iran.

In late 1985, our green-pad business started slowing down. I was only manufacturing the pads a couple of days per week or when we had orders. And to make matters worse, some of the basic ingredients and materials we used to make our product were no longer available, which was causing the quality of our product to deteriorate.

My brother decided it was time for him to try something new. He had long been interested in computers. He most certainly would have studied computer science if he weren't denied access to higher education, as all Baha'is in Iran had been (and continue to be) since 1979. So he handed over the running of the family manufacturing operation to me and a close friend of mine, even while we were busy going to high school. He then invested some of the money he'd made into opening the very first computer shop in Shiraz, selling Commodore 16s and 64s, as well as the early British-made personal computer, the Spectrum 48.

As part of that, he asked me to come on board as his employee at the new shop as well. And I did. It was yet another set of challenges and responsibilities, which I enjoyed. I loved the challenge of being involved in two businesses, and the responsibility of having so much to do.

I know that might seem far-fetched to some readers. As I've learned since becoming a parent myself, most eighth and ninth graders in other countries have a hard time waking up for school in the morning. They aren't responsible for making their own lunches, let alone running one business while working for another, and certainly not while going to school and getting good grades at the same time. All I know is that this was my reality. It's what our family needed to do to survive, and what I needed to do in order to keep going while so many challenges surrounded us.

People also wonder how we managed to go essentially unharmed while so many other Baha'is were jailed, or killed, and so many Iranians were sent to war or killed as a result of the bombings of the cities. I do not have an answer to these questions. Clearly, many Iranians survived, and we did as well. I believe, as all Baha'is believe, that we are put on this planet for a reason, and that each of us is supposed to use our unique skills and individual minds to serve humanity and the planet in a meaningful way. So perhaps destiny had other purposes for each of us that had not yet been fulfilled.

A big part of my job for the computer business was one that my brother no longer felt safe doing himself: traveling to Tehran to purchase computers and software. It simply wasn't safe for someone his age. So, to reduce his risk, he stayed in Shiraz, and I took those business trips to Tehran and back by myself, often flying. That was not a common way people traveled within Iran back then, and because of the war, there were sometimes terrible delays. But Tehran was the only place where we could get those computers.

I knew the city well, and at thirteen and fourteen years old, I was still young enough to move freely throughout the city unharmed. I did so while regularly passing banners hung from buildings with a picture of Ayatollah Khomeini on them that read: "Our leader is that nine-year-old boy who killed himself to destroy a tank." This often accompanied another quote from the Ayatollah that was plastered all over the country: "War is a blessing!"

During this period, the Iranian government had launched a successful volunteer militia called the Basij. This militia enlisted anyone, old or young alike, who wanted to join the fight against Saddam Hussein. These volunteers, including boys as young as nine years old, were to be sent to the front lines to charge at Iraqis in human wave attacks and to clear land mines in suicide missions. Those who fought and died were considered martyrs, hailed for making the ultimate sacrifice as a means of showing their dedication to God.

The war was changing. What was once a necessary defense against Hussein's unjustified attacks was turning into a political tool to be used by the Islamic government.

At times it felt like I was living in two different realities at the same time: one filled with everyday life—going to school, running errands, making money—the other, a world I did not recognize, understand, or want any part of.

I did my best to stay grounded in what felt right to me. And it was not easy. There was little escape from the fear and oppression on all sides.

Even the simple escapes from everyday life that so many of us take for granted were not easily available. The only two channels on television were government-controlled stations full of propaganda and imagery sanctioned by the Islamic regime. Movie theaters, the few that existed, showed only Iranian films. The only radio channel available was run by the government and was used as a propaganda machine as well. The only way to listen to news that was more reliable was to use shortwave radios to pick up broadcasts from outside our own borders.

To make matters worse, music was banned in Iran. Not just Western music. All music, except for Muslim prayer music, or propaganda music that glorified war and the fighting against infidels, particularly against Israel and the U.S.

My cousin Shahram, who was now living in Modesto, California, and going by the name Sean, wrote letters about all of the things that were happening in America in the mid-1980s, including the music that was taking over the airwaves. Madonna and Michael Jackson were huge at the time, and occasionally we'd glimpse certain images of these superstars and/or a bootlegged recording of one of their songs would find its way into somebody's hands and get played in an underground environment, maybe in the back of some store. I and everyone around my age was interested in their music, and we would have loved to listen to their albums, but there was just no way to get our hands on it. Even if Sean tried to mail me a cassette directly from America, I wouldn't receive it. All mail was searched and scanned for illegal contraband, which meant that cassettes coming from America were confiscated before they ever reached our home.

One day, Sean had an idea. Instead of sending me a cassette, he decided to take one of his cassettes apart, roll the tape inside into a single reel, place it in an envelope, and send it to me—just to see if it would make it past the inspectors. And it did!

I received the reel of tape and wound it into a blank cassette shell that I took apart in my bedroom, and when I popped it into the cassette deck, I heard Michael Jackson's *Thriller*. In Shiraz! I cannot tell you how freeing and amazing that music was. Soon after, he sent me some Madonna, and I swear, on some unconscious level, listening to all that American music gave me hope that a better life might exist, somewhere, somehow, in my future.

But joy and hope weren't the only things that music awakened in me.

Our tape deck was a double-deck unit, with the ability to make high-speed copies. And that gave me an idea: What if I made copies of these tapes and sold them at my high school?

I made a few and sold all of them the next day. Word spread, and suddenly everyone at school wanted a tape of their own. So I made some more. Sean sent me more music, and I made and sold more of those bootlegged tapes. Was that a dangerous thing to do? Yes! We were all searched before entering school, and bringing in contraband of any kind was punishable—not by suspension, but by arrest and solitary confinement. But the underground economy in Iran was thriving, and before long, I had a thriving business of my own. I truly do mean "thriving." In terms of buying power in Iran at that time, I was making the equivalent of around $40,000 a year—by the time I was fifteen years old.

That was a very good thing, because the knockoff Scotch-Brite business that had made everything possible for our family was growing tougher and tougher to sustain. Supplies grew difficult to find. Crackdowns on Baha'i-owned businesses kept happening more frequently. And while the computer shop was doing okay—not only by selling computers but by renting Atari games and game consoles to families to enjoy twenty-four hours at a time—every day seemed filled with more and more danger. At any point, that business could get shut down. And at any point, my brother easily could have been arrested and thrown onto the front lines of a war.

It felt like the walls were closing in.

Despite the love we all had for Iran, not only as our home but also as the birthplace of our Faith, my brother began to wonder if there was a future for him there that didn't end with an early death.

In 1986, a lot of other Baha'is had similar thoughts. They were leaving the country in increasing numbers. More and more Western countries were concerned for the safety of Iranian Baha'is—countries that included the U.S. President Ronald Reagan himself spoke out about it, and his administration opened up channels for Iranian Baha'i refugees to gain safe passage to America. Those channels were not easy to navigate. Just finding a way out of Iran was a journey marked by the possibility of being shot at every turn, and even if that journey was successful, it would be followed by all sorts of international red tape—assuming whatever country you escaped to didn't send you back.

I remain in awe of the overwhelming majority of Baha'is who chose to stay. The ones who never gave up and chose to simply continue to exist in post-Revolution Iran. History will certainly remember the sacrifices they made and the impact of their sacrifices on Iran and Iranians of all walks of life.

But after many conversations, my parents and Farhang decided that the life he wanted, the life he deserved, especially the higher education he wanted, just couldn't be found in Iran. Whatever risk he had to take in order to escape and find a better life would be worth the price. Together, they paid the equivalent of $10,000 to smuggle my brother out of the country. It was a challenging thing for my parents and Farhang to find "smugglers." The only illegal thing my family had ever done was to operate a business without a permit at a time when permits were denied to them because of their Faith. Neither my parents nor my brother had ever dealt with people involved in illegal activities such as smuggling. And I can hardly imagine the fear they must have had, to trust that these smugglers would follow through on their word and get their oldest son to safety. But what choice did they have? There was no legal way for my brother to leave Iran. The government made sure of it.

It all happened rather quickly, so quickly that I couldn't quite wrap my mind around the idea that my brother would no longer be there.

In June 1986, my parents handed my brother off to smugglers who promised to get him into Pakistan. For days we waited to hear from him. The agony when no word came is difficult to describe.

But then, a week later, a telegram arrived. My parents unfolded the document and were so relieved to read the contents: He'd made it. He was in Quetta, Pakistan. The journey was very difficult, he said. But he'd made it!

My parents shared the good news with Addy and her husband, and that was all they needed to hear. They had two young children by then, and they were terrified to raise them under the increasingly fearsome leadership of the Islamic Republic. One month later, the four of them escaped to Pakistan, too.

I stayed focused on getting through high school while concentrating on my entrepreneurial hustles. For instance, before he left, my brother told me he was going to sell off the assets of his computer store to help pay for his journey. Knowing that meant the end of me having any sort of employment at his shop, I asked him if I could make copies of all of his software first, and of course he said, "Yes." So I held onto my brother's software, and every time a new computer shop opened, I paid the owners a visit and sold them copies. I made good money. For a teenager, I was rich! And making that business work was nearly as fun as playing Monopoly.

I went out and bought myself a motorcycle. It was really more of a glorified scooter, but still, it was mine. It was faster than walking, and it gave me the freedom to get around Shiraz so much quicker than I ever could before then. I was able to buy myself some new clothes and new shoes. But mostly, I just saved the money I made. I never wanted to lose the security and freedom that came from having some money stashed away.

Yet, no matter how much money I made, I couldn't ignore the fact that there were so many things that money alone could not buy and could not fix. More and more, the life I thought of as "normal" was gone, and it became clearer and clearer every day that that life was never coming back.

I missed my brother. I missed my sister, too, and the togetherness of the family we once had. Sure, we had spent the last two or three years separated by hundreds of miles in Iran. But we still saw each other pretty often. We could travel to Tehran whenever we wanted. Now? We were spread over two different countries, not knowing if we would ever see each other again.

I wanted my family to be together again.

I wanted to be able to live in peace.

I wanted to attend a university once I graduated from high school.

And I was starting to doubt whether any of these things would ever be possible in my country again.

REFLECTIONS ON CHAPTER SIX

When did you first feel the desire (or need) to make money for yourself? What did you hope that your money would buy?

Did you ever have an idea for a new business or an original product? What did you do with that idea? What drove you forward and kept you inspired to make it happen? Or, what stopped you from going after it?

Do you see any holes in the marketplace that need filling right now? A product people need, a type of store or service that's missing from your neighborhood, town, or region? Maybe even the world? Have you thought about what it would take to fill that hole yourself?

If a change in government suddenly caused the world to close in around you, how would you and your family survive? How far would you be willing to go to protect yourself and your children? If that meant smuggling your own children across the border to another country in the hopes of finding something better, would you do it?

CHAPTER SEVEN

THE GREAT ESCAPE

L istening to American music and watching American movies while longing to escape the toll of the seemingly never-ending struggles in our daily lives made me long for something new. I decided I wanted to learn how to play the piano. My brother had bought me a small electronic keyboard during one of his trips to southern Iran before he left, but with no music education in our schools, I didn't have a clue about how to play the thing. So I sought out someone to teach me.

I found a piano teacher right there in Shiraz. He was a Jewish man who taught lessons in the back of his shop, away from view, in a spot where the music couldn't be heard from the street.

I started seeing him once a week, and after about ten lessons he said, "You're not learning anything. What's going on? Are you practicing?"

I told him I was trying, and he asked, "What kind of keyboard are you using? Do you have a picture?"

"No, but I'll bring it here to show you next time."

"Bring it? How small is it?" he asked.

I walked in for my next lesson and pulled the keyboard out of my bag. It couldn't have been more than five inches wide and twenty inches long. It was basically a toy.

"That's not a piano!" the teacher said. "You can't learn on that."

Since full-size keyboards were difficult to find and too expensive to buy, I asked, "Well, what's an inexpensive instrument I could learn instead?"

He convinced me to buy a guitar from him. A used guitar, which was somewhat bent after being stored in a moist area for probably years, so it was even cheaper. And he began teaching me how to play it.

Music was illegal, which means walking down the street with a guitar case slung over my shoulder would have put a great big target on my back. So I didn't do that. I hid the guitar in a big laundry bag and hoped no one would stop me to ask what I was carrying.

Why would I take that big of a risk just to play some guitar? Why did we and so many other families take any of the risks we took in post-Revolution Iran?

Because people cannot live without joy. It's not possible. History shows us again and again that threats of jail or fines imposed by an unjust government, or the threat of attack or bodily harm, or of having your property confiscated or stolen, or even the threat of death itself will not stop people from finding a way to do the things they love, which includes things like playing music.

Eventually, I connected with a family friend who played the mandolin—a guy who used to play with one of the top recording artists in all of Iran before the Revolution. With no exaggeration, the artist he played with was like the Michael Jackson of Iranian music, and it was so much fun to learn songs from him. He taught me the chords to pop songs I liked to listen to, and he was very patient with me. This I know because, honestly, I didn't have the genes to be a musician. My timing was always off. To this day I can barely clap along in time with a crowd at a concert. But regardless, we had fun making music, and we got really close. In many ways he became like an older-brother figure to me, especially with my brother and sister so far away.

This guy was Baha'i, and one day his nephew disappeared. In reality? His nephew was killed at the direction of a Muslim cleric, and when my friend started asking questions about it, he was arrested and accused of being a spy for Israel. (That was often the charge laid on Baha'is, with no evidence or proof whatsoever. It was something the government started using as an excuse to arrest and kill Baha'is once there was some international pressure for them to stop.)

The Revolutionary Guards kept him in solitary confinement, in complete darkness for months, in a cell with three inches of water on the floor at all times.

When he was released from prison, he was never the same.

I think the music we once shared, which lived in his heart, died at the hands of his captors.

It was hard to find joy and keep playing guitar when I no longer had anyone to share it with. I couldn't join a band. I couldn't play music with anyone outside of my home. The experience of it got pretty lonely after a while.

And with my siblings gone, I felt pretty lonely already.

More and more, it felt as if the walls were closing in. On me.

The older I got, and the older I looked, the chances of me being arrested and sent to the front lines grew every day. I realized it was one's duty to serve his country. We had been attacked by Iraq, and our sovereignty as a nation was at stake. But the thought of going to battle was terrifying. And the thought of having to join an army for a government that did not necessarily believe I had a right to live seemed, at best, odd. Still, as Saddam Hussein's bombers targeted more and more cities, killing thousands of civilians, it felt that the war was coming to us.

Meanwhile, the government showed no signs of stopping its aggression toward Baha'is—and when certain individuals at my high school learned that I was Baha'i, I was targeted once again, much like I was back in Hashtgerd. I was continuously beaten up.

The government made strange decisions, for seemingly no reason. For instance, allowing Iranians to play chess and backgammon again after banning all such games for the first half of the 1980s. Why these games were now suddenly not an affront to Islam is anyone's guess, but it showed the unilateralism of the power of the Shia Muslim regime and their sharia law in Iran: The supreme leader decided whatever he wanted to decide. Period.

There was no chance I would be allowed to go to a university. There was no chance of me starting a legitimate business, which meant anything I wanted to do to make money would have to be done in the shadows—and any endeavor that was pursued in such a manner offered little security, as we soon found out.

By the beginning of 1986, our Scotch-Brite knockoff business had been shut down, which meant my dad had to find another way to make money. The business he stumbled into? Socks. He found big wholesalers of socks, and people who were making socks, and shops that needed the inventory, and he quickly became known as the sock guy in the bazaar. You wanted socks? You talked to my dad.

His ability to move on and find a new way to make a living so quickly was admirable. But as I approached my sixteenth birthday, I couldn't help but think, *Is this what my future is gonna be, too? Selling socks, and doing so without a license?*

We received telegrams every few weeks from my brother and sister, who were both in Pakistan and going through the long process of applying for permanent refugee status that might allow them to immigrate to the U.S. They kept encouraging me and my parents to follow in their footsteps.

My parents did not want to go. They felt as if leaving their country was a matter of giving up—a matter of letting the Ayatollah and his cohorts win. They did not want to give up on their country. But six months after Addy left, my parents sat me down and asked me point blank, "Do you want to leave?"

What choice did I truly have? What future possibly existed for me in Iran?

A future without the ability to gain any higher education was bad enough. But what fate was waiting for me in the months and years ahead? Getting arrested and maybe tortured? Facing death in the war? Death at the hands of some mob? Death by decree of the government?

"Yes," I said to my parents. "I mean, I don't want to leave. But what else can I do?"

The thought of putting my fate in the hands of smugglers terrified me. I was still just a teenager. I didn't want to leave my parents and certainly couldn't imagine navigating life in an unfamiliar country without them. I was also scared to leave them behind and potentially never see them again. Just the thought of it made me feel guilty, too, knowing how difficult it would be for them, especially my mom, to say goodbye to their last remaining child.

Just after we had this discussion, the Universal House of Justice issued a statement lovingly advising that Iranian Baha'is not leave the country. Their letter was in line with what my parents felt, that staying put was the best way to show the government that the Baha'is were here to stay. It was important for us to be there to serve the country and its people. So we put any plans for my escape on hold, at least for the time being.

It was during this time when a friend of mine from school, one of my classmates, decided to enlist in the Basij, the voluntary militia set up by Khomeini to aid in fighting the Iran–Iraq War. This friend, like most Iranians, wanted Iran to win what he thought was an aggression by Iraq against Iran. He wanted the war to end, as many of us did, but his primary reason for volunteering was simple: If you volunteered, it would nearly guarantee your acceptance into an Iranian university. We had both heard stories of Basijis, mainly made up of teenagers, being sent to the front lines and used in "human wave attacks"—in which these volunteers would walk forward, side by side, not unlike British forces during the American Revolutionary War, in long straight lines. Human sacrifices to the greater good. But this friend felt it was well worth the risk, for the sake of our country and the sake of his future. After all, he said, many Basijis were given other tasks, working far from the front lines, guarding checkpoints at different spots within the country alongside the Revolutionary Guard, and he was sure he would be given one of those.

He was a wonderful, genuinely nice person. He loved practical jokes. One time he borrowed my jacket, brought it back, and there was a frog in the pocket. That's just the sort of person he was, always laughing and joking around.

He left Shiraz feeling hopeful about his future, and within a month, he was sent back in a body bag.

This wasn't a stranger or a friend of a friend. He was a friend of mine. A classmate who hadn't even turned sixteen yet. Someone just like me. And he was gone.

It was the last straw for me.

I didn't want to wait any longer. I didn't want to meet a similar fate.

My mother took me to Tehran, where we met with another Baha'i family who was already in the process of figuring out how to get their son safely out of the country. For the purposes of this book, I'll remember the son as Omid.

The landscape and the dangers were constantly shifting as the government was cracking down on smugglers, so we weren't able to hire the same people who had helped my brother and sister and her family. But my mother took the lead in figuring it all out. She had always been a person who got things done, and it was so impressive to watch her in action—at a time when she was getting ready to send her youngest child out of the country, knowing there was a very real possibility that we may never see each other again.

As a mother, she was trying her best not just to get me out, but to find a trustworthy smuggler, if such a thing existed.

I honestly don't know how she did it. I don't know if I would have the strength to do the same for my own children. All I know is it took a toll on her. My mother was only fifty-four, and the stress of life in Iran had caused her to look like a much older woman. Her hair was all gray. Her stance was weakened. It made me sad to see the effects on her physical appearance.

But that June of 1987, she found a smuggler who promised to take me safely into Pakistan. She made all the arrangements. We went back home to Shiraz for a few days so I could say goodbye to my father—and I honestly don't remember how that goodbye went. Somewhere in the trauma and surrealness of it all, my mind seems to have blocked out that moment. To have blocked out the sadness of it. To erase the very memory of the look in my father's eye as he sent his youngest son on a journey from which he might never return.

All I remember is that my mother and I went back to Tehran and stayed with a cousin for a couple of days. And on the final night that we were there, a person who represented the smuggler came to visit us and give us our instructions.

My mother wanted to accompany me on the journey for as long as possible, she said, just to make sure I was safe for as long as she could. The smuggler strongly advised against it and thought we should say our goodbyes in Tehran, but my mother insisted. So he agreed my mother could accompany me on the first part of the journey, on the long bus ride to Zahedan, a town close to the border of Pakistan. "But you cannot sit together on the bus," he said. There would be many checkpoints along the way, and we were not to interact, at all, or we would raise suspicion.

He also insisted that, once we reached Zahedan, which was a well-known artery for people escaping the country, I could not hug my mother goodbye.

"Do not touch her, shake her hand, anything. Don't even look at her in any way that could raise suspicion," he said. "Members of the Basij patrol the streets of Zahedan in plain clothing. You won't be able to tell who's who, and they will be looking for people like you."

"Can you do that?" he asked us. "Are you sure?"

My mother and I both agreed, and she handed him the equivalent of about $10,000—trusting that the payment would buy my escape and safe passage.

It was around 5 PM when he left. It was July 4. The night was warm, and it doesn't get dark until late in Tehran at that time of year. So I told my mom, "I'm just going to take a walk."

I strolled the streets of Tehran for the better part of the next five hours, just reminiscing, and thinking, *I will never be back here. To this city I love. This city I know so well.*

I walked by a movie theater and decided to go in. *This is my last chance to see an Iranian film*, I thought. Movie theaters in Iran were an experience. They were busy, and since Iranians like chewing seeds as a snack, the floors were covered with shells that everyone in the audience spit out. Sometimes seeds or shells would hit you in the back of the head.

No one got mad about it; it's just how it was. I sat there in the dark, watching the flickering light make its way through the cigarette smoke and illuminate the screen, knowing I would never have this experience again..

It was getting late, and I knew my mom would be worried. It seems funny to me now, to think that she would be worried I was out until late, when soon she'd be handing me to smugglers on a journey that, if it went as planned, would see me going to a foreign land. But I did not want her to worry more than she already was, so I wandered back to my cousin's home around 10 PM, knowing that every step I took was the last I would ever take in this city.

In the morning, we took a taxi to the bus station. We had to catch an 8 AM bus out of one of the three major bus terminals in Tehran, this one in the southern part of the city, which felt like it took a very long time to drive to. I stared silently out the window the whole ride, looking at the buildings, the streets, the people. It was nothing like the journey we were about to take: twenty-four hours across the Emptiness Desert, to the town of Zahedan, not far from the point where the borders of Iran, Afghanistan, and Pakistan meet.

My mother and I did not sit together on the bus. As the smuggler had instructed us, we did not interact, in order to avoid any suspicion. Omid and his father were there. Omid and I were going to leave the country together, so I sat with him.

Three hours from Tehran, the bus entered Dasht-e Lut—the Emptiness Desert—one of the hottest and driest spots on the planet—a landscape of constantly blowing, shifting salt sands that have more than once reached a surface temperature over 159 degrees Fahrenheit.

If you've ever seen the original *Star Wars*, it looks like the surface of the planet Tatooine.

At times, the bus had to slow down and navigate through areas where the sand had completely covered the road. And every once in a while, the bus would stop completely—for checkpoints, bathrooms, or Islamic prayers, which would sometimes be accompanied by a chance to get something to eat. At checkpoints, members of the Basij or Revolutionary Guard came onto the bus, asked questions, took some people outside, then let them come back up, or not, and the bus would leave again. It was completely nerve-wracking every time we stopped, as we sat silently and tried not to draw any attention to ourselves. The whole idea of check-points and people being taken off public transportation or out of their cars, with or without reason, had become a fact of life in Iran by then. But on this route, it was particularly tense, because this bus was headed toward a border town where unrest was common.

I was wearing long pants, sneakers, and a long-sleeve shirt, because after the Revolution in Iran, men did not wear short sleeves. And all I had with me was a little duffel bag. By little, I mean you could probably have fit two soccer balls in it, and it was half empty. What do you take on a journey when you don't know where you're going, or if you'll ever make it to your destination? What's essential? I didn't know. I didn't bring nail clippers, or toiletries, or any of the things one might take on a vacation. This wasn't a vacation. I didn't know what to take, so all I took was a pair of pants, a couple of shirts, and no personal items at all but a toothbrush. Oh, and some cookies. I didn't know how long the trip would be, what access we would have to food, and whether or not I would be willing to eat the food that was offered (for fear of foodborne illness on the long desert route, and eventually, hopefully, in a foreign land). So I decided to bring cookies, and promised myself I would wait to eat them until I thought I could wait no longer.

I did take some money, which was hidden in different places—in my shoes, sewn into the bag, sewn into the lining of my pants—so even if somebody found some of it, they wouldn't find all of it. I didn't have that much, but in the craziness of leaving, I wasn't thinking straight. Almost all of the money I brought consisted of U.S. $100 bills, which would be diffi-cult to use for any small purchases and would disappear quickly if I tried to buy anything from anyone who wouldn't or couldn't make change.

We finally reached Zahedan around 8 AM the next morning. It looked like something I'd seen in movies from the Old West. All the buildings were khaki colored, covered in sand and dirt, and there were no trees. The bus stop wasn't paved. It was basically a turnout with a shack meant to shield waiting customers from the searing sun. That was it.

When I stepped off the bus, I walked toward the street, just as I had been instructed to do. I hardly looked at my mom, and I definitely did not touch her. I remembered the instructions we had been given, and quietly feared that every other person I saw on the street could be a plain-clothed member of the Basij.

Each step I took felt heavy, as if every inch of distance I put between me and my mother carried me light-years away from the only life I had known, not only from Iran, but from the safety and protection I felt under the watch of my parents. Everything in me wanted to stop, turn back, and go home. But I couldn't. It wasn't the right thing to do. We knew that. We had wrestled with this decision for many months. And stopping now would have raised suspicion anyway, which meant my mother and I could both be arrested. It was too late to change our minds. Too late to turn back now.

As soon as I reached the street, a car stopped. A white Paykan, a relatively new-looking Iranian-made car. The driver looked at me and nodded, and I climbed into the back seat, along with Omid, and as soon as he shut the door the car sped away.

I turned and looked back and saw my mom standing there, just staring at the car, and I could tell that she was crying out loud on the inside but could not show any emotions. We made eye contact for a moment—at least that's how it lives in my memory. The sun on the window was probably too bright for her to be able to see my face inside that car at all. But in my memory, we made eye contact for one brief moment before that car made a left turn, and my mom disappeared behind the buildings of that dusty town. For all I knew, I would never see her again, and I cannot even describe what that felt like—because none of it felt real. It's almost as if my mind and body rejected the idea that such a thing could ever happen.

Instead, I remember thinking how bad I felt for her—that she would have to get back on that bus, in that emotional state, and sit without showing any emotion to anyone for another twenty-four-hour ride back to Tehran, followed by another long trip back to Shiraz. I knew that whatever pain and loss I was feeling was nothing compared to hers. Can you imagine living under a government that would cause so much harm to its citizens that a mother would even consider handing her own children off to a smuggler, in the middle of a desert? What had Iran's cruel government done to make a mother feel that doing that was safer than keeping her youngest with her? (Later on, I heard that my mom got off the bus in Tehran and got lost. In her painful emotional state, she couldn't find her way. She wandered the city. For hours.)

The sadness I felt sunk deep into the pit of my stomach, as I closed my eyes and prayed that my mother would be okay.

Just a few minutes later, the Paykan stopped on the outskirts of Zahedan, at a house with a traditional, walled interior courtyard. The gate opened, we drove inside, and the gate was locked tight behind us. Omid and I were quickly escorted to a room where we were told we would wait until nightfall. Persian rugs covered the floor. There were blankets and pillows neatly piled on top of each other in a corner to be used at night for sleeping, as was the custom in traditional homes. There were no beds. There was no other furniture.

We sat with our backs to the wall, and occasionally the people in the house offered us some food and water. The bathroom was located in the courtyard, and we had to ask permission to use it so they could make sure nobody from the outside was watching.

Inside that bathroom, cockroaches crawled everywhere. Big ones. I counted at least ten as I went, as quickly as I could.

I only asked to use the bathroom once.

Right around sundown, the smugglers brought in another group of escapees: four Jewish girls. The youngest was about my age and the oldest was probably in her early twenties. They were well dressed, and these girls had huge amounts of luggage, big bags filled to the max.

Judaism was a religion officially recognized by the Iranian government. Jews were allowed to travel and carry passports. They had entirely different reasons to secretly escape from Iran than the Baha'is did. Perhaps they were from a wealthy family. If they were stopped at an airport or bus terminal and suspected of leaving the country permanently, there was a good chance that the government would have stopped them and seized all of their assets. I'm not sure for what reason these particular girls were there. I didn't ask.

I just knew, instinctively, that a bigger group meant a bigger risk. Suddenly, and starkly, these girls had raised the stakes.

With nothing much to do in that room, Omid and I made a habit of looking through a high window into the courtyard whenever we heard someone approaching. And in the glow of the setting sun, as the girls rearranged their things, we looked out the window and saw one of our smugglers do his Islamic ablutions and start saying his evening prayer.

From the way he stood and the verses he recited, I realized he was Sunni, as were most people in that part of the country. The fact that our smugglers were Sunni and the Iranian border guards and military were Shia Muslim made this clandestine operation that much more dangerous, too. Our smugglers could have been targeted for any number of reasons above and beyond the illegal job they were doing for us.

For a moment, a knot of fear cinched tight in my stomach.

What if this doesn't work? What if we don't make it?

We were about to illegally cross one of the most dangerous borders in the world. Fear was natural. But the fear isn't what I remember the most. I just remember the sadness.

There was nothing I could do about it. There was no turning back. Even if there were some way I could, I knew that would not have been the right choice.

As darkness set in, one of the smugglers came into our room.

"Come," he said. "Time to go."

He escorted us all outside, where a four-wheel-drive Grand Cherokee pickup truck was waiting. It was raised up higher than a regular one, with big tires. He asked the girls to lie flat in the bed of the truck, where he covered them with a thick tarp. Then he asked Omid and me to sit in the cabin with him and the driver. We were jam-packed into the front bench seat of the pickup as he drove out of the courtyard and onto the highway bound for Pakistan, where he floored it. I couldn't see the speedometer, and it was an old truck, so maybe it felt like we were going faster than we were, but I had never been in a vehicle traveling that fast before.

He was speeding with good reason.

Everyone understood that if we were spotted, we would be instantly identified as smugglers and escapees.

The tension in the truck made it feel like the air around us had thickened.

We were traveling as fast as that truck could go, and I could see a bend in the highway up ahead. A spot where the road turned sharply to the right. This wasn't a broad, four-lane highway. It was a two-lane highway. I wasn't sure the truck would be able to make the turn at that speed, but the driver didn't slow down. At all. We got closer and closer and my whole body tensed up. I dug my fingers around the edge of the seat and held on for dear life, and when we reached the corner, the driver didn't even turn the wheel. He turned off the headlights and kept going straight, right off the road, flying at full speed out into the desert, bouncing over bumps and gullies and rocks with nothing but the light of the moon on the sand to guide our way. We were thrown back and forth in our seats, but he never looked back, and never let up. I could only imagine how terrifying it must have been for the girls lying flat on the truck bed in back, unable to see.

There was no vegetation, anywhere. No lights up ahead or to either side. Just rocks and desert, like the surface of Mars, and the faint black silhouette of a mountain range in the distance, cutting into the dark night sky.

I knew that we were close enough to the border now that if we were spotted, the Guards wouldn't stop us to ask questions; they would shoot our vehicle on sight, most likely with rocket-propelled grenades.

Roadkill. That's the word that kept going through my mind, over and over. Roadkill. We could easily become roadkill. Nobody would know what happened to us. They would blow up our vehicle, bury our bodies in the desert, and our parents would never know. We would just vanish.

We drove on quickly, bumping and bouncing for what must've been an hour and a half, and then, all of a sudden, the driver hit the brakes. We slid to a stop and a man came running up to the driver's side of the truck. I don't know where he came from. Possibly a hole in the ground?

He told the driver that there were Revolutionary Guards in one direction, but not the other, so we sped off in a new direction, careening over the unmarked landscape until we stopped again, and another man came out from nowhere to point us in the best direction again. Then again. At one of the stops, the second smuggler removed the tarp and told us to climb in back with the girls, where Omid and I squeezed in beside them under the cover of darkness, like sardines in a can.

We finally stopped at the edge of an embankment, and the smugglers let us sit up. We all peered into the darkness, and in front of us, a few hundred yards away, ran a highway. From that distance we could see the border guard installations, their official four-wheel-drives patrolling a mile or two stretch from left to right. The guards drove back and forth, almost pacing the road, looking for anything suspicious.

While we sat there, the smugglers told the girls that they had to get rid of most of their luggage to lighten the load for the upcoming portion of the trip. I wondered why they didn't mention that back in Zahedan. Surely, they knew where they were taking us.

At first, the girls refused.

"Then we'll have to leave you here in the desert for a day or two," they told us all, "and we'll come back with more help to carry everything."

No one could survive in that desert for a day or two.

We all knew what they meant.

They would never come back. They would leave us to die.

The girls had no choice. They left most of their belongings behind, knowing that the smugglers would surely come back later and collect the precious things they had carried from home, either to take for themselves or to sell for more profit than they were already making from our desperate situation. Or maybe the things they were carrying were the very reason they were choosing to leave the country in this way in the first place, rather than leaving legally. I would never know.

As we sat near the road, the smugglers waited and watched. They familiarized themselves with the timing of the border patrol. Once they saw an opportunity, they said, "Hold on." They put the truck in neutral and we silently rolled down the embankment and straight across the road.

That's when the second smuggler jumped out and grabbed a broom that was lying beside me. I watched as he swept away the dirt tracks our truck had left on the asphalt. He jumped back in, the driver turned the key, and we sped off into the desert. We all stayed sitting up in the back of the truck at this point, and I didn't see any headlights coming from the road behind us.

We'd made it without being spotted.

Everyone exhaled.

From there, the trackless, rocky terrain started to turn mountainous, and after thirty minutes, we reached a rough and narrow trail that the truck could no longer navigate.

As we climbed out, we saw six beat-up dirt bikes, each with a driver, waiting for us. The six of us got on separate bikes with one tiny bag each latched to the back, and we held on for our lives as we sped off through the hills. Without any headlights, we wove through rocky ravines, deep sand, and salty dry soil, dust filling our noses and mouths. The roar of the motorcycle engines echoed out into the empty desert, hopefully far enough away from anyone to be heard.

Finally, beat up and exhausted from all the pounding on our bodies, we stopped at a rugged, mountainous place where even the bikes could go no farther. There were two more people waiting for us there, in the middle of nowhere, at what must have been sometime after midnight.

"What's happening?" the oldest girl asked.

"From here, we go on foot," they said.

I looked up at the moonlit, steep, nearly sheer wall of the canyon in front of us and thought, *This trip is about to get much harder than I ever imagined.*

The smugglers told us the wall had been created by government bulldozers and dynamite to make it impossible for people to climb.

Clearly, they underestimated just how badly some people wanted to leave.

We had to claw our way on our hands and knees, with loose dirt and rocks tumbling down all around us as we dug in our fingernails and ascended.

We were all young and fit, and we eventually made it to the top, panting and gasping for breath, filthy, but with our hope alive. Squinting into the distance, I saw nothing but bare mountains, stone, and sudden sharp crags pointing up into the night sky. There wasn't a plant or a tree growing anywhere.

"Is this the border?" one of the girls asked.

The smugglers just shook their heads and pointed forward, toward even higher peaks.

"Go," they said. "We must go."

The smugglers hurried us along, never allowing us to stop for rest and only occasionally offering us water from one small jug, which we all shared, from which they insisted we drink sparingly. We used no lights, not even a tiny flashlight, only navigating by the dim glow of the moon.

Somewhere along the narrow passageways, I asked one of the smugglers how much longer we had to go.

"About fifteen minutes," he said in a thick Baluchi accent that I could barely understand.

Thirty minutes passed. I asked him again, "How much farther?"

"Fifteen more minutes," he said.

I kept asking, and we kept walking.

Five hours later, we emerged onto a vast, flat plateau. We were famished, dehydrated, completely drained, and covered in dirt.

As the wind blew across the sand, we collapsed. We all just fell to the ground, on the hot desert floor. Two smugglers, two boys, and four girls, watching the sun rise in front of us, knowing that its heat would soon kill us if we weren't rescued.

I asked one of the smugglers, "Why didn't you tell us we would be hiking for five hours? Why wouldn't you tell me the truth about how much farther we had to go?"

"I had to break the news to you in pieces," he said. "Anyone can hike for fifteen minutes at a time, but if you knew the hike was going to be five hours, the weak would have given up and been left behind to die."

I'm not sure I want to know the story of how he came up with that approach. But it worked.

As we sat there, resting, an hour went by, and the sun rose higher in the sky.

"Why are we just waiting here?" I asked.

"Trucks will come," he said.

"When?"

He didn't answer.

I am going to die here, I thought.

Then I spotted something. Dust rising into the air. In the distance, two vehicles were speeding through the desert.

We all sat up. Soon, we could make out the details of two Toyota pickup trucks headed our way. It wasn't until they were close enough to see through the windshields that I noticed that the steering wheels were located on the right-hand sides of the vehicles, rather than the left.

It was July 7, 1987, and I knew we'd made it to Pakistan.

The drivers pulled up and asked us to get in.

With hardly an ounce of strength left, I stood up, knowing that any one of the smugglers could easily kill me right there for the money I carried and the clothes in my bag, and there wouldn't be anything I could do about it. I couldn't fight. I couldn't run. I had no defenses. I was an illegal immigrant in one of the most treacherous parts of the world, and I was completely at their mercy.

But I also knew I had escaped Iran.

And I prayed that mercy would be shown.

CHAPTER EIGHT

A NEW HOPE

We piled into those two Pakistani pickup trucks as if they were lifeboats—Omid and I in one truck, the girls in the other. And the smugglers drove us away across a roadless, trackless, somehow hauntingly beautiful desert.

The landscape here was different than it was on the other side of the mountains. No rocks or gullies. Just a vast expanse of sand as far as the eye could see, relieved by nothing but blowing dust and the increasingly distant mountains behind us. If you've ever seen *Lawrence of Arabia,* or *Indiana Jones and the Temple of Doom,* or anything set in the Sahara, you can probably visualize what it looked like.

The metal bed of the truck was scorching hot, yet even with the dust filling my nose and the sun piercing my skin, I was relieved to be moving again—and not on foot. I felt the hot wind on my face and silently wondered where these smugglers were taking us, and what would happen next.

I knew anything could happen, but I wasn't prepared at all for the sight that appeared in front of us about an hour into the trip: a fort, perched right in the middle of the Pakistani desert.

Like a mirage or a film set, it looked like something out of a different century—maybe because it was from a different century—with high walls reaching twenty-five feet into the air, a turret on top (like you'd see on a castle), and huge wooden gates, which were opened just for us. Yet outside, as we were driving in, I noticed a metal Coca-Cola sign, faded and pockmarked by years of blowing sand, its metal hooks screeching and screeching as it rocked back and forth in the wind.

Inside, there were people going about their business, taking hardly any notice of us. They were washing clothes, and I don't even know what else. But the fort featured two stories of rooms facing the center, and they all had metal bars on the front, like jail cells. I have no idea who owned it, why it was there, or what its purpose was, but the smuggler put Omid and me into one of these cell-like rooms and said, "Wait."

The girls were nowhere to be seen. They must have taken them somewhere else.

I hoped they were okay.

At one point, someone brought us some food. It didn't look clean to me, and I couldn't risk getting sick, so I politely said, "No thank you." I think the person understood Farsi because he turned and walked away with a shrug. I then proceeded to eat the cookies I had stashed in my bag.

I assumed our journey was near its end, so I ate every one of them.

It was the first thing I had eaten since leaving the hideout in Zahedan.

Nearly five hours later, the driver of our truck came and told us it was time to go. He walked us through the gates, where a bus was just pulling up in front of the fort. It didn't look to me like there was even a road there, and I wondered how such a rickety old bus could make it through the middle of the desert. And why?

The bus was built of wood over a metal frame. It belched black smoke from its tailpipe, and it was full of people, and baggage, and rugs, and tools, and chickens, and goats, and what seemed to me like all sorts of illegal contraband. It was so packed full of people that some were standing, and some were even sitting on the roof as it pulled to a stop.

I noticed there were no women on board. Only men.

A few of them got off and took their things as our driver explained he would be right behind us, watching out for us the whole way. "It's safer for you to be on the bus," he said, "because you're in Pakistan now, and you're illegal."

"Where are we headed? Is it far?"

"Less than twenty-four hours," he said. "Now go. Go!"

Omid and I were able to find seats on one of the hard wooden benches, engulfed by the smells of farm animals, cigarettes, and body odor. I still didn't know where we were going. The driver never fully answered my questions. But I stuck my head out the window and looked back as we drove away, and sure enough, the Toyota was following close behind us.

The road this bus drove along was not much more than an unmaintained path of old tire marks compressed in the sand, and the bus moved so slowly that I could've jumped off, jogged along beside it, and hopped back on at any point on the journey.

Still, it was better than walking.

After traveling all afternoon and all through the night, the bus came to a halt just after sunrise.

There was a lot of commotion. Finally, someone came on board and told us that the Pakistani police had set up a checkpoint a few miles ahead.

"They will search this bus for anything illegal—including people," he said.

A whole bunch of passengers, mostly Afghans, stood up, grabbed whatever they had, and climbed off the bus as fast as they could. We felt we had no choice but to follow. After all, we were the "illegal people" the man was talking about.

They all started walking in one direction, toward the mountain range, as if they had done this before. *How do they know which direction to go?* I wondered. *Why are these Afghans even here?* I would later learn that this route was part of the largest drug trade in the region, moving heroin from Afghanistan through Pakistan and out to the rest of the world. So I suppose that was a good enough reason for some of those folks to not want to be searched.

Our smuggler parked his truck and told us to go with the group, which looked to be a total of about twenty men.

"Cross over the mountain range and the bus will pick you up on the other side," he said.

"How far is it?" I asked.

"It'll take you about five hours, but there's no other way," he insisted. "Go. Stay with the group," he said. "And be careful. It's going to get hot."

Five hours. Again, five hours. I wish he had told me it was only fifteen minutes!

I had no choice but to go. I knew that if the police found us, they would immediately arrest us and send us back to Iran—where the criminal penalty for illegally leaving the country could have been execution.

I didn't want to think about it. If I had focused on the worst possible outcome at any point during this journey, there is no way I could have made it. I had to think about my future and remind myself that I had little hope for a positive future in Iran. There was no point in worrying about what might happen if my escape didn't work. It had to work. I had to stay optimistic. One foot in front of the other.

After about an hour, we came to a small stream. The water was muddy and murky, but everyone bent down and started drinking. They asked me to do the same. We didn't speak the same language, but there were enough similarities between our languages that I understood what they were saying. And I refused. They promised that I would be sorry for not listening to their advice, but the water was not clean. I was sure of it. I didn't want to get sick.

I should have listened. With every passing minute of that hike, the temperature went up.

At first, I perspired profusely, soaking through my clothes, but after an hour or so my clothes dried out and my sweat glands closed up. Three hours in, every step made me weaker. I could feel myself faltering. My lips dried up and cracked. My head ached. My feet felt like fire. I started falling behind the group. Dizzy and fatigued, I realized that I was about to collapse.

Collapsing would have equaled death. No one could have or would have carried me. We were traveling as a group, but within that group, each one of us was fighting for our own lives.

Just as I was about to fall over, when I felt I couldn't take another step, I saw a small oasis on the side of the rocky mountain. There was one tree, the size of an average apple tree, with water sitting under it. I don't know where the water had come from, or why it had not evaporated in that hot sun, but I walked to it. I practically crawled the final steps. I lay down flat on the ground and put my mouth in the three-inch-deep water. That water was full of worms and bugs and all kinds of other moving stuff, but I didn't care. I drank as much as I could, and I don't think anything has ever tasted better to me in my entire life.

I don't believe in miracles, but I don't know how else to explain the existence of that oasis. I don't recall whether anyone else stopped to drink from that pool at the bottom of the tree. The thing is, I don't know if that actually happened to me or if it was some sort of hallucination. Either way, I managed to stand up after taking that drink, and hike for another two hours.

At that point, we came to a spring where pure, clean water flowed from inside the mountain, and everyone stopped to drink. And though we didn't speak the same language, the smile on everyone's face after drinking our fill marked a shared sense of accomplishment that I would never forget.

It was only a short walk from that spring to the spot where the old rickety bus was waiting for us as promised.

We drove on from there, into the night, spotting only a few other cars the entire time we were on the road—until the bus came to a stop again. This time, there must have been forty cars in front of us and to the sides. A pileup. There was apparently a battle up ahead, one in which government forces were trying to search whatever the smugglers in front of us were smuggling. All of a sudden, all of these guns came out on our bus! A whole group of Pakistanis and Afghans got out and ran ahead to fight. One of them who spoke Farsi asked, "Do you want to join us?"

"Nah, we're good," we said. "We'll just wait here."

The battle went on for a couple of hours. One of the men came back with a wounded leg. But the people in nearby villages, which we could not see, were apparently very friendly with the smugglers. The smugglers treated them well, and they were good to them in return. So a few of them came out and brought us a big dish of rice to share. It smelled of smoke, like it had been cooked over an open fire, and everyone dug their hands into this one big dish.

It was the only food I'd eaten since the cookies, and I was grateful for every bite.

Before long, we were on our way again, with no interruptions for another few hours—until we were stopped at a checkpoint with no warning. This checkpoint was different. They didn't seem concerned with the Afghans, and the Afghans didn't seem concerned with them. But one of the guards came on board and started asking me and the other boy questions in Urdu. Neither one of us understood what he was saying, which made him angry. He ordered us to stand up, and he forced us off the bus. He took us into the police station—and the bus drove away without us.

I tried to stay calm and hope for the best. What else could I do?

You can't allow fear to consume you in the middle of the journey. I think of soldiers on the battlefield and have often wondered if they're actively worried about dying while others are falling around them. Being in this situation, being smuggled out of one country and illegally entering another, knowing that I could be sent back and executed, I think my answer to that question is "No." Once you're in it, you cannot help but mentally prepare for the worst, and once you do that, the meaning of "danger" and our sense of worry changes. Dramatically.

Instead of worrying, you just do the next thing. And the next.

One foot in front of the other.

Fifteen minutes at a time.

At first, they told us to sit on a bench, under the watchful eye of a soldier who kept his gun pointed at us the whole time to make sure we wouldn't run. Where would we run to? I thought. After a while, I asked if I could go to the bathroom. I didn't have the right words, so I just sort of gestured until the soldier understood. He pointed me in the right direction and let me go. I found that interesting. He didn't follow me to the bathroom. He didn't make any sort of a verbal threat. I think he probably came to the same conclusion I had: Where would we run to?

Or maybe he already knew what was going to happen next.

When I came out of the bathroom, our smuggler was there.

"Let's go," he said.

"What?" I asked. "How?"

"I took care of it," he said. "Come on."

We climbed into the front seat of the truck with him, and he explained that all the policemen wanted from us was a bribe. He had paid it. That was that.

He drove quickly and caught up to the bus. He flashed his lights, and the bus pulled over so we could get on again. From there, we rode on the same hard wooden bench, on the slowest bus on Earth, until we finally arrived at a bus station in Quetta sometime early the next morning.

What we had been told would take less than a day was almost three full days in total.

I had to go to the bathroom again and wished I hadn't: That bus station was the dirtiest place I had ever seen, times ten. The bathroom was basically a shack with a hole in the ground, through which the deposits of many years of usage were all piled up. Imagine a bus stop bathroom in any major city. Now, imagine if that bus stop had never been cleaned. Ever. That's how filthy this bathroom was.

Our smuggler took us from there to a motel, which looked about as well maintained and full of unsavory characters as the bus, only without wheels. He walked us inside, right up to the front desk, where he told the manager, "They're Baha'is from Iran."

The manager nodded, and the smuggler turned to us and said, "My job is over. Good luck," and he turned and left.

The manager took us to a room and said, "Don't come out. Don't ever come out. Lock the door from inside."

He closed the door, we locked it, and we collapsed. There was only one small bed. There were cockroaches scrambling across the floor. It didn't matter. We were safe. We were out of the sun. We could rest.

As the constant pressure and tension of the journey slowly released from our bodies, the room itself came into focus, and we realized that there were notes carved into the walls all around us.

Notes from other Baha'is who had made this journey before us. The words of survivors, like me and my traveling companion who were about to start our lives anew away from the oppression and hatred that had held us down for so long.

My experience, which had seemed so strange, so difficult, so impossibly hard, and at times just surreal, had been repeated many times over. A river of Baha'i refugees was flowing out of Iran, and this motel was a safe, sandy shore.

As we were reading those notes, the manager came back and told us that we could make one phone call each.

My brother and sister were living in Lahore, on the other side of Pakistan near the Indian border. They didn't have a phone of their own, but their landlord did. They had sent the number to my parents via telegram before I left, and I carried that number with me through the desert and over the mountains. I could not wait to make that call.

I reached their landlord and asked him to call my siblings so I could speak with them, and he did. It was so good to hear their voices, and they were so relieved to hear mine. I asked them to send a telegram to our parents to let them know that I had arrived safely in Quetta, and they promised they would. And they told me how much they looked forward to seeing me as soon as I could arrange to catch the train to Lahore.

The manager then let me use the washroom—the single, shared shower that was available to guests in the entire motel.

I wasn't even sure how many days had passed. Was it five? Six? I had not changed my clothing in all that time—not since leaving Tehran. I hadn't eaten anything but a few cookies and some rice. I'd been through hell. I mean, I was as dirty as anyone can ever be. Stepping into that shower and letting the water run over me, watching the coating on my skin turn into mud as it streamed from my body and ran down the drain, was maybe the best feeling I had ever felt. I put on my one change of clothes and stuffed my dirty clothes into my duffel bag, and even after all I had been through, that was all it took for me to feel renewed and ready to tackle the world.

I had no idea how it was possible for a body to recover so quickly after going through so much—after consuming maybe three hundred calories total in the course of five days.

But it can. And it does.

No matter how difficult the journey, and how big a toll it may take, it is possible—and maybe even inevitable—that we come out the other side feeling renewed. That is the power of the human spirit and our ability to adapt and overcome challenges, at least for a finite period of time. Survival is a primal instinct, and our ability to overcome is immense—somehow larger than we ever know, until we're faced with no other choice.

That afternoon, I had one small meal of yogurt and bread. And I felt full.

The next day, a member of the Local Spiritual Assembly of the Baha'is of Quetta showed up. He told us that we would be staying in that room for one week. He said we could not leave the room unless we were escorted by a member of the Assembly. He also gave us some Pakistani clothing, the long, traditional clothes that Pakistanis wear.

"I will come back here tomorrow," he told us, "and I will take you to the UN office."

We ate twice that day: yogurt and bread, with the addition of some rice. We were told we would be fed the same twice a day while we were at the hotel, and that was more than enough for me. I was perfectly happy just to have enough food to survive.

It was odd to be trapped inside a locked room. From the small and partially blocked window, we could see the hustle and bustle of sidewalks and streets full of people. It was difficult to just sit there and not go stir-crazy. But the two of us had listened and obeyed at every step of the way, and we had made it. We were alive. We were in touch with our families. Whatever we had to do to get through this final stage of the journey was worth it.

The next day, dressed in our Pakistani clothes, Omid and I were taken to the local office of the United Nations High Commissioner for Refugees (UNHCR). It was a temporary outpost, set up to handle the enormous influx of refugees not only from Iran, but also from Afghanistan, which was occupied by the Soviet Union during this time.

While we were waiting in line to speak to an official, who did we run into but the four Jewish girls who had joined us during the first half of our journey. They looked cleaner now, and we looked cleaner, and even though we hadn't had much of a chance to get to know them through talking at any point during this whole experience, it was as if we knew them well. We had been through the most amazing and harrowing journey of our lives together. We hugged each other. We said how glad we were to see each other.

"We're the lucky ones," the oldest girl said, and we all knew exactly what she meant. By then, we had all learned of people whose journeys out of Iran hadn't ended as well as our own. We all had friends and family who were left behind in Iran, and many of them were in danger.

At certain times, after certain events, be they tragedies, traumas, or even shared moments of awe and joy, there's a feeling of human connection that exceeds anything that can be put into words, a connection that crosses all borders, all religions, all nationalities, all beliefs. It doesn't even have to be spoken to be shared.

I wonder sometimes why it's so hard to recognize that connection in our daily lives. Why do we have to wait for such extreme circumstances to arise in order to recognize what's real?

The girls were already on their way out, onto a new life in Israel. Jewish Iranians were granted easy and quick access to resettlement in Israel, if that's what they wanted. So they were processed and they had to go. We hugged them goodbye, and just like that, they were gone. We never saw them again.

Finally, after responding to questions and filling out some paperwork ourselves, a UN officer gave us each a paper that granted us temporary asylum in Pakistan.

"How long is temporary?" I asked.

"Basically, until your case is proven and approved," she said.

All they needed to prove was that we were, in fact, Baha'is. Since Baha'is choose to be Baha'is (or not) at the age of fifteen or older, there was actually a registration process we'd gone through with our local Assemblies. After the Iranian Revolution, the records of Iranian Baha'is were sent out of the country for safekeeping. The UN would now need to reach out to Baha'i organizations outside of Iran to confirm that our names had been registered—a process that could take many months. But once that confirmation was attained, we would be granted permanent refugee status and could apply for asylum in a country of our choosing—or at least out of those countries that were open to accepting Baha'i refugees. In the meantime, this piece of paper he handed me meant I would be free to stay in Pakistan without getting arrested.

Of course, the letter of the law and the execution of the law are two different things, as they often are for minority populations almost everywhere. We were warned by other Baha'is that the police in Pakistan wouldn't always honor a person's UN refugee status, so we should keep out of trouble and avoid any sort of confrontations with the Pakistani police if possible.

Compared to the pressure we had been under to avoid being spotted during our escape, that warning seemed fairly easy to heed.

After a week spent in the motel and getting the rest of our affairs in order with the help of the Local Spiritual Assembly, we went to the train station to embark on the next part of our journey: a trip across the entire length of Pakistan, from the westernmost side to the easternmost side, near the Indian border, all the way to the town of Lahore, close to Kashmir. That trip would take another twenty-four hours, on a train that, much like the bus, was overcrowded with passengers—a train that would go so slow it felt as if you could hop on and off it without getting hurt, which made stops in just about every town along the way.

To help ensure our safety, the Local Spiritual Assembly, or LSA, had facilitated the purchasing of tickets for the two of us, along with two other Baha'i refugees who had been staying at the hotel, to travel in a private cabin. That's not as luxurious as it sounds. There was no air-conditioning, and by the time we neared the end of our twenty-four-hour train ride, the white Pakistani clothing I was wearing had turned yellow from the dust and dirt blowing in through the window.

Finally, we were almost there. I was so excited to see my brother and my sister and her family. I could hardly believe this part of my long journey out of Iran was almost over.

The train made a stop, just one station before Lahore—and all of a sudden there was a knock on our cabin door.

What now, I thought.

The door opened—and it was my brother.

With only one train per day coming from that part of the country, he had figured out when I was arriving and had gone ahead to the station before Lahore to surprise me. It was one of the biggest shocks and surprises of my life.

More than a year had passed since I'd seen him. He was much thinner. He told me he had survived a bout of malaria during our time apart. From the stories my dad told me of his work with the health department in the 1970s in Iran, I knew how awful malaria could be. My brother seemed very weak, and he looked, for lack of a better word, like a refugee.

But he was alive. So was I. And we were together.

My journey out of Iran wasn't quite finished. Many months of waiting and worrying lay ahead. And there was always the fear that something could fall through or go wrong, or that something terrible might happen to our parents, who were still refusing to leave Iran.

But in my brother, who showed up out of the blue to surprise me on the very last leg of my train trip through Pakistan, I caught a glimmer of hope.

A new hope. For an entirely new life.

REFLECTIONS ON CHAPTERS SEVEN AND EIGHT

What would it take for you to begin the journey toward something better for your life?

Have you ever said goodbye to your parents or loved ones for an extended period of time? What was it that pushed you to take that difficult journey? Was it by choice? Was it by necessity? Do you regret taking that step, or was it one of the best things you've ever done? (It is entirely possible that it's both.)

When you think about where you are in your life today, did you ever think it would be this hard to get here? If you had known how difficult the journey would be, would you have taken the same road, or tried some other way?

We've all overcome obstacles and difficulties, large and small, to get to where we are. Does knowing that you've overcome difficulties in your past make it less scary to think about overcoming them in the future? In other words: Do you draw strength and confidence from the accomplishments you've made on your own personal journey so far? And if not, why?

"Suffering is both a reminder and a guide. It stimulates us better to adapt ourselves to our environmental conditions, and thus leads the way to self-improvement. In every suffering, one can find meaning and wisdom."
—Shoghi Effendi

CHAPTER NINE

CHOOSING HOPE

When my brother and I met the Nasdaq president, he handed each of us a small glass globe featuring the Nasdaq logo alongside our AutoWeb logo—like little trophies we could place on our desks to mark the occasion. Our new CEO was ushered from there into an interview with CNBC and other financial news programs, and a few other meetings, followed by more celebratory events, while my brother and I picked up our luggage from the hotel and were chauffeured to JFK.

It wasn't until we settled into our cushy, first-class seats on the plane that I opened a copy of the Wall Street Journal and noticed the headline: "AutoWeb Worth More Than Rolls-Royce."

I showed the article to my brother and we both smiled.

The headline was based on the share price we had set the night before the launch. Not our opening price, which was nearly double, or our closing price, which was nearly 50 percent higher than that. People would ask how such a thing could be possible, but we knew: AutoWeb represented the future. Something bigger than just one company. We were disrupting and changing one of the biggest industries on the planet. Our valuation represented what was possible.

We had expected a successful IPO, but as we sat there figuring out what our combined 40 percent personal stake in AutoWeb was worth at the end of the day, we came to an amusing conclusion: "Together, we can afford to buy this airline."

After we landed in San Francisco, I climbed into another black car to be chauffeured back down to earth—back to my humble house in the Bay Area. The driver had NPR on the radio, and a commentator was talking about this successful IPO and how it was the most-traded stock ever in a single day.

He was talking about AutoWeb.

We weren't just big news to the business press in New York. We were big news everywhere.

And yet, I didn't think things would change much for me. At least not anytime soon.

Though I'd been pushed out as CEO, I was still a member of the board and AutoWeb's management team, which meant that I wouldn't be allowed to sell any of my shares for quite some time. I was excited and happy about our big day, sure, but I didn't feel rich. I was only rich on paper. We had a business to run. We were still small and scrappy. We had so much work to do, and so many things left to figure out. It had been an amazing experience to witness our IPO, for sure, but I was ready to get some sleep and get back to work—and I was already imagining the progress we could make by putting the proceeds from the IPO to work.

Our IPO day gave us much more than a valuation, a stock price, and some notoriety: We had raised $85 million in cash for the company. It felt great knowing that we now had the capital we needed to build AutoWeb into something truly amazing—to disrupt the industry on a massive scale and fulfill all of the potential that my brother and I, and Wall Street, and our employees and clients, all saw in this company.

The next morning, before I left for the office, I got a call from Credit Suisse: "We want you to know that you now have access to a $4 million credit line. It's available to you for any reason, whatever you want, at any time."

I guess it was naïve of me to think my life wouldn't change. In reality, everything had changed.

It is amazing to think how drastically our lives can change entirely, from top to bottom, in a matter of hours, days, or weeks. We forget this sometimes, imagining that things are "just the way they are," or being lulled into routines, when in fact, the only constant in life is change itself. Whether changed by choice or changed by circumstance, there is always the possibility that tomorrow our lives will be entirely different than they are today, and there are really only two ways to approach this possibility: with fear or with hope.

Looking back, I think the one thing that allowed me to survive and thrive through so many unexpected changes in my life is simple: I chose hope.

After sixteen years spent as an Iranian citizen, protected and cared for by my parents, all it took was one decision and a difficult five-day journey to throw me, helpless, into the arms of the world. I was now a young man without a country, completely at the mercy of the patience of our Pakistani hosts, the efforts of the UN, and the love and support of my fellow Baha'is.

When I first arrived in Lahore, my brother, our sister, her husband, their two children, and I all lived together in an area called Gulberg—the six of us in one small room on the second floor of a house filled with other Baha'i refugees. Soon, we were able to improve our situation a little bit when one of the other refugee families left for their new country, allowing my sister's family to live in the original room as a family while my brother and I bunked in the room that had just become available next door. At one point, there were about fifteen of us Baha'is all living on the second floor, spread across four bedrooms, sharing one kitchen and one balcony. The bedroom my brother and I were in was between the other bedrooms, like a hallway that connected our shared patio to the stairs that would take us downstairs in and out of the floor, which meant we had no privacy. But we made the best of it.

We couldn't hold jobs. We couldn't go to school. All we could do was wait for our permanent refugee status to be granted so we could apply for asylum in another country—and then, in many of those countries, we would only be allowed to enter if there were citizens willing to sponsor us.

There were about a thousand Baha'i refugees in Lahore, and a majority of those I met were ready and willing to accept asylum wherever they could find a sponsor. Me? I had my heart set on going to the U.S., and waiting on news about my status from the UN was agonizing.

Thankfully, there were lots of Baha'is our age in Lahore, and lots of families, too. And overall there was a relative sense of safety. Not all Pakistanis liked the fact that we were there, of course, but we didn't face the sorts of daily threats that we did in Iran, and certainly not the type of government-sanctioned hatred that we had endured at home.

Home. That word weighed heavy. I didn't have a home anymore.

None of us did.

I was happy to be back with my brother and sister, but the fact that our parents had stayed behind grew more worrisome with every passing day. We sent them telegrams and practically begged them to join us. But they refused.

They wanted to stay where they were, to be of service to Iran.

While we waited—and worried—we were lucky enough to have access to two different Baha'i centers in town with plenty to do to keep us busy. There were also centers we could visit that were run by the Germans, the British, and the Americans—all of them offering language classes and more to help ease our transitions. I preferred the American center, not only because that's the country where I was set on relocating, but because it was nicer than the others. It had air-conditioning. They held movie nights. They had all sorts of books available for us to read, and I enjoyed going there right from the start. Interestingly enough, they were open to us, but not to Pakistanis. I think it's because some of the books and movies they offered had potentially R-rated stuff in them, and they weren't about to offer those "corrupting" influences to local citizens. But we were foreigners, so they didn't have to follow the same rules with us.

One interesting experience in Lahore was going to the movies. The theaters were filled with mostly men, and the movies were heavily censored. When a woman would show up on-screen, the audience would go crazy, clapping, stomping, and making "whoop" noises. I saw a James Bond film that year, *The Living Daylights*, and you should have heard the noise when one of those Bond girls showed up on the screen!

I supposed I should have spent most of my time in Lahore learning English, but instead, I played a lot of cards, and from time to time I played with a Ouija board with some friends. It was a homemade board, but still, we ended up having a few unexplainable experiences, which I won't get into.

From one of our housemates, I learned how to use a hand saw and surgical knife to carve wood into a miniature version of what is often called the Lotus Temple—a beautiful Baha'i temple in India that is world-renowned for its architectural significance. I was able to sell those carvings as souvenirs to other Baha'is who were on their way to their new host countries. It was the only entrepreneurial endeavor I attempted during my time in Pakistan.

About seven months after my arrival, in early 1988, my sister and her family received acceptance from the U.S., along with sponsorship from a Local Baha'i Spiritual Assembly on the island of Petersburg, Alaska. It wasn't exactly where my sister and her family had dreamed of moving, but it was in the U.S. They were ready to leave. They were ready to set down roots and stop living in the in-between. So they moved from one of the warmest places on the planet to one of the coldest, in February, during the time of year when it stays dark in that part of Alaska nearly twenty-four hours a day.

They didn't write back with complaints, though. They wrote back to tell us what a great experience they had. It wasn't just the Baha'is who welcomed them, they said. The whole town welcomed them. The whole island welcomed them!

They were happy. They were free. They felt they were finally making progress in life. And they were praying for us to make our way to the U.S. as soon as we could.

My brother and I were able to move into their old room, which finally gave us more space—even though we were still sharing a room. But what's amazing to me is that my brother could have left Pakistan around the same time as our sister. He had already been there a year and a half. His permanent refugee status was set, and he already had sponsors lined up as well, from the Local Spiritual Assembly of the Baha'is of Kake, Alaska. But my brother refused to go. Instead, he added me as his underage sibling on his own application, so we wouldn't be separated again. That caused him to be stuck in Pakistan longer than he would have been if he had simply gone alone, but it also moved the process along a little faster for me, for which I was grateful.

My permanent refugee status came through just before my sister left for the U.S., and it was now time for me to get my immigration status figured out. So I traveled to the American Embassy in the city of Islamabad, where I was greeted at the door by a U.S. Marine.

"Why are you here?" he asked.

"I wanna go to the U.S.," I said in my very limited English, thinking to myself, *Yeah, you and everybody else.*

To my surprise, without hesitation, he invited me to step inside.

This was the Ronald Reagan era, so the mood toward me and my fellow Baha'i refugees was welcoming. All I had to tell them was, "I'm a Baha'i, and a refugee—here's my paperwork," and the U.S. Embassy immediately got me a lawyer, an American lawyer, at no cost to me, to help me complete my case to be presented to the ambassador.

At this point, my cousin Sean, who had been in America for a few years and had become a U.S. citizen, stepped up and offered to sponsor my brother and me so we could immigrate to his new hometown, where my aunt and uncle also lived, in Modesto, California.

A couple of months and a whole bunch of paperwork later, I went for my interview at the embassy, and they said, "Okay, as a refugee escaping religious persecution you are officially being offered permanent residency

by the United States, which means after five years you will have the opportunity to become a U.S. citizen."

I get emotional thinking back on it, because that was the first time
I had experienced human rights in my life. What an incredible feeling.
I mean, this country that I had read about, and admired, and dreamed
about—this country agreed to take me in, a teenager who was driven out
of his own country. I threw myself at the mercy of the world, and the U.S.
said, "Yeah, we'll take you in, we'll support you, we'll give you a chance
at a new life."

In the Baha'i Faith, it is prophesized that America has a spiritual destiny. It is America that will ultimately lead humankind to a higher state,
as it will grow beyond material riches and spread the spiritual message the
world badly needs.

Abdu'l-Baha himself prayed for America during his visit to Chicago
in 1912: "O God! Let this American democracy become glorious in spiritual degrees, even as it has aspired to material degrees, and render this just
government victorious. Confirm this revered nation to upraise the standard of the oneness of humanity, to promulgate the Most Great Peace, to
become thereby the most glorious and praiseworthy among all the nations
of the world. O God! This American nation is worthy of Thy favors and is
deserving of Thy mercy. Make it precious and near to Thee through Thy
bounty and bestowal."

The fate of this country is intimately intertwined with what Baha'is
believe is the ultimate destiny of the peace and oneness of humankind.

Baha'is believe that in order for this country to live up to its potential, it will have to experience challenges and struggles. Just like people,
countries also become a better version of themselves as they are chastened
through their tests and difficulties. So the destiny of America will be found
in its ability to make it through the fire, because it has the potential, the
foundation, the roots, the spirit, and the ability to dream a better future
that will ultimately guide humanity through the challenges we will face
along the way.

The U.S. already serves as a beacon of hope to people all over the
world, and I experienced one of the reasons why firsthand: This country

took me in. To take me and all of the refugees that the U.S. takes in requires a deep-rooted level of goodness. A goodness that exists at its core, even during periods of political unrest and division.

The offer of permanent residency was just the beginning of the goodness I experienced.

One thing the U.S. Embassy did not provide was funding for our flights to America. So, once again, we were at the mercy of the world—and a group of Americans were the ones who came through for us. A nonprofit organization called Catholic Charities, based in New York, paid for our flights. I never met a representative from their organization, and we didn't have to jump through hoops or fill out a million forms or promise anything in return for their generosity. They had simply set up a program to help Iranian Baha'is on their journeys, and that funding was there waiting for us as soon as we cleared our immigration status with the embassy. The only thing they asked in return was that someday we pay them back, when and if we were able, so they can continue their support of refugees in the future.

It's difficult to explain just how much that gesture affected me.

It was an affirmation of a generosity that exists in the world, and especially in the U.S., that rises above and beyond any of the difficulties or challenges we face. It was a gift, not made because of a religious affiliation or a political belief or anything else, but one given freely to support the dignity and human rights of a persecuted people from a far-off land. It was an expression of faith in action. How beautiful is that?

As our travel date approached in that late spring of 1988, there was really only one thing that weighed heavy on my heart: my parents.

My brother and I made one last plea. "We're going to America! All of your children are now going to the U.S. Please, come join us," we begged.

My father, especially, struggled with the idea of "giving up"—as if choosing to leave Iran was personally letting the Islamic Republic government "win." But once he knew that all three of his children, as well as his grandchildren, were going to live in the U.S., he finally saw things differently. My parents prayed together and agreed that the best way they could continue to offer service to the world was not to stay in a country that was holding them down, but to join their family in the land of the free—to offer up service in the U.S.

In the weeks before my brother and I were set to leave Pakistan, my parents sold everything they owned and decided to follow in the footsteps of their children. Out of the past, and into the future—both leaving their elderly moms and siblings behind in Iran. They did so knowing they would never see them again. They would not even be able to attend the funerals of their moms or siblings in the years ahead.

At first it was difficult for me to imagine how my parents could possibly make the trip—not only emotionally, but physically—in the back of trucks, up steep climbs, on motorcycles, and then on foot, for five-hour treks through the mountains and the scorching desert heat. But I also knew the challenges both of them had endured before I was born, which meant that, deep down, I believed that they could do anything.

It had been ten months since we'd seen each other, and nearly two years since they had seen my brother. Their drive to get to us and the power of their faith would carry them through.

In May 1988, they let us know the day they were leaving, and since we both knew how long the journey took, we anxiously awaited their phone call from the hotel in Quetta. On the fifth day, we were on pins and needles, so anxious to hear from them that we stayed close to the landlord's phone just waiting for their call. But the call never came. There was no telegram. Nothing. We were helpless, with no one to reach out to.

A sixth day passed. No call.

A seventh.

My brother and I were terrified that something had gone wrong, that our parents had been arrested—or worse. I couldn't help but think of how frail my mother looked the last time I saw her.

Eight days passed. Then nine.

It was ten full days, and still no word. My brother and I were at our wits' end trying to figure out what to do. Could we somehow contact the smugglers ourselves? Could we retrace our steps and go find them? The idea that we might never hear from them and might never know what happened to them sank hard in our stomachs.

And then, as luck would have it, on the tenth night, while on our way home, a Baha'i boy ran up to us on the street: "We just dropped your parents off from the train station!"

We ran back to find them in our room on the second floor, looking tired and haggard. I had never seen my father with a beard before—and I had never seen two people look more overjoyed to see their own children walk into a room. They had made it! We had all made it! And that surprise reunion was made all the sweeter by another surprise: They were not the only two people we recognized when we stepped foot into that room. My best friend and his mother from Shiraz had escaped along with them!

The four of them recounted their journey out of Iran, which was marked by more difficulties than either my brother or I had faced. At one point they were nearly caught, and the smugglers hid them in a barn under a pile of hay so they wouldn't be seen. They held their breath while the guards drove past them. But they made it.

We were able to spend three weeks together in Lahore before my brother and I headed for the airport in Islamabad, carrying one small suitcase each. It was maybe the happiest three weeks of our lives up until that point, knowing that we'd all survived, and that soon, as long as all went well, we would be together again. Our family. In America.

REFLECTIONS ON CHAPTER NINE

I want you to think back on a moment, or moments, in your life in which everything seemed to change overnight, or in a matter of just a few days. Was it a negative experience or a positive experience? Or maybe you've experienced both.

Did you cause that massive change yourself? Or did someone or something else cause that change to happen?

How did those changes affect you, both positively and negatively?

Knowing that such changes can and do occur, and that life can alter course dramatically basically overnight, are there things you would like to change? Is it possible that whatever's holding you back from making those changes can be overcome more quickly than you ever imagined?

Are you holding on to a past that is no longer serving you? Or are you moving into a future that could be brighter than you even dreamed?

PART II
THE PROMISED LAND

"The more difficulties one sees in the world the more perfect one becomes. The more you plow and dig the ground the more fertile it becomes. The more you cut the branches of a tree the higher and stronger it grows. The more you put the gold in the fire the purer it becomes. The more you sharpen the steel by grinding the better it cuts. Therefore, the more sorrows one sees the more perfect one becomes ... The more often the captain of a ship is in the tempest and difficult sailing the greater his knowledge becomes. Therefore, I am happy that you have had great tribulations and difficulties ... Strange it is that I love you and still I am happy that you have sorrows."
—Abdu'l-Baha

CHAPTER TEN

FREEDOM

On June 17, 1988, my brother and I said goodbye to our parents and left Lahore for Islamabad.

On June 19, we boarded a flight on PIA, the Pakistani airline, to Karachi. After a five-hour stop, we flew from Karachi to Bangkok. From Bangkok (after seven hours there) we flew to Tokyo. And from Tokyo we boarded a Northwest Airlines 747 bound for San Francisco.

There were a number of us on that flight: refugees from all different countries and backgrounds, all on our way to the U.S.—each of us carrying a white bag with a blue logo on it marked with the letters "IOM." The bags were provided to us by the International Organization for Migration, a branch of the UN that has helped refugees from around the world for decades. The bags were used to hold our important documents so we would have them at the ready as we passed through all of those airports on our flights from country to country—to serve as a sign to keep us all together and to let others know that we weren't just everyday passengers, but people who had fled our own countries, seeking safety and a chance at a future.

After crossing the International Date Line in the middle of the Pacific, which was like traveling back in time and erasing the nearly twenty-four hours we'd spent in the air and at airports across the globe, it was the morning of June 20, 1988, all over again as our 747 started its initial descent into San Francisco. Once the pilot made the landing announcement, people started opening their window shades, and sunlight filled the cabin. I was seated in an aisle seat in the middle section on that big wide-body plane. I couldn't see anything. After a few minutes, I couldn't take it anymore. I put my hands on the armrests and lifted myself up a bit, craning my neck to look out the windows as the plane turned and banked to the left. That's when I caught my first glimpse of the rolling golden hills shrouded in patches of fog and the sun sparkling on the water. I said to my brother, "Oh my God. That's America. We made it! We're here!"

I thought about how many hours I had spent watching poorly copied VHS tapes of American movies and listening to bootlegged cassettes of American music, and how many years I'd spent reading about this country and looking at maps of this country. I could name most presidents, going all the way back to Washington, Adams, and Jefferson. I knew the states and many of the capitals.

I mean, come on; pinch yourself, Payam. This is America, and we're about to land!

"Sir . . ." one of the flight attendants said to me. I couldn't understand any of the other words that came out of her mouth, except for "please." Then she pointed to my waist and made a motion with her hands, and I said, "Oh!" and nodded my head.

I sat back down and fastened my seat belt, and she smiled and nodded.

Then I sat there, and sat there, craning my neck each time the plane turned, trying to see whatever I could see, my right knee bouncing up and down in excitement.

When we touched down and started taxiing to the gate, my stomach was doing backflips. And when we finally disembarked and walked into the terminal, I experienced something really strange: Nearly everyone I saw looked Chinese. Behind the counter, in the waiting area, everywhere I looked. *What's going on?* I wondered. *Did we land in the wrong country?*

I would quickly realize two things: One, there were a lot of people of Chinese ancestry living in San Francisco (and, apparently, working at the airport); and two, Americans don't have a specific look. That is one of the most beautiful things I would come to learn about this country: It is filled with faces of every color, from every imaginable background, from all over the world.

And now? This country included me.

Getting through customs at the San Fráncisco airport was remarkably easy. "Welcome to America!" the agent said—a phrase that caused me to choke up then, and now, and every time I hear it from an agent at passport control, every time I return to the U.S., to this day. And before I knew it, my brother and I were standing in this glassed-in, high-ceilinged terminal collecting our suitcases. Just a few minutes later, we were hugging our cousin Sean. I can't even put into words how good it was to see him after all those years. He looked so different—older, sure, but also, American. I know I just said Americans don't have a look, and that's true, but he was dressed in jeans, sneakers, and a beige T-shirt with some movie-related print on it that I didn't recognize, and he carried himself in a way that seemed to blend in so comfortably.

In a matter of minutes we were outside, headed to the parking garage, walking past so many beautiful cars with California plates on them, and breathing in the salty San Francisco air mixed with jet exhaust as it blew in through the open structure.

"This is it," Sean said, in Persian, as we approached a brand-new, metallic-blue Chevy S-10 pickup.

"Wow!" I said. "This is yours?"

"Yup. Don't be too impressed, though. I was totally taken advantage of. It's a lemon."

"A what?"

He laughed.

"That's what they call a car here when it's no good, like, when it has all kinds of problems, one after the other."

"A lemon?" I asked again.

"Lemon," he said in English, then in Persian.

"Why a lemon?" I asked.

"I don't know!" he said, laughing. "There're so many weird sayings here. You'll learn 'em."

We threw our two small suitcases in the back, and the three of us climbed onto the bench seat in the front. It was the first pickup truck I'd ridden in since I'd made it out of the desert in Pakistan, and this experience could not have been any more different. Sean turned the radio on, and we smiled as a bunch of pop songs blasted through the speakers. He turned the dial and there was station after station, all of them playing music that sounded better than anything I'd ever heard—in part because all I had heard since I was eight years old were bootlegged copies of copies of cassettes!

As he pulled out onto the highway, I could hardly believe how big and clean and amazing everything looked. The freeways had so many lanes! He took us over the San Mateo Bridge, which is the longest of all the bridges in the Bay Area, but not the prettiest. To this day, I prefer to take visitors over the Bay Bridge, a more awe-inspiring experience where you get to the see the San Francisco skyline—but I wouldn't learn about that view for a few months.

Because there was no GPS in those days, Sean got a little turned around at first, which meant we circled around a little as we took a few wrong turns. Sean said that he lived in Modesto and didn't make it to San Francisco often. I think that's why he chose to take the San Mateo Bridge—so he didn't have to drive through busier freeways to the Bay Bridge, where he was even more likely to get lost.

The first place he took us (once he figured out which way to go) was some sort of refugee assistance organization in Stockton, where he said we had to take care of a few important documents. I was so jet-lagged from more than thirty hours of flights that I still don't fully understand what we did there. But he made it clear that was the first place we had to go, so we went along with it. What I remember most is that this official building looked more like a residential building to me, in a newly developed area. It had a green, manicured lawn in front that was prettier than any front yard I had ever seen.

From there, we headed straight to Modesto, another thirty minutes away.

As much as I thought I knew everything about the U.S., my idea of what an American city looked like came from pictures and movies set in places like New York, Chicago, and Los Angeles. The only other images I had were from extremely rural settings, like what you see in old Western movies and things like that. So when Sean said, "This is it. We're in Modesto!" I had no idea what to think.

We drove in on a four-lane, two-way street, passing gas stations, small strip-mall plazas, stretches of small single-family homes built out of wood or stucco, apartment buildings that were only two stories high, and many empty lots. No high-rises. No sidewalks full of well-dressed people rushing to work. Instead, I saw a few shirtless men, some of them barefoot, walking on the side of the road drinking straight from big two-liter Coca-Cola bottles (or the cheaper version, Shasta). There were train tracks and farm equipment, but there were cars everywhere, intersections with streetlights, and all sorts of perfectly spaced telephone poles carrying wires down every single street. Phone and electrical wires that connected to every single home.

"You guys must be hungry," Sean said.

"We're starving!" we answered.

"Well, you're gonna love this place," he told us as he pulled his truck into a Jack in the Box on Coffee Road. I didn't know what to make of the place at first. We didn't have any sort of franchises or chain restaurants in Iran. People think McDonald's exists pretty much everywhere, but we didn't have any McDonald's, not even in Tehran. Perhaps there were some American chains that I never visited as a young child, but if there were, there was no American presence left at all after the Revolution. Our hamburger joints were little individually owned shops. So this place I'd never heard of, with its big, lit-up signage and oversized windows, and even its own parking lot, was a first for us.

With Sean's help I ordered an Ultimate Cheeseburger. I had never tasted anything with so much melted cheese on it in my life. I loved it!

My brother offered to pay using the only money we had: a grand total of $75, which Sean himself had sent us before we made the trip.

"No, no, my treat," Sean said.

Honestly, I was kind of glad he paid, because the total for the food was $17. That one meal represented more than 20 percent of all the money my brother and I had.

This is not gonna be easy, I thought.

Then, Sean took us home. He still lived with his parents, who were my aunt (my mom's sister) and her husband, in a small home not unlike many of the others we'd passed that day, not far from the Jack in the Box, just off Coffee Road. The house was probably about thirty years old with four small bedrooms. His parents were both still at work when we arrived. I wanted to go right to sleep, but we waited for his parents to get home, and I was glad I did. It was good to see them after all those years, but I was so tired I couldn't even hold a conversation. I excused myself, went to one of the beds Sean said we could use, crawled under the covers—and didn't wake up for sixteen hours.

I wasn't just tired. I was soul tired.

Sean's house was the first comfortable setting I had slept in since I left Iran.

From the moment I woke, though, I was ready to get started on my new life. After eleven months spent waiting in Pakistan, I didn't want to wait one minute longer. The way I saw it was this: My job was to get a job, and then to continue my education. I had things to do now and there was no more time to waste.

My attitude was important, because our uncle told us he was happy to have us, but we could only stay for twenty days. After that, we needed to get our own place to live.

He worked as the facilities manager at an apartment complex nearby, and he told us, "I'll help you get a place there. I will sign the credit application, and I will lend you money for the deposit, but you guys need to make enough between now and then to start paying your own rent."

The next day, Sean took us to the nearby town of Ripon, where a friend of his was able to offer us jobs at a silk-screen printing shop. Because my brother was older, he offered him a full-time position. But for me, all he had available was a few hours here and there. I knew I would have to find a second job to make ends meet, but I didn't care. I was happy for the work.

Our uncle also gave my brother a car, so we could get back and forth to work, and my brother immediately got his driver's license. The car was an old, faded burgundy Mercury Zephyr that had been totaled. Nearly a quarter of it was gone. Just gone! When my brother drove it, it made a lot of screechy noises. But it ran, and it got us to Ripon and back until my brother could afford a car of his own—for a grand total of $400. (When he did, he sold the Zephyr for $160. That's all that car was worth.)

The rent in the apartment our uncle helped us into was $340 per month, and after twenty days, the two of us combined had earned enough to pay the rent with about $50 left over. It was a one-bedroom apartment, unfurnished, with old shaggy green carpet and a popcorn ceiling. We had nothing, but we went around to some garage sales and managed to pick up a sofa (with one of its springs popping out) and a few other things. And just like that, we had our own place.

Right after we moved in, Sean offered me a job at a place called Pizza Palace, where he'd recently been promoted to manager. The owner used to run a Little Caesars franchise, but decided to open his own shops instead. This man was an entrepreneur, and he'd managed to open three locations in the area, which impressed me.

His slogan: "Why buy pizza from a Hut when you can buy it from a Palace?"

I didn't know what Little Caesars or Pizza Hut were and wouldn't learn until later, but I was very thankful for this man and his openness to hiring both Sean and me.

The pay? Minimum wage, which was $4.25 an hour at that time.

I tried to stay in the back and just work in the kitchen, or clean, but no matter how hard I tried, I ended up having to deal with customers.

I mentioned earlier that I barely spoke any English when I came to the U.S., right?

Sean taught me to answer the phone to take orders, and say, "Hello, this is Payam," but no one could ever understand what I was saying. So he said, "From now on your name is Patrick. Just say, 'Hello, this is Pat,'" and I tried. "Hello, this is Patrick . . ."

It didn't help much. Even if they could understand my name, I couldn't understand what they were asking for on their pizzas. For example, in my first week or so, a customer came in when I was alone in the shop and asked for extra potato sauce. I asked him to repeat what he said, and I was sure I heard him correctly: He wanted more potato sauce on his pizza. I had never heard of such a thing.

"No potato sauce," I said.

"What do you mean you don't have potato sauce? This is a pizza place, isn't it?" the customer said. "Where's your chef? Let me talk to him."

I knew the word "chef." This was a pizza place, not a fancy restaurant.

"No chef. Only me," I said.

The guy started to get really mad—until he finally pointed to the red sauce near the edge of the crust on a pizza, and it dawned on me that I was mishearing or misinterpreting what he was saying. He wasn't saying "potato." He was asking for extra tomato sauce!

Thankfully, we were able to have a laugh over it, but I dreaded every time I had to take an order.

Funny thing about being put into such an uncomfortable position is that the experience forced me to learn English under intense pressure. Anyone who's ever worked in a pizza joint and felt the wrath of an angry customer when you mess up their order knows what I mean by that. The pressure forced me to learn as much English as I could really quickly, which gave me a little bit of a head start before school started in August.

Plus, it all seemed pretty easy compared to what I was up to just one year earlier, when I made my way across the Emptiness Desert and into Pakistan as a refugee. It was hard to believe how much my life had changed in just one year.

I had no idea what to expect the first time I walked into Beyer High School, the "Home of the Patriots," with its red, white, and blue color scheme and a picture of an eagle on the sign out front. But the thing that made my eyes pop wasn't the way kids dressed, or any sort of mean words or bullying of any kind (at least none that I could understand). It was seeing boys and girls making out in the hallways between classes. There were couples French kissing, and I mean really digging in and going for it, right in front of everybody! I had never, ever seen that sort of behavior in my life, from teenagers or adults. It was definitely a culture shock.

The concept of "freedom" here extended much further than I ever imagined, as if the concepts of boundaries and privacy were all just sort of thrown to the wind—as if anyone, even kids, was free to do whatever they wanted. I wasn't sure if I liked it or not. It was certainly something I would have to adjust to.

Gym class was a bit of a culture shock, too. Everyone went into the locker room and got naked to change into gym clothes. I remember thinking, *There's no way I'm doing that!* And I didn't. I always got changed in the bathroom.

Modesto wasn't the most diverse city then, with a population that was mostly two races: white and Hispanic. There were not many Black kids and only a handful of Laotian and Cambodian kids who I saw in my English as a second language class. I can't even say for sure that "ESL" was the name of that class. All I knew was that it was filled with nothing but us foreign kids, and that whatever they were doing to try to teach us all English at the same time didn't click with me. Instead, every day, I would write down words that seemed important, and I would take that list to work after school, where I would ask Sean to teach me what those words meant. Learning in context that way was pretty effective for me as the year went along, but the first few months were a real struggle.

I was able to do math just fine. But everything else was hard—especially since I was enrolled as a senior, and the school wouldn't to allow me to graduate without taking certain courses, including U.S. history and U.S. government. These were required courses for graduating from high school, and I couldn't understand what the teacher was teaching. Even the simplest things confused me. I remember taking a test and one of the questions asked if something "increased" or "decreased." I knew one meant up and the other down, but I didn't know which was which, so I had to get up and go ask the teacher. Thankfully, the teacher helped.

Lots of people were willing to help.

Nearly everyone I met here was helpful and kind to me, right from the start. Even when I couldn't speak the language, and when I clearly stood

out as someone "different," they were never mean to me. The last time I
was enrolled in school, in Shiraz, every one of us had to be searched every
morning on the way into the building. I would have to watch my back
and go out of my way, constantly changing my route on the way home
after school to avoid being beat up by one or more of my classmates, just
because I was Baha'i. I had to keep a low profile to avoid any confrontations with police or the Revolutionary Guards. I lived with the constant
fear of being targeted or arrested every day, just for what I believed. And
that was on top of worrying that some Iraqi jet might drop a bomb on our
neighborhood at any random moment.

Here? Life was so free from the noise of fear and anxiety that, no
matter what happened, or how hard it was, it all felt quiet and peaceful
by comparison.

I took every day as it came, while feeling very grateful to be alive
and welcomed by this country. But I was still a teenager. The last thing I
wanted was to feel embarrassed, and while I was learning how to speak
English—and, basically, how to be an American—embarrassment just
seemed to find me.

For example, one day I woke up with bumps all over my skin. I had
no health insurance, which meant I had no choice but to go to the emergency room at the nearest hospital to find out what those bumps were.
I waited for hours before finally seeing a doctor who revealed that I had
chicken pox. He said that I wouldn't be able to go to school for a week.
When I called the school to tell them, I mistakenly told the office that I
had been diagnosed with "smallpox," which apparently caused a small
uproar at the school. I'm pretty sure they held an emergency meeting
to discuss whether or not to quarantine students and teachers from the
classes I attended, and there were more than a few people who panicked
over the idea that this foreigner was bringing diseases into the country.
Finally, someone from the school called me back to clarify the diagno-
sis, and everybody calmed down. But I made language mistakes like that
pretty often.

Because I couldn't really talk with my classmates, I usually sat alone
and read books during lunch. One day, the principal saw what I was

doing and said, loudly, "You all should learn from this student. See, he's reading, even during lunch!"

I didn't want that kind of special attention. In fact, I kept so quiet for the first few months of school that, one day, a guy next to me in art class leaned over and asked, "Are you mute?"

"No," I said. "No English."

The kid shrugged his shoulders, like it was no big deal. He wasn't looking to pick on me. He was truly curious why I never spoke.

Others were curious about the way I dressed.

I mentioned that I came to the U.S. with nothing but one small suitcase. In that suitcase I had two pairs of pants (one of which I did not like at all), one extra pair of shoes, and I had a couple of shirts. That was it. So I wore the same pair of pants to school every day, and one day, one of the kids asked me, "Were you in the military in Iran?"

"No," I said. "Why?"

"Those are military pants, right?"

I laughed a little. They were sort of greenish in color, so I could understand why he might think such a thing.

"No, I just don't have other pants," I said.

"Oh," he replied.

That was it. He didn't make fun of me for it or start talking about it with other people.

Like I said, just about everyone I met was kind.

Not having enough money to buy new clothes was a little embarrassing. Not knowing the language was difficult for me every single day. But I never looked around and thought, *I'm starting at a disadvantage* or, *I'll never catch up to my peers*. I was happy to be here, to be free from persecution, to be around family again—not only Sean and his parents, but my sister and her family as well, who moved from Alaska down to Modesto just a couple of months after we arrived.

There were three Persian Baha'i families in Modesto, and the rest were American Baha'is. There were maybe one hundred of us in total, and the Baha'i community was very welcoming. I can't even put into words how good it felt to know that no one here held any sort of hatred toward us for our beliefs. I was told that there were some churches in the U.S. that labeled the Baha'is as a cult, which couldn't be further from the truth, but I never faced such an accusation directly. No one set out to attack or hurt us. There were no rocks thrown at any of the Baha'is I met, and I did not have one negative run-in with anyone in Modesto over the expression of my beliefs.

Freedom of religion in the U.S. was real. And it was wonderful.

I could not wait for my parents to come and experience that freedom for themselves—having no idea how long it would take before they would be allowed to move here from Pakistan. Especially after the Reagan years came to an end, as George Bush won the election that November. Even that was kind of exciting, though, because it was the first time I had witnessed a democratic election choosing the president of a country. It was only a matter of time before I would be old enough and eligible to vote in an American election myself. A free election, in a democracy. What a privilege that was!

I had long believed in my heart that the U.S. was a great country, and now I was experiencing that greatness firsthand. Sure, I was struggling. I was broke all the time, living in a run-down apartment with old shag carpet, working two minimum-wage jobs after school, every day, every night, and every weekend—fifty to sixty hours a week, with no overtime pay. But after all I had gone through on my life's journey so far, working hard came easy. The promise and hope of my future here made it worth overcoming any obstacles I would ever encounter.

I wish every kid in every high school in the U.S. could appreciate how great the opportunities here really are—that, instead of feeling overwhelmed by the challenges of just getting by (as big and as real as those challenges are), they could feel empowered and inspired by the freedoms they've been given.

Freedoms that I knew, all too well, should never, ever be taken for granted.

REFLECTIONS ON CHAPTER TEN

Have you ever thought about the freedoms you have? Have you ever taken time to reflect on and appreciate those freedoms and what they mean to you? (If not, please do!)

Have you ever felt an obligation or, better yet, the inspiration to take advantage of the freedoms you have, especially to do something more with your life and your life's work?

If starting something new feels daunting, think about this: Have you ever started over? In a new town, a new school, a new country? Have you ever taken on a new sport or a new instrument? Or learned a new skill (including a new language) that was totally outside of your comfort zone? Every new endeavor, from new relationships to new jobs, brings you face-to-face with a daunting learning curve. But if you've faced any of these sorts of challenges before, you obviously made it through them or you wouldn't be here reading this book. There is power in that: the power of knowing that you are capable of learning new things, overcoming great changes, surviving against the odds, starting over . . . the list is long.

Take a moment to think about some of the challenges you overcame as a child, a teen, a student, a new employee, and so on. Write them down. Then ask yourself: What did I learn from those situations? How did I change? How did my life improve because of what I overcame? (Even if all you learned is, "I never want to do that again!" it's still a worthwhile lesson.) Recognizing your own history and knowing these answers can help give you hope—and maybe even some courage—as you face new challenges and set out to make positive changes in your future.

CHAPTER ELEVEN

AMERICA 101

M y first few months in the U.S. reminded me of some important life lessons I'd learned so far. One of the biggest was this: Once we've endured real hardships, everyday challenges become smaller and easier to overcome—even if they're seen as "hardships" by the society that surrounds us.

For instance, Modesto is a car town. You can't really get around that city without a vehicle, and a lot of people take pride in the vehicles they drive. This is the city where George Lucas was raised, where he got the inspiration for his 1973 film, *American Graffiti*, from the cruising that happened every Friday and Saturday night on the main drag through the center of the city to downtown. I had been fascinated by cars since I was a little kid, and I was instantly attracted to the car culture of Modesto. It was amazing to me how many people owned really beautiful automobiles. It also amazed me that, in America, boys and girls could cruise up and down the street in those cars, with guys leaning out of windows and unabashedly trying to pick up as many phone numbers as they could from the girls, who were also cruising—where those girls were free to hand out their numbers and flirt right back.

Most people considered it a hardship to not own a car in Modesto. Yet there was no way I could afford one when we first arrived. I think my first paycheck from Pizza Palace was $92 (minus taxes). It would take a lot of paychecks to earn enough to pay for rent, food, school-related expenses, and other necessities, and to save up for a car. But to me, that wasn't something to complain about or think, *Oh, poor me. I'm pretty much the only senior at Beyer High without a car to drive.* No.

Who has time for complaining when the opportunity to make that dream come true is right there in front of you?

Getting a car wasn't impossible. It would just take some hard work. It was a goal I set, something I wanted to achieve, and something I was willing to work hard at achieving. For the time being, all I could afford was a used bicycle, which I found at a garage sale and rode everywhere, rain or shine, back and forth to school and to work, many miles every day. Was that a hardship for me? Especially after all I'd endured on my journey so far? No! I was grateful that I had a bicycle, and very grateful that I had a job.

The owner of the Pizza Palace was a guy named Wayne Wilder. And the first time I got paid, I went straight to his office, where I shook his hand and said, "Mr. Wilder, thank you for the paycheck."

He looked shocked. I don't think anyone had ever done that to him. But that's how I'd been raised. If somebody does something nice for you, you thank them. And, of course, I always called him Mr. Wilder, not "Wayne." Respect for elders is a must. I'm sure he was thinking, *Who is this guy?* But that was a good thing. He noticed me. He very quickly saw that I was both hardworking and grateful to have the work. In my experience, bosses rarely forget that sort of thing.

It was strange when I looked at how some of the other employees behaved. No matter how busy or slow it was in the shop, they moved at the same speed. Half the time they had one hand resting on the counter while the other was spreading cheese on the dough, as if they were about to fall asleep. I was the opposite. I wanted to do well, to follow in Sean's footsteps, to get promoted to manager myself one day, and hopefully to get a raise. To get the orders right and make the customers happy, too.

I liked it when they smiled as they walked away from the counter and couldn't understand why some of the other employees seemed to have none of that motivation.

In the Baha'i Faith there is truly high regard for work. Abdu'l-Baha wrote, "Work done in the spirit of service is the highest form of worship." I love this quote. It's not only about putting worship into action, but about how we approach all work. Any job can be done as a form of worship, as long as we do it with the spirit of service to others. To me, this means that regardless of how we feel about a job or even an employer, we have a higher responsibility to do it well—a responsibility that is spiritual in nature.

I couldn't understand the lack of enthusiasm many students showed at school, either. Teachers rarely ignore or fail to reward a student who's enthusiastic, respectful, and wants to learn. So, to me, asking for help, no matter how embarrassing it seemed, was always better than staying silent and never giving myself the opportunity to learn something new. For example, one day in art class, I needed a marker—and I had no idea what markers were called in English. But for some reason, I thought I knew the word in French: *Magique*. That's the word we use in Farsi. (It's confusing, right? But stay with me here.) Since I was learning that "que" wasn't often used in English words—English uses a "c" or a "ck," and the "g" in the middle of a word usually sounds like a "j," and some words are similar between French and English—I went to the teacher and confidently said, "I need a magic."

She looked at me really weird, and said, "What are you talking about?"

"Magic?" I said. "I need a magic."

I made a drawing motion, and she got it. "Oh, you need a magic marker," she said. "Here you go."

I did my best to not let any sort of embarrassment stop me. Instead, I read lots of books and asked for help, and went to my cousin every single night with a new list of words and phrases to learn—and by December, I was acing every class. My GPA was a 4.0!

Once it made sense to me, I loved my U.S. history class. I loved learning about the Civil War, and how so many white Americans sacrificed themselves to free the slaves. I was astounded by Abraham Lincoln's Gettysburg Address, which he wrote on the way to the event, and which truly seemed divinely inspired to me. You could say that all of this made me a bit of a nerd, but it was all so fascinating. What a country this was. We would use No. 2 pencils to fill in multiple-choice answers to tests on Scantron cards, which was just the coolest thing. I studied really hard before every test and would always get 100 percent. The one time I didn't, I asked the teacher why—and he realized that the answer to one of his own questions was wrong. He had input the answer incorrectly into the machine. My score was actually 100.

Once I got the hang of everything, I was sure that graduating from high school wouldn't be a problem. So I concentrated on my goal of getting my license and buying a car. I also decided to invest in something that was really important to me: my teeth.

In Iran, I was too afraid to go see a dentist because they don't numb their patients. They probably do now, but they didn't back then. They would literally give people root canals without any sort of anesthesia or novocaine. That's just the way they did things, which is unbelievable to me now. Pulling and drilling teeth without numbing the patient sounds more like some kind of torture than a proper medical procedure—like what the mafia would use to get somebody to talk.

My teeth were in need of some work by the time I came to this country, so I saved up a bunch of money just for that and went to a dentist in Modesto. (I'll never forget his name, but for the sake of not turning this into gossip and backbiting, I won't print his name in this book.)

After he performed an exam and told me what work he thought I should have done, I told him that I only make $4.25 an hour and asked him, "How much of that can I get done for, say, $1,500?" That was a ton of money for me, but with what I had saved, and figuring the work would be done over the course of a few months, that was the budget I could work with—as long as he let me pay for some now and some later.

He seemed fine with that plan and said, "For $1,500, you can get these fillings done, and then this one, which requires a root canal." (Remember this was 1988 and medical procedures were much cheaper back then.)

We set a timeline. We got started. I biked there to see him, rain or shine. It didn't matter if he performed a root canal, I had no choice but to bike back and forth and empty my pockets to get each procedure.

He started with the fillings, and then he did the root canal, which was a two-part procedure. Once he was done with part one, he put some filler and gauze in the hole, and I was supposed to go back a few days later to put a crown on it. But when I went back for the crown, he said, "Sorry, your money has run out."

"What?" I said. "We had a deal."

"Well, your money has run out. It's so much more money for the crown than I had initially assumed, and that will have to be paid up front."

"I don't have it," I said. "You know I don't have it. We had a deal to pay over time."

"Sorry," he said. "I can't do it." And he didn't!

So I had to live with that hole in my mouth for the next couple of months until finally I went to another dentist and had the tooth pulled. (Years later, my gums started to turn black. The clinic at UC Davis initially thought I might have cancer, but then it became clear that the discoloration was from the poor-quality fillings this dentist had given me. I had to have every one of them redone.)

It was the first time I felt taken advantage of in America. I couldn't understand it. This dentist was an immigrant himself. He had been so cordial, and then turned so cold and mean. I had only experienced that sort of a turn in a person once before. In Hashtgerd. At my school. Only this time, I had no idea what this dentist's motivation was (besides financial gain at any cost to a teenage patient). No idea why he would do this to a kid who was trying to support himself, who had no parents to defend him and keep him safe from harm. I just had to live with the consequences of being too trustful, and to learn to be more cautious when I made deals with someone like that in the future.

They say what doesn't kill us only makes us stronger, right?

Aside from the dentist fiasco, my life in Modesto just kept getting better.

In November 1988, I achieved a major goal when I passed the test and earned my California driver's license. I then went out and bought myself my very first car: a rusty burgundy 1981 Ford Pinto for $680. Armed with all sorts of Armor All polishes and protectants, I spent hours polishing it up, trying to make it look better than it did. But no matter what, it was still a Pinto. It wasn't much of a cruising car, that's for sure. But that wasn't why I bought it. I bought it because I was tired of riding my bike everywhere and wanted the all-American freedom that only a car provides. It was a reliable car. I not only took that car to work and to school, but one day drove it all the way to Pasadena and back—nearly five hours each way. I didn't know anyone in Pasadena. I just did it because I could. I was free to travel and loved knowing that I could drive anywhere for the price of a few gallons of gas. Is there any better feeling than being able to go where you want to go, whenever you want?

Perhaps I should have saved a little more money before I started driving, though, because I wasn't prepared for the cost that would come when I got my first ticket. I did not pay attention to somebody crossing the crosswalk. They had not stepped into the crosswalk yet, but they were about to, and I did not stop—and there happened to be a cop right there who decided to pull me over.

The ticket was $500.

It felt like I was playing the worst game of Monopoly ever. As if I had bought all kinds of hotels, and then I drew the card from the deck that made me pay taxes on all of that property, all at once. In the game, if you don't have the cash, you have no choice but to sell properties to other players for whatever you can get until you have enough to pay off the tax bill. That's kind of the real-life situation I was in, only I didn't have anything to sell—and I wasn't willing to sell the car.

When I went to court to try to figure out why the fine was so large, the clerk told me it was mostly because my car was not insured. "Well, I for sure cannot afford insurance now!" I said. "The fine is almost as big as the price of the car!"

Once I was in front of a judge, I all but begged him to reduce the fine, but he said there was nothing he could do. I was guilty, and that was the fine set by the State of California. The only thing he could allow was a payment plan, so I agreed, which meant I had to work extra-long hours to pay off that fine over time.

I took it as another hard lesson learned. A car that that seemed like a pretty good bargain turned out to be very expensive for me. Maybe I should have slowed down and fully understood just how expensive own-ing a car could be before committing to driving everywhere. But in the long run, it was still a small price to pay for the freedom gained by having a Pinto to call my own.

The learning curve that came with just about everything in America was large. With big freedoms and big opportunities, that's just the name of the game. And more learning curves definitely revealed themselves as the end of my senior year approached.

By the spring of 1989, my English was pretty good. I had learned fast and could almost hold my own in a conversation.

My GPA was a solid 4.0.

I had no social life, mainly because I worked so much and, well, because of my English. The Beyer Senior Prom came and went, and I don't remember hearing a word about it before it happened. Which means I certainly didn't find a date or go to the prom myself.

And while many students were talking about how excited they were to get their acceptance letters from colleges and universities, I realized I had missed out on all sorts of application deadlines.

With my grades and my compelling history as a child refugee, I prob-ably could have applied to and been accepted at any number of major universities, maybe even on scholarship. But I didn't know a single thing about where those universities were, how to get in touch with any of them, or how the application process even started. I didn't even know there was a difference between them. To me, a four-year degree meant a four-year degree, as it did in Iran. I didn't understand that there was any difference between Harvard and a place like Fresno State.

The real problem was I didn't have a mentor.

The reality is, a large portion of my student peers in Modesto in 1989 did not care about college. I actually remember people postponing college so they could work to buy or pay off a truck.

There was no one in my family or at the print shop or at Pizza Palace to tell me that a place like Stanford was nearby, maybe an hour-and-a-half drive from Modesto—or to make me realize that UCLA and other great schools were located not far from Pasadena, where I'd already driven to on a random road trip. I had no clue there was this thing called "Silicon Valley" and the tremendous opportunities in the tech world that were starting to unfold basically just up the road. And for some reason, no one at Beyer High School led me down any of those paths, either. You would think that someone with a 4.0 GPA would get some college guidance from a teacher or a counselor. Then again, maybe they all assumed someone with grades like mine must already know what they're doing. Or maybe they underestimated me as a recent refugee. I don't know.

At that point in my life, the outskirts of Modesto were just about as far as I could see. I did not feel that this one city represented all the possibilities in the world, but I did not consider moving to one of the big cities I'd seen in the movies, either. To me, Modesto looked okay. Compared to anything I'd known or anywhere I'd been, I thought, *You can have a decent life here.* Not that I didn't dream of having an incredible life, or expect a lot out of life. I knew that I wanted to live a life of impact, and I also knew that moving wasn't something to be scared of. It wasn't a big deal to me now. But at that point, Modesto felt like enough for the time being.

The only college I knew anything about was the one that was a mile or so from our apartment building: Modesto Junior College. So that's where I made plans to go in the fall, to study chemistry with thoughts of becoming a doctor.

Graduating high school in America felt like a really big accomplishment. Beyer was a big school, with somewhere between three hundred and four hundred people in my class, so it was a large ceremony—and thankfully my English was strong enough that I could understand what was happening, and even what was said in the speeches. My sister and her husband came to see me graduate, along with Sean's parents. And before that, Sean's parents came out for a special awards night, where I was given a $300 scholarship from the Martin Luther King Foundation. One would have thought that award was meant for a person of color, but they saw me as someone worthy of support. I was so proud, and so amazed that this organization was handing me money to help pay for college when I didn't even ask for it. I was grateful.

I only wished my parents could have been there to witness it all.

I missed them so much.

There was very little time to celebrate, though, because $300 would not come close to covering tuition, let alone books, on top of my regular living expenses, and the additional dental work I needed, and the ongoing payment plan on the traffic ticket. So I made up my mind to get another job for the summer.

My brother had been offered a second job at a local gas station, making $7 an hour for taking a late-night shift, which sounded pretty great compared to $4.25. But on his first day, the owner showed him where the baseball bat was located, and the handgun. "Just in case there's any trouble," he said. It turned out that the previous employee who held that shift was no longer there because some drunk guys came in past 2 AM, got angry when the employee wouldn't sell them alcohol (after the California cutoff time for alcohol sales), and threw the employee through the window!

Despite hearing that story, I also needed to make more money, so I went out and got a late-night gas-station job. On the first night, a fight broke out, and the manager tried to get me to go break it up. I quit the next day and never even collected my paycheck for the shift.

Instead, because I was planning on studying chemistry, my uncle put me in touch with a friend who worked in the chemistry lab at the local cannery, S&W, which just happens to be the biggest cannery in the world. There was a Persian guy there who hired me on the spot and gave me a graveyard-shift job in the lab. That meant that every day that summer, I worked at the Pizza Palace in the afternoon until closing and then at midnight went to the cannery and worked until 8 AM.

I would go home, sleep, and then go back to the pizza place, and so on.

When school started, I didn't want to give up the money I was making. I didn't like being hand-to-mouth all the time. So I asked myself: "Can I do this without sleeping, so I can have the income?" And I decided, "Yes, I can."

I would arrive at Modesto Junior College by 9 AM, giving myself time to shower and change for my first class; then go to Pizza Palace right after classes ended in the afternoon; then go to the cannery at midnight, work until 8 AM, and head straight back to school; then the pizza place, then the cannery . . . day after day, basically without sleeping at all. I would catch little naps in the hallway before class, or overnight during breaks between activity in the chemistry lab, and that was it. I was a zombie. I tried drinking coffee, like lots of other hardworking people, but the caffeine didn't seem to do anything for me. It still does nothing for me. So I just trudged through and kept up that schedule—until I couldn't.

One of my responsibilities at the cannery was to control the chemistry of the apricot juice, which they turned into apricot juice concentrate. There were three 4,000-gallon tanks on-site, and every three or four hours they would be filled. My job was to go to those tanks, take a sample, take it to the lab, and do some measurements to figure out the formula for the chemicals I needed to add to the batch so all the imperfections would then come down. We would then drain those imperfections out and take the rest of the apricot juice, let's say 3,800 gallons, concentrate it into maybe 50 gallons, put it in a barrel, and ship it. So those barrels were valuable. I mean, 4,000 gallons of apricot juice is really valuable.

I got so used to doing it that sometimes, in between testing and draining, I found that I could catch a couple of hours sleep. But I didn't have an alarm clock, and one night, I overslept. When I woke up and saw what time it was, I ran to the tank room.

"What did you do with the last tank?" I asked the crew.

"Since you didn't show up, we just used the formula from the last tank. But it's a mess. Look at it!" they said.

Of course it was a mess. The chemistry of every batch is completely different, since the fruit comes in from different orchards.

"Oh no," I said. "Oh my God!"

I took a sample of the mess and ran it to the lab, hoping I would be able to add some more chemicals to fix the problem. I went back and forth, and kept adding more chemicals, but it didn't work. We had to drain four thousand gallons of apricot juice and throw it away.

They didn't fire me, but that was my clue that maybe I should have fewer jobs while going to school.

I decided to keep the cannery job during the week, since it paid more, and to only work at the Pizza Palace on the weekends. Mr. Wilder was fine with that since the shop was only busy on the weekends anyway. Of the three locations he owned, the location he asked me to work at was the worst. There were occasional weekdays when the shop only made $50 in sales, in total. There were whole months when he only pulled in like $1,000.

After settling into a better routine between work and school, I saw what an opportunity he had to market the Pizza Palace to students and others living and working in the area. I offered Mr. Wilder my time and creativity to do some marketing and promotion work, to help drive up business by offering to hand out flyers on campus and place them on cars. I didn't expect him to pay me any sort of hourly wage for that work. "I'll do everything myself," I said, "and in return, I would only ask for 10 percent of the increase in sales that my marketing and promotion brings in."

For the life of me, I could not understand why he said no. It would have cost him nothing up front, and it would potentially have brought in a whole lot of new business. He seemed happy just running things his way, or maybe reasons unknown to me prevented him from giving up any percentage of profits—even profits that were nonexistent without my marketing efforts.

It's funny how businesspeople view the "cost" of things sometimes. Even in this highly entrepreneurial country, so many people seem averse to taking a risk, even when, in reality, the undertaking represents no real "risk" at all. I guess it's all a matter of perspective. Compared to the costs and risks associated with trying to do business as a Baha'i in Iran, hardly any business venture in America seems either costly or risky.

One thing I recognized early on, though, is that "reward" should always be measured in more than dollars and cents. No matter what sort of work we do, the "cost" associated with any job involves some amount of risk and reward. Working at a pizza place is low risk, but also low income. But working at a chemistry lab comes with a different type of cost: the safety risks.

One of the chemicals we worked with was highly concentrated hydrochloric acid. It came in big barrels, and if you weren't wearing the proper protective gear, a single drop of it—or even the mist from the cloud that emerges from the top when you open a barrel—could burn holes right through your body. One of my jobs was to dilute that hydrochloric acid with specific formulas. When I did it, I was always alone in the lab and dressed in what looked like a space suit. (I wish we could have had access to gear like that in our manufacturing warehouse in Shiraz.)

One night, it was really hot, and my goggles fogged up. So I lifted them for a second just to try to clear the fog—and some of that acid splashed into my eye. It burned like a miniature blowtorch. I closed my eyes, tight, and went running toward the spot where I knew there was an eyewash station on the wall. The station was empty. Panicking, I cracked open my other eye just enough to exit the room and run to the on-site nurse's office. She looked at my eye and washed it for me, but then sent me off to the hospital.

She didn't call an ambulance or give me a ride or have anyone else on the overnight shift give me a ride. She just said I had to go, which gave me no choice but to drive myself, in my Pinto, with one eye closed.

The hospital washed my eye again and said there was nothing else they could do. If there was long-term damage, I would have to address it later on.

A week later, S&W sent me a check for ninety-eight cents—to reimburse me for the mileage to the hospital and back. That was the only money I ever received from that incident. I had a spot on one eye that remained for years, until it turned into a cataract. It was early onset, and

the outer lens of my eye grew so clouded that I had to have the lens sur-
gically removed.

Risk and reward. The real "costs" of doing business or working a
job. By the fall of 1989, I was learning all sorts of new things—far above
and beyond anything that can be learned in a classroom. It was like going
through some sort of an Americanization boot camp.

Even with an acid burn on my eyeball, I was grateful for every bit
of freedom and opportunity I had. I was making money. I was going to
school. I was free to practice my Faith.

I felt like I was becoming more "American" by the day.

REFLECTIONS ON CHAPTER ELEVEN

What was your attitude toward work when you were a teenager? Did you do your best, or did you try to do as little as possible?

What are some lessons you learned at work that you never learned in school?

When it came to your post–high school plans, did you have any guidance? Did you have a mentor? Or were you left to figure things out on your own?

Knowing what you know now, how might you have done things differently back then if you'd had the chance?

While none of us can go back in time for a do-over, did it ever occur to you that "knowing what you know now" can be applied to finding ways to make positive changes in your life, career, or business endeavors going forward? The knowledge we gain on our journeys creates new opportunities for us, all the time. It's up to us to recognize those opportunities, to embrace the gift of the knowledge we've gained, and then—the most important step—to act.

CHAPTER TWELVE

BECOMING AMERICAN

O
n Sunday mornings, I came into the Pizza Palace a couple of hours before opening to start preparing dough. Half the time I was by myself, or there was just one other person there. The radio would be on, and we'd listen to Casey Kasem's *American Top 40* countdown. The music of Billy Idol, Debbie Gibson, MC Hammer, and Bon Jovi kept my mind busy, occasionally interrupted by loving messages from a boy to a girl, or vice versa (which I loved).

It seemed as if everyone listened to that show in the 1980s. Everyone paid attention to what the number-one song was. Listening to pop radio, in general, created a sort of common language for American teenagers in those days.

Kasem sounded like a Persian name to me, which I thought was cool. The last name Kasem was not uncommon in Iran, although it was pronounced "Ka'zem." In reality, this famous radio host was of Lebanese American descent and had grown up in Detroit, but I didn't know that then. I just liked listening, and I liked the message he shared at the end of the show, signing off with the words, "Until next week, keep your feet on the ground and keep reaching for the stars."

That was just the sort of all-American attitude I could get behind.

With my much-improved English and a growing sense of self-confidence, I carried that attitude into my pursuits at Modesto Junior College (or MJC, as we all called it) starting that fall semester of 1989. It was my very first semester—the one in which I worked one too many jobs back to back for the first few weeks—and I enrolled in twenty credits' worth of courses. Twelve credits were considered full-time enrollment, but I was "reaching for the stars" and wanted to learn as much as possible about everything and get through college fast. I was eager to get the most out of life.

I also decided to get a little more involved and connected with the student body than I had been in high school, and in order to accomplish that, I joined the International Club.

MJC had more than twenty thousand students, including a lot of foreign students. I liked the diversity of the school from day one and thought the International Club, which boasted nearly four hundred members, would be a great place to get to know some people.

After staying quiet for so long during my senior year of high school, it felt good to get involved in a club where I fit right in. More than that, the experience gave me a boost in self-confidence, which was something I needed as a young adult.

When it came time to elect officers, I ran for president—and won! It was huge for me, in every way, and I immediately felt a strong responsibility to do right by all of my fellow international students. First and foremost, I noticed that the club didn't have much in the way of financial resources. To me, that lack of funds was not a positive reflection of who we were, especially when considering how some people viewed foreigners—as if they were a drain on society. I didn't want anyone to think this about us at school. So I decided to engage my entrepreneurial mind.

"Let's do things differently," I told the group. "Let's make some money."

We started brainstorming some really fun fundraisers, and the first one came together shortly after we returned from Christmas break: We decided to sell and deliver flowers on campus for Valentine's Day, and the sale was a big hit. We followed that up with an International Food

Fair, where we served foods from around the world, and barbecues on UN Day and Earth Day. Someone mentioned a governmental body called the FCC, which oversaw radio stations in the U.S. According to FCC rules, radio stations had to offer a portion of their advertisement space for free to promote charitable organizations and nonprofits as part of their licensing agreements. So we went to the local radio stations and asked if they would help promote our events. They agreed without any hesitation! Suddenly we were getting advertised on the very same radio stations that all the kids on campus and in the broader community listened to, and that increased the attendance at every event we held—which brought in more money than we ever expected. The radio stations even came out to cover the barbecues and other events, broadcasting live with their local DJs right on campus.

That spring of 1990, we put on a talent show, and nearly a thousand people showed up and bought tickets. Suddenly we were flush with cash. So, as a way to improve relations and outreach on campus, we started offering seed money to other clubs and groups with some of the money we raised. People came to us looking to start a new organization or saying that their existing clubs needed some money for a good cause, or whatever it was, and we were able to grant them what they needed.

We also treated ourselves to some pretty amazing outings. We were able to cover the cost of taking everyone in the club on a trip to Disneyland.

Disneyland!

None of us had to pay a dime out of pocket for the trip down to Anaheim, or the tickets—any of it. If I hadn't been a part of that club, I don't think I ever would have set aside money for a day full of fun like that. There were too many important costs I needed to cover with the earnings from my jobs. But because I was in school, and because I had stepped up with the support of my fellow students to change the trajectory of this club, I was able to experience that amazing theme park alongside all of these other students, many of whom had never experienced anything like that, either. It wasn't an extravagant trip. We rented a school bus with uncomfortable seats to make the 350-mile trip in one day, leaving at 4 AM and returning around midnight. But we all had an amazing time.

We took the group on a white-water rafting trip, too, which was fun and exhilarating. I had never experienced anything like that before. This brought us all closer together, which made the group even stronger. It also made us realize what we were capable of and what we could accomplish when we were united. Unity is a foundational value, and our successes in the club furthered my belief in how organizations, businesses, families, and more can all prosper when people are unified.

I didn't know how to swim. I had never learned. But the white-water rafting trip didn't personally scare me much. Something else did: Speaking in front of others. I was still nervous about my English and had so much to learn, so in preparation for the talent show, I decided to challenge myself: As president of the International Club, I had to give a speech in front of the whole auditorium. I didn't have any nice clothing to wear, so I went to Mervyn's (a pretty big chain in middle-class areas back in the day) and used my cousin's store card to purchase some nicer pants and a couple of shirts. I also bought a black suit that came in a box. (I paid the cost of those clothes back directly to the store over time, and never missed a payment—since that would affect my cousin's credit.) I borrowed a tie, and only had white exercise socks to wear, but I did my best!

I was trying to be cool and look professional. Imagine: a black suit that didn't fit me well, with the sleeves rolled up (yup), and a colorful shirt with a thin black tie and white socks, kind of like Michael Jackson. I badly needed fashion advice.

More importantly, I took a class on public speaking just for the occasion. I worked on my ability to communicate. I memorized what I was going to say, and by the time the big day came I was so confident that I did not rehearse. (Big mistake!) As I stepped onto that stage in front of almost a thousand people, the lights turned on, and I was blinded. I could not see the audience—and I forgot everything. I could not remember a word of my speech! So I stumbled a bit, and improvised, not very eloquently, and I don't even know what I said. But at the end, the audience applauded, the show began, and the rest of the evening went off without a hitch. The event was a hit, and the club made a ton of money, so I called it a success.

Failing to give the speech I'd memorized didn't matter as much as the fact that I had set out to do it. Challenging myself to get better and then standing on that stage was a big step for me. The fact that it didn't go so well wasn't a step backward. To me, it was an important part of my journey forward, toward embracing a life that would allow me to have an impact in every way I could. After all, standing up, giving a speech, leading with confidence—these are all skills that are necessary if you want to have any level of influence.

Having a full-time work schedule on top of twenty credits was sort of crazy now that I look back on it. But I still found time to go hang out at Denny's with friends, or to go see movies at the Briggsmore 7, where you could watch two second-run movies for $3. We could hang out and listen to live bands at the Red Lion Inn some weekend nights. And there was always cruising downtown on McHenry Avenue late nights on Fridays and Saturdays.

Not wanting to miss out on that experience, I sold my Pinto and traded up to a 1976 Camaro—a car with a powerful engine that (apparently) was so cool that one day when I was coming back from work (and not looking particularly put-together), a girl in a nearby car got out of the passenger seat, ran into my lane, and handed me her phone number through the window.

That summer, I went on a couple of dates. Dating wasn't common in Iran, and it wasn't allowed after the Islamic government was established. There was courtship, which meant that you were courting someone for the sake of marriage—not the American (or, more-generally, Western) idea that you could just explore, date, go to dinner and a movie, or even hook up without any intention to settle down with that person. I didn't have much interest in dating, to be honest, and didn't really have time for it. Plus, I never did (and still don't) believe in casually "hooking up"—far from it. But to dip my toe into dating made me feel, again, just a little bit more American than I was before.

Speaking of which, it was during this same period when my brother decided to Americanize his name. He started going by Frank, which is how everyone knows him to this day. The name "Pat" or "Patrick" never felt right for me. Sean and some of my friends tried calling me that name for a while, but I just didn't like it. I insisted everyone stick with Payam. I figured I could still be an American without having an American-sounding name, and I was right. What's an "American" name, anyways?

I didn't keep the Camaro for very long. After the Gulf War started that August, gas prices went through the roof. The Camaro ate through gas and cost way too much to fill up. So I sold it for $1,200. With gas prices as high as they were, I thought, *I go to Modesto Junior College. It's only two miles from home, and then two miles to work. I can walk it. I don't need a car!* That lasted for about a week before I went out and bought a car that was better on gas, but still super cheap. Then I sold that car a few months later and tried something new.

Buying and selling cars became a bit of a hobby for me. Over the next three years, I bought and sold sixteen different vehicles, almost all of them for less than $2,000. I learned how to do some basic things to keep those cars working, going to junkyards to get parts, replacing headlights, and making simple fixes myself for a fraction of the cost of bringing them to a repair shop. I drove everything from a Nissan Pulsar to a Datsun convertible pickup truck (that's a pickup with a retractable, soft-top roof), complete with a giant, booming speaker system behind the seats. I even made a profit on some of them after cleaning them and fixing them up a little bit.

Still, as I grew into this new American persona as a Camaro-driving, Denny's-dining, sometimes dating-now-and-then kind of guy, I was a serious student—and a bit of a loner. I liked hanging out in the library and reading, especially at the historic Modesto town library or the library at MJC. It was there where I learned that the entire library system in America was essentially created by one man: Andrew Carnegie. Before that, I assumed that libraries were just a part of the local fabric of government services that citizens were afforded in the U.S. But the library system wasn't formed by the government. It was essentially formed by this one man, a wealthy man, who wanted to do something impactful. In the late 1800s and early 1900s, Carnegie donated something like $40 million to pay for nearly 1,700 new library buildings in communities all across the U.S. I didn't know much about the man or how he made his money, but it really opened my eyes and sort of blew my mind to think about the long-term impact one wealthy individual could choose to have on this country, and on the world. It's a lesson that stuck with me and, coincidentally enough, fell right in line with some of the lessons I had learned as part of my Faith.

Acquiring wealth is not frowned upon by Baha'is. On the contrary, living in the full abundance of God's grace during our time here on Earth is perfectly fine. Abdu'l-Baha himself stated that "wealth is praiseworthy in the highest degree, if it is acquired by an individual's own efforts and the grace of God, in commerce, agriculture, crafts and industry." The only caveat is that such wealth must serve humanity, to "enrich the generality of the people," and be expended for "philanthropic purposes" and "the promotion of knowledge."

It's hard to think of a more powerful, philanthropic effort to promote knowledge than the establishment of free libraries all over the country.

Being a Baha'i served as the foundation of my identity, and that has never changed. I think I'm a very practical guy. I see the Baha'i Faith as providing humanity with the best path to true happiness, joy, and living a life of impact. I often tell people that the world is better off today because Jesus sacrificed himself two thousand years ago. The spiritual beliefs, values, and ideals we believe to be so universal today did not come out of thin air. Religions brought those to us, and many sacrificed in order for these values to be viewed as universal. Baha'u'llah similarly sacrificed himself so humanity would be on a better path. It's up to us to study his writings and give it a chance. But again, we often prefer to learn the more difficult way.

In my late teens, living on my own, there were plenty of people around me who were partying all the time, and the peer pressure to have a beer or puff on a joint was real. That lifestyle simply wasn't something that interested me. I have plenty of close friends who choose to drink or smoke a joint. It simply isn't for me. I want to have an alert mind; I want there to be guardrails in my life that will protect me against vices, whatever they may be.

That doesn't make me perfect or better than anyone else, or anything like that. But there is another element: After years of facing persecution and risking my life on a daily basis for the sake of my Faith, why would I ever consider throwing it away for the sake of a drink, a puff, or a pill?

Was it difficult to resist the temptation and the peer pressure in college? Honestly, no. Not at all.

Again, once you've experienced real difficulty in your life, these sorts of daily "struggles" and "difficulties" seem small.

And also, I would see what those decisions would often lead to, and that's not what I wanted for me. I was too busy trying to make a life. I didn't have the luxury to numb myself.

I'm glad I didn't have that luxury.

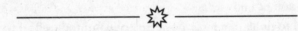

In the fall of 1990, my brother and I received some wonderful news: Our parents had finally been cleared to come to the U.S.!

It had been two-and-a-half long years since we had seen them, and it's difficult to describe the amount of joy and excitement we felt as my brother and I drove to San Francisco to pick them up in Frank's Honda Civic. Just like when Sean picked us up, we got lost trying to make our way home, but we eventually made it back to Modesto—where my mom saw her sister for the first time in ten years.

Finally, our whole family was together again.

My parents, my brother, and I all moved into another apartment in the same complex where Frank and I had been living. My sister and her family also lived only about two miles away. Our new apartment was a little larger, somewhat nicer, two-bedroom apartment, but still pretty run-down. It didn't matter. We were all so grateful to be alive, to be together, and to be starting our lives all over again in the U.S.

Given my success in running for president of the International Club, I decided to take an even bigger leap in my second year: I ran for student body president. There were four other candidates, but the most serious contender was a girl named Kendra. Here I was, this Persian-looking young man with an unusual name, broken English, and a very thick accent, up against a highly qualified, all-American redhead. I campaigned hard while remaining civil and loving toward all of my opponents. And while my English wasn't quite as good as I thought it was (as I found out when trying to express myself during debates), I did okay when making individual speeches, handing out flyers, shaking hands with students, and getting my fellow International Club members to spread the word about our success with the club.

In a constituency of twenty thousand students, I lost to Kendra by less than twenty votes.

To me, that was a huge win.

My self-confidence had grown, along with my overall Americanness. When I wanted to make some extra money toward the end of that school year, I even went out and did what so many American teens did during that era: found a job at the mall. Specifically, at RadioShack.

The chain-smoking manager of the place bragged that he made $2,000 a month, which sounded amazing to me, and I loved the fact that we would make a commission off of every sale we made. But the manager didn't give me any training, and I didn't know the first thing about what I was doing in that store.

One day, a man came in asking for a CB radio.

"I don't think we carry those," I said.

"What? Yeah, you do. They're right there," he replied, pointing to one of them on the shelf directly behind me.

"Oh," I said. "Then sure. Which one would you like?"

He started asking questions about which one had what features, and I'm thinking, *Dude, I didn't even know we carried them, so I don't think I'm gonna be able to help.*

How can any business expect to succeed when their employees aren't trained and mentored?

Despite my cluelessness, and through no efforts of mine, sales during the Christmas season went through the roof. I was excited by thoughts of how much money I was going to make before realizing that RadioShack reduced its commission rate during Christmas sales. On top of that, the day after Christmas, a lot of people started returning their gifts—and with every return, the company took back our commissions. The way it was going, I was going to owe money to the store! After doing the math, I realized I was earning less than I did making pizza. So I quit.

It had been fun to hang around the mall. It was the only place a girl ever asked for my number outside of the time a girl ran up to my Camaro at a stoplight to give me hers. "For my friend, over there," she said. So I gave her my number. Since dating was not a priority for me, I wouldn't ask anyone out, and I'm still surprised that girls every now and then were interested in offering their phone numbers to me. I was far from stylish, and one could not really consider me cool. Not that I wasn't trying.

Working at a mall could be costly. You're surrounded by shops full of stuff that tempts you every day. For example, that December, on the same day the girl asked for my number, I decided to buy this cool leather jacket from the leather store. It cost something like $250, which I couldn't afford all at once, so I put it on layaway.*

I made small payments on that jacket for months. By the time it was mine, it was summer. It was hot, so I never wore it. When the weather cooled off again, I decided I didn't really like the jacket anymore, which means it was a complete waste of money.

That was the last time I ever put anything on layaway.

It was all a part of my learning curve.

Of course, my parents faced a learning curve, too. In some ways—setting aside the fact that it's more difficult for an older person to

---

* If you're not familiar with what "layaway" is, it means that the store would hold the item for you as long as you made a minimum payment every so often. They did so without charging any interest, so once it was paid off, the item was yours.

learn a new language—they had it easier than we did, simply because my brother and sister and I were there to help them through everything, and to help them understand everything. But some lessons on life in America they would learn on their own. And my dad started out with a big one.

My dad was fifty-six when he arrived here, and like many from our part of the world, his teeth had been badly neglected for years. He needed work done, and after hearing about my experience at the dentist, he went to a different dentist than the one I had seen.

This one was worse.

This particular dentist had some sort of a chip on his shoulder from the start.

While my dad was in the chair getting his first filling, the dentist asked him some pointed questions, like, "Why are you in this country?"

My dad answered honestly, joyfully, speaking through his numbed-up lips. He let the dentist know he was a refugee who had fled religious persecution in Iran, and was grateful to be welcomed into the U.S., where his children had immigrated as well.

The next time he went, the dentist's questions turned to things like, "Why are you people taking away our resources?"

The third time he went, my dad came back to the apartment a few hours later—and all of his teeth were gone. Every single tooth in his mouth. Gone. The dentist had pulled every one of them.

Blood was still trickling out of his swollen bottom lip when he walked through the door, and my mom went crazy. "What has happened? Why? Why?!"

"The dentist said none of my teeth were fixable," he said. "They all had to be pulled."

"Even if that's the case, there was no reason to pull them all at once!" she said.

She was right. There was no good reason.

Our father's smile was forever changed, as was his ability to eat properly.

I found it remarkable that his first negative interaction with anyone in America happened to be with a dentist, just like it was for me.

He would eventually see a different dentist to get a full set of dentures, but they never fit him well. He's struggled with them ever since.

In retrospect, we should have sought legal advice and maybe even filed suit. It would then have been up to the legal system to decide if that dentist did anything wrong or not, and whether compensation was in order. Perhaps if we had shared our experience with the city attorney, the justice system would have decided if what he did had broken the law. But back then, as new immigrants, we were a little bit afraid about what to do. Did we have the right? Could we say something?

Separately from the legal issues of what the dentist did, one cannot help but wonder if what he did was driven by prejudice. There are prejudiced people in the world. There is no question. But you know what? I feel that often we are too quick to call people prejudiced, to call people bigots, and to cancel them and label them, and so on. So I don't want to go there. As a proponent of peace and unity, it is of no value for me to label, condemn, or spew hatred toward others. More often than not, what we need to stay focused on is us and what we can do to make positive changes in the world.

The same year I arrived in the U.S., Michael Jackson released a powerful song called "Man in the Mirror." And the message found in his lyrics resonated with me: If we want to make the world a better place, we have to start with looking at what we can change in ourselves. It is similar to a lesson that Mahatma Gandhi taught, which is widely quoted (and sometimes misquoted) in memes and on inspirational posters. But it is also a lesson that is found in the writings of the Baha'i Faith, including this passage by Abdu'l-Baha from Star of the West: "Whenever you recognize the fault of another, think of yourself: What are my imperfections?—and try to remove them. Do this whenever you are tried through the words or deeds of others. Thus you will grow, become more perfect. You will overcome self, you will not even have time to think of the faults of others."

I cannot help but apply that lesson to this situation with my father.

Embracing this lesson does not mean that justice isn't important. It does not mean that the government shouldn't ensure that people have safety in their lives. All it means is that as an individual, I prefer not to focus on the kinds of things that could make me feel like a victim.

My father was in a vulnerable position, and for whatever reason, he was harmed.

He would learn to be far more cautious when choosing health care providers, and more outspoken in defense of his own body and health in the future.

He would put it behind him. A lesson learned. And we would all grow wiser because of it.

The junior colleges in California have an amazing program with the University of California system that allows any student with a GPA of 3.5 or higher to be automatically accepted into the UC system. You simply need to sign a contract in advance and then deliver on your grades.

Just as I did in high school, I worked hard to keep my GPA as perfect as possible. And I did. Therefore, from MJC, I now had the option to complete a four-year education at either UC Davis or UC Santa Barbara. I was accepted to both, but I didn't know anything about the city of Santa Barbara. Years later, I would visit a friend in that beautiful coastal town and kick myself for not knowing better—UC Santa Barbara was on a beach, and (if I may add) seemed to be populated by some of the most beautiful women I had ever seen. But at the time, I looked on a map and saw that UC Davis was located just outside of Sacramento, a lot closer to Modesto, and therefore closer to my family. So, in the fall of 1991, that's where I chose to enroll.

I would end up loving Davis, and that's where I would earn my degree in three years (because of my community college credits).

As I mentioned earlier, though, I often learned more outside of the classroom than inside. And there was one more very important lesson I learned before I completed my two years at MJC, a lesson that I think is important to share.

Somehow, around everything else on my schedule, I managed to set aside enough money and carve out enough time to take a Shotokan Karate course.

One day, the sensei, an African American Shotokan master, asked me to break a board. I tried a few times, and I couldn't do it. It hurt my hand something awful.

"The problem is," he said, "you're thinking defeat. You're not thinking about the fact that your hand is going to be on the other side of the board."

No kidding, I thought. All I was thinking was, *My hand really hurts!*

"Just focus on the objective. See your hand on the other side of the board. Imagine what that will feel like. How good it will feel, knowing you did it—knowing that you accomplished your objective."

My objective, I thought. I wasn't thinking about the objective.

I listened to him. I changed my attitude. I visualized my hand on the other side of the board. I made myself believe, "Yes, I'm going to do this!"

I focused. I concentrated. I took a deep breath and exhaled slowly. I breathed in again, tightened my muscles, and exhaled with a yell as I struck the board with this new mentality—and it broke.

I was astounded.

Optimism worked.

I believed I could do it, and therefore, I could.

That's when it hit me: This was the final piece that was missing; the last step I needed to take in order to make my way forward, purposefully, in this country. I needed to believe that I could, and therefore, I would. Whatever it was. Whatever I dreamed. Whatever I wanted to achieve or accomplish was possible as long as I visualized the objective before taking action to make it happen.

"I believe I can, and therefore, I can."

This is the core belief, the particular optimism rooted deeply in the American Dream that sets this country apart from the rest of the world. It is this belief that allows people here to create and build and thrive in ways that they might not anywhere else, even when they've started with nothing.

After breaking that board, the triumph of optimism swelled in my core.

I let every bit of that feeling stitch the torn fabric of my heart and fill up the loss of leaving my country behind.

I would have to wait two more years to become eligible to take the test and get sworn in as an American citizen.

But on that day? The day I learned just how powerful optimism can be?

That's when I became an American.

REFLECTIONS ON CHAPTER TWELVE

Do you remember the first time you challenged yourself to step out of your comfort zone in a meaningful way? What was the result? How did it make you feel?

When was the last time you challenged yourself to step out of your comfort zone?

When thinking about what my dad went through with the dentist, does it remind you of a time when you or someone you loved was taken advantage of in some way? How did you handle that experience? Did you enact revenge, take your complaint to higher authorities, or find a way to make peace with it and move on, maybe a little more cautious about your dealings in such matters in the future?

Knowing that optimism is, ultimately, at the root of what it takes to dream bigger dreams and accomplish new things in life, how often do you think about ways to remain optimistic? Do you find yourself falling into patterns of believing that you can't? (It's okay! We all do sometimes.) If so, what would it take for you to discover or to rediscover—and reclaim—your optimism? It could be as simple as reminding yourself, daily, of what I believe to be a fact: "I believe I can, and therefore, I can."

CHAPTER THIRTEEN

PAINTING A FUTURE

After nearly three years in the U.S., I had barely traveled anywhere outside of California. I had attended events in Phoenix and Las Vegas, but without any free time to explore those cities. I had driven down to L.A. and back in my Pinto one day, and I had taken a bus to Anaheim to go to Disneyland with the International Club. I had traveled up to Sacramento to check out UC Davis, and gone a little farther north, too, to Chico, to visit my brother, who was enrolled as a computer science major at Chico State. One day, I took a trip over to Tahoe, where I had the opportunity to see that beautiful lake, along with some snow. But that was about it.

So, in the spring of 1991, after my second year at the community college wrapped up, I decided to take my very first vacation. Three friends from the International Club and I rented a Toyota Corolla and set out to see as much of the U.S. as we could. Ten states in ten days, with a goal of visiting every national park we could.

We hit Mt. Rushmore, Devil's Tower, Monument Valley, the Grand Canyon, Arches National Park, and Yellowstone, making this whirlwind loop that took us all the way up to Cody, Wyoming, and back—this motley crew, including a friend from Japan, one from Guatemala, another from Germany, and me. We all looked different. We all had different accents.

We each carried a grand total of about $300, which meant we couldn't afford to stay anywhere other than inexpensive roadside motels. But we did it, and it was one of the best things I had ever done. The national parks were more beautiful than I could have imagined, even after reading so many books and seeing pictures of some of these places going all the way back to my childhood. And the experiences we had were nothing we ever could have planned, in part because they were driven by the people we met along the way. In Cody, for example, we stood out. As soon as we stopped the car, we could tell the locals were thinking, *Who are these people?* Not just because of our varying nationalities, but because we were four odd-looking people from California, which seems about a million miles from Cody, Wyoming, in every way you can think of. But some of the kids in town started talking to us and helped us figure out what to do with our one day in town. We ended up going to a rodeo—a real-life, all-American rodeo—which was one of the coolest experiences ever.

Road tripping became one of my favorite styles of traveling from that summer on. And it set me up well for the experiences I would have over the next three years, as I split my time between weekdays at school at UC Davis and weekends home in Modesto—with a lot of time in my various cars or trucks in between.

The move from Modesto to a real college town and real college dorm felt like a major step up in my life. Davis is a leafy, Northern California exurb of Sacramento, the state's capital. The town wraps around the school, and most of the 68,000 people who live there either work, teach, or study at UCD.

Davis has a smaller population than Modesto, but somehow it feels more cosmopolitan, probably because of the university and its intellectual atmosphere. It was there where I began to meet the sort of aspirational go-getters and change-makers I had imagined Americans to be. The university and Davis itself had a real buzz, a hum of activity and ambition, as if the people at the university somehow had bigger plans for the future, and those plans gave the place a sense of import and consequence.

I went to UC Davis as a chemistry major with the goal of going into medicine. I thought I wanted to become a surgeon, which my parents would've really liked. Since they had both worked for hospitals, they looked at it as a noble profession. I thought the money would be good, too. But it wasn't long before my old entrepreneurial dreams started to erase my desire to work in the medical industry.

One of my wealthier friends at school asked me one day, "So, what are your financial goals? How much do you want to make after you graduate? How much is enough for you?"

"Well," I said, "I think I'll be disappointed if I don't make $100 million within ten years."

"Get outta here!" he said. "First, that's not gonna happen. But second: Why? Why do you want that much money?"

"To give it all away," I said.

The interesting thing is I fully believed I'd achieve that. I wasn't kidding. I wanted to make money. Lots of money. It was a motivator for me. And a big part of that motivation was because I wanted to have enough money to make an impact—to make the world a better place.

I was a long way from any of that, but the thought of it, the dream of it, the vision of it kept me going. I did not want to be poor, and I no longer wanted to struggle financially. At all. The idea of becoming wealthy was a major motivator for me. After all, in the U.S., you gain influence in one of two ways: being a celebrity or being successful in business. I couldn't even pronounce the word "celebrity."

Becoming wealthy would not be easy, and I accepted that. I embraced the idea of working hard for what I wanted to achieve—knowing full well that the results of my efforts might not be seen right away. The road to wealth is a journey. No one said it would be an easy one.

I loved the following quotes from George Bernard Shaw: "Imagination is the beginning of creation. You imagine what you desire, you will what you imagine and at last you create what you will." And: "People are always blaming their circumstances for what they are. I don't believe in circumstances. The people who get on in this world are the people who get up and look for the circumstances they want, and if they can't find them, make them."

So I worked every night and weekend to make ends meet—every vacation period, even spring break—anytime I wasn't in class. And even after all of that, I was flat broke most of the time. I remember going to the ATM to get some cash one day, but I only had $17 left in my account. The machine only dispensed $20 bills. I was too embarrassed to go into the bank and ask for a measly $10, so, more than once, I reached out to my brother at Chico State for help. If he had it, he would send me a single $20 bill in the mail so I could eat. I didn't care for ramen, so my poor-college-kid meal of choice was potatoes. I didn't like bacon or sour cream, and didn't want to spend what little money I had on toppings anyway. So I ate potatoes plain. Sometimes a week at a time.

There were other times when my brother called me for help, and if I had it, I'd drop a $20 bill in the mail to him. We were both going to school full-time while working nonstop, and barely able to get by. I rarely had time to go to parties, or concerts, or just to hang out in the quad like other students did. I could only imagine what my college experience would have been like if I came from a wealthy family, or if my education were free, paid for by the government or scholarships or other sources. It's mind-boggling to think about how many students like me could benefit from free higher education, and how much the world would benefit from the higher education of all of those students if they weren't forced to study while under so much financial stress.

Having said that, though, I don't think I would trade my struggles for any of that. Those difficult days were all part of the tapestry that has made me who I am. And I am grateful for that.

The schedule I kept never really allowed me to settle into the communities of either city, which made me feel like a bit of a nomad. But I also realized pretty quickly that the hourly jobs I held at Pizza Palace, the T-shirt shop, and even my time at S&W were not giving me the experience I needed to advance professionally.

Moving to Davis to go to university there also meant I needed to find a job closer to school. So I went to the student employment office to see if they could help me find something more suited to my future.

At first, I looked for a job in my chosen field. I thought working in a chemistry lab or a hospital would be a good idea, but that didn't happen. I learned that graduate students were far more likely to get those jobs than an underclassman like me. But I also knew that my eventual professional life might include managing. I had managed a few employees at Pizza Palace, at least at a rudimentary level, and I liked it. So I asked about managerial positions that might be available, and that's when I first learned about a company called Student Painters.

The goal of the Student Painters program was to train and develop college students into young entrepreneurs. They were a house-painting company, but instead of hiring students on an hourly basis to grab a brush and paint houses for them, the company trained entrepreneurial-minded students to become managers and business professionals, so they could go out, market and book paint jobs, and hire and manage teams of painters on their own and produce tens of thousands of dollars in house-painting revenue in a summer. It sounded perfect.

I applied for the opportunity at the career center, and then a manager named Tim Karman called me. He asked me to meet him at Theta Xi Fraternity house close to campus—an interesting environment for my initial job interview. Tim and I got along great from the moment we met. To this day he is a close friend. He is now the Global Head of Internet Investment Banking at Royal Bank of Canada. In fact, many of the successful Student Painter hires did well later on. It was a great training ground, and also a great way to filter hard workers and those with entrepreneurial spirit from others.

When I first encountered them, the Northern California branch of Student Painters had about one hundred college students as managers during its peak summer months, and about 1,500 painters. So my first job was to come on board as a rookie manager—to work during the spring to market our house-painting services to homeowners and landlords, to give free estimates, and close the sales. Then, during summer, I would hire painters and manage jobs from start to finish.

There was no salary—my income would depend entirely on my own hustle, creativity, and work ethic. I would only make a profit if I could run a profitable business. Working on commission—or, to be more accurate, on the profit margins left over after deducting a 25 percent royalty to the corporate office plus the cost of labor and materials—seemed a little risky, but I was up for the challenge. The good news: I didn't have to pay them anything to join as a temporary franchisee. Such a deal, right? Some might look at it as a bit of a scam, hiring young workers to go out and promote a company's services without any guarantee of pay for the time, effort, and investment in supplies they put in, while the company itself takes no risk beyond the cost of training the hired managers/franchisees how to sell and manage job sites. But I saw it as an amazing deal with lots of potential upside, and I didn't mind the risk.

After Tim interviewed me, I was sent up the ladder for an interview with a regional VP. He hired me, and then the company trained me. They taught me how to generate house-painting leads, how to give estimates to homeowners, allowed me to use their brand, offered a warranty on the jobs I would finish, and provided me with insurance coverage, too. Most importantly, I had mentors—successful veteran Student Painter managers and entrepreneurs who had started out the same way. I could rely on their advice and counsel. My primary mentor was Tim. One of the company's mottos was "show them, don't tell them," which meant mentors were expected to get out in the field and show us how to give estimates, book jobs, manage job sites, and so on, and not just tell us in theory. Tim did that, and he was great at it.

I was hired in fall of 1991, went to training in February of 1992, and my preseason for estimating and booking for the summer began in early spring.

I was confident that I could give out estimates, book the house-painting jobs, hire the painters, and manage them as they painted the homes. I would be good at all of that. But once things got rolling, I began to realize how difficult it would be to turn a profit. Student Painters took 25 percent off the top of each job I booked. I kept 75 percent, which sounded terrific until I had to settle my bills. You wouldn't believe how much paint costs! After I paid my painters—typically three of them on each job—I had to pay off the paint store account for all of the supplies, plus my marketing costs, and my own expenses, too, one of which was trading in my car for a truck so I'd be able to get all the paint and equipment where it needed to go.

It started to become clear that many Student Painters managers would actually lose money over the course of a summer. I couldn't let that happen. I had already quit my other jobs in order to give my all to this!

At our biweekly managers' meetings, where we'd bring all the checks we had collected during the prior two weeks and get our payroll done, I could tell which of the rookies weren't succeeding—they usually had paint all over their clothes. They were trying to cut costs by doing some of the manual labor themselves, and it wasn't working. Trying to be both the entrepreneur and the manual labor was just not the right strategy. The more they tried to cut costs, the more money they lost. So I figured out what I needed to do: focus on selling jobs and managing painters, not painting. I had to build a sales pipeline. That meant really hustling for estimates.

Reviewing my statistics with Tim made it clear that I was booking only 10 percent of my estimates. That was much lower than the average. But then again, considering my accent, my poor English, the way I dressed and looked, I think I did pretty well! The good news was that I now knew my primary driver: I had a 10 percent close rate, so the rest was simple math.

If I kept my estimate pipeline full and continued with that tiny 10 percent conversion factor, I could still make money. My average job paid about $1,500. When all was said and done, I could turn a 25 percent profit. So, by the end of summer, if I wanted to make $20k for myself, I had to produce about $75,000 in sales. That meant I had to book fifty jobs, which at a 10 percent closure rate meant that I had to go out and give five hundred estimates.

That's a lot of estimates! To get there, I figured I had to source at least 1,500 leads.

I quickly learned that selling was all about transferring enthusiasm and building trust. I also learned that because I looked like a foreigner, and talked like a foreigner, I would have to work harder than many of my peers in order to make a sale. So I tried to psych myself up before every estimate. I'd listen to Anthony Robbins or Wayne Dyer on the way to the address. I'd crank up my favorite music before I stepped out of the truck.

That summer I had the worst closure rate of any manager I knew. I also got chased by dogs at people's homes, and managed to get stung by bees on jobsites on multiple occasions—nine times at just one of them! But the experience taught me an important lesson: If I wanted to make a certain income, I had to first know my numbers, then find out what it would take to drive that income, and then take the hard steps to make it a reality. It was just like putting my fist through a board: I had to set an internal goal for myself, to see my objective, clearly, and then meet it. If I didn't hustle on the front end by giving estimates and booking jobs, my life would suffer on the back end.

Somewhere in the process of building my pipeline, I heard a quote that inspired me. I'm not sure who said it first, and in trying to find its origins I've come across similar quotes from George Bernard Shaw and Winston Churchill. But it goes like this: "Some people dream of great accomplishments, while others stay awake and do them."

I was determined to stay awake and "do."

The fact that I started out with a bottom-of-the-barrel close rate didn't deter me. It actually was liberating to know what the path to making my desired income looked like. I now had a formula that would lead me to $20,000 in income. It motivated me to work harder, and longer. I had to figure out what it took to close a sale, and how I could generate enough leads to give five hundred estimates. Some of the better Student Painters managers had 40 percent close rates—they really knew how to close a sale! I envied their ability, since it meant they could earn more with less work, and I tried to learn how to do that from my mentors. To make matters worse, my geography was Modesto, where average job sizes were only $1,500 while many other managers in places like San Jose had job sizes of over $2,500 to go along with close rates that were much better than mine, which meant that with a fraction of estimates and jobs they could produce the same amount of revenue as fifty jobs in Modesto.

But I didn't let that stop me. I started picking up self-help books, business books, and specifically "how-to-sell" books, reading them cover to cover. It marked the beginning of a lifelong habit that would keep me motivated in all sorts of different environments.

During the hot summer of 1992, I wrote five hundred estimates, and sure enough, my meager 10 percent close rate held true. We ended up painting fifty homes—not bad for less than ninety days. I tried to keep three painting jobs going at the same time, at all times. And at the end of the season, I'm happy to report I made my goal. I earned $20,000 in profit—enough to cover tuition and basic living expenses for the upcoming school year.

Thank God.

Despite the long hours dedicated to Student Painters, I worked hard at my schoolwork during my second year at UC Davis. And I did well in chemistry—until I took organic chemistry. I wasn't a fan. Then I had to take physical chemistry, I didn't even know what it was, and it turned out to be the most difficult thing I've ever encountered in my life. I quickly started to question my commitment to becoming a doctor—especially as it applied to making money. Making money is not a good motivation for going into medicine. So, at the end of my first year at Davis, I changed my major.

Environmental causes were gaining more and more attention in the early 1990s. There was all manner of renewed interest in clean energy and recycling. College students across the nation were celebrating Earth Day every year, and I thought, *Maybe I can start a business to ride this positive wave.* Not "get a job," but "start a business." That's where my mind went.

I changed my major to environmental toxicology, thinking I could gain the right foundation to start a business with an end goal of cleaning up superfund sites and other environmental messes. There was still a lot

of chemistry to take, but it wasn't physical chemistry—and the end goal
was much more aligned with my entrepreneurial aspirations. So I felt I
could put up with it until I made it to graduation. But that's all it became:
an act in "putting up" with something. School wasn't fun for me. My
classes seemed more and more irrelevant, filled with information I would
never really use in life. And it was exhausting. If I could go back, I'd study
literature, English, journalism—something that could make me a better
communicator (a life skill that I wished I were better at).

What fired me up was being an entrepreneur.

Still, I was determined to graduate with a degree—and that would
take me one more year.

At the end of the Student Painters' 1992 season, the company named me
Rookie Manager of the Year. I received that award at a dressed-up gala
in Lafayette, California, in the fall of that year, and they also promoted
me to district manager—the job that my mentor, Tim, used to have. The
upper managers let me know that they didn't give me the award or the
promotion because of any particular talent or aptitude I had over my
peers, but more because I just plain worked harder than most people. I
was proud of that.

As a district manager in 1993, I still did not have a salary. Instead, I
would earn a percent of my team's sales (above a certain threshold), which
meant I no longer had to go out and get chased by dogs and stung by bees.
I hired other people to do that part of the job, and I served as their mentor.

One of the rookie managers I hired was a guy named John Truchard,
who to this day is one of my best friends. John was born on the Fourth
of July, in Texas, and seemed more American than George Washington to
me. I almost felt bad that his mentor had to be me, this foreigner with a
thick accent! But I guess it went okay, because in his very first summer,
his close rate was nearly 50 percent. It was ridiculous. Only in my dreams
could I achieve that.

Over the course of my final year at UC Davis (1993–1994), Student Painters promoted me again, this time to general manager. I became responsible for recruiting a larger group of managers in many cities, and I would continue to get paid a percentage of the business those managers generated once my teams started painting in the summer after graduation.

I'll admit that I learned quite a bit more in years one and two with Student Painters than I did toward the end, but no matter what, I gained an enormous amount from the experience. It taught me how to manage people, how to make a profit, how to manage P&L (profit and loss statement)—not in the abstract in some classroom, but through the actual work of running a business that was tough to run: a business with almost 100 percent employee turnover each year, since most painters and managers we hired only lasted one season, and a business that called for intensive training and oversight, since inexperience is no excuse in a job that directly interfaces with customers. You can't just go around messing up people's homes.

The money I earned from that job contributed to something meaningful to me as well: It allowed me to pay back the cost of the airfare that brought me to America. I never forgot the generosity that brought me here, for free, courtesy of Catholic Charities. So I paid them back in small increments, whenever I could afford to, knowing that the money I sent them would be donated to another refugee in the future. It was gratifying to be able to pay that back, and to pay it forward at the same time.

Making the decision to go to work for Student Painters was what I like to call a "life moment"—a turning point that changes the direction of your entire life. It was the moment I chose to take a job that would benefit me far beyond anything a simple hourly paycheck ever could—an entrepreneurial job that would provide me with experience and a new sort of education that would take me into all sorts of people's homes, and a courtroom, and into paint stores, and to new cities, teaching me more than I could ever have learned in a classroom alone. And then it helped me learn to mentor others, not only to develop their own capacities, but to get my goals achieved by motivating others to hit their own targets. To learn how to manage, how to hire, how to motivate, how to think like an entrepreneur . . . it was the experience of a lifetime.

Working for Student Painters taught me that I could effectively and profitably run an American business. And that gave me the self-confidence to think about starting my own.

REFLECTIONS ON CHAPTER THIRTEEN

What are some "life moments" that stand out from your own journey so far?

Can you imagine what your life would look like if those moments didn't happen?

If you went to college, are you one of those rare individuals who pursued a career in your chosen major? Or did you move in a different direction after graduating? Why did you make that decision? And are you happy with the decision you made? If not, what would it take for you to change direction again?

What are some of the lessons you learned from your first job during and/ or after you completed your education? How important was it to gain that experience, and how has that experience served you since?

Did you love the work you were doing then?

Do you love the work you're doing now?

CHAPTER FOURTEEN

DECISIONS, DECISIONS

My decision to take a chance working for Student Painters was an easy one. Relying on my own entrepreneurial spirit to pay my way through school might be considered a big risk to some people. But it didn't feel that way to me. It felt more like an opportunity. I didn't hesitate to apply for the job, and I jumped in with both feet after my very first meeting.

I didn't agonize over the decision.

I didn't weigh the pros and cons for days or weeks on end. I just went for it. Nor did I spend any time struggling over the decision to continue with Student Painters after graduating college. I had just graduated from a well-known program at UC Davis, and I'm sure I could have found a job at any number of major corporations that were seeking fresh-faced environmental toxicologists. But I made my decision quickly and without a second thought.

I firmly believe that being decisive is a virtue and that being willing to make decisions with limited information is key in life. I find that more damage is done by being indecisive than by making wrong decisions.

A decisive person will have the ability to make even wrong decisions right over time, while the indecisive person will get stuck in paralysis.

Decision-making is important, and by the time I reached my early twenties, I had developed a two-step style of decision-making that still serves me well to this day:

One: Decide, and decide quickly. (In hours, when possible.)

Two: Don't agonize about the inevitable obstacles ahead.

For the first part, I'm not sure what in my background or upbringing led me to feel this way, but I cannot stand the idea of taking too long to make decisions. What's the point? I don't find being too cautious anything to be proud of. I see people paralyzed by decisions. How often do we see guys who have dated a girl for years and still cannot make up their mind whether to marry or not? How many people share ideas they have for a business, which they've been thinking about for years, but still haven't taken action on?

The way I see it is this: Once you gather enough information to make a decision, the process of gathering more information is only going to have a marginal impact on your eventual decision. So why bother? Just decide. Decide quickly. Move forward. Whatever happens next is exactly what's supposed to happen.

As for the second part, we cannot let the fear of what might happen or what might go wrong—or how impossible it might be to achieve—stop us from moving forward. Yes, obstacles will happen. No one said big goals would be without risks. In fact, the bigger the goal, the bigger (and more numerous) the risks. The key to making anything happen is to have the perseverance, the commitment, and the resourcefulness to look at those obstacles as inevitable and expected rather than as roadblocks. Look, if something is easy and has few to no obstacles ahead, then chances are it is not a big deal and not worth agonizing over anyway. So what we are talking about here are big and potentially life-changing decisions.

Perhaps because the types of decisions my family was all but forced to make in my early life were so big, they made everything else seem small by comparison. I didn't let the cost of going to college while I had no money stop me from going to college. I didn't let the dangers and risks associated with escaping Iran deter me from taking that journey. So why would the risks associated with other decisions in life turn into roadblocks? Risks exist, no matter how much you try to anticipate them or avoid them. Sure, if we decide too quickly about getting married, that could end in divorce, but the same is true for those who spend many years dating before marriage.

There is risk in any potentially life-changing decision you make, and you cannot de-risk completely. Therefore, I tend to believe there is by far more risk associated with being indecisive than by being decisive.

I'm not suggesting that we keep our heads in the sand and ignore the signs that we should not be wasting our time by committing to something that has a very high likelihood of failing. My point is that fear of potential unknowns, obstacles, and risks should never overtake our ability to decide in the first place.

I realize looking back now that having confidence in my own decision-making by the time I hit my early twenties was a skill that allowed me to move a little faster (and worry a lot less) than some of my peers.

And that skill would become more and more valuable with every passing year.

I graduated from UC Davis in June 1994, just a few weeks after my brother graduated from Chico State with his degree in computer science.

I felt like I'd reached the top of a mountain. I could not wait to put on my cap and gown and pick up my diploma. In Iran, I had been denied all access to higher education simply because I was Baha'i. Here? I had gone to school, all on my own, and worked hard every step of the way. It was a major accomplishment—even if my degree wasn't exactly in line with what I wanted to do with my life. I had a deep sense of gratitude for the U.S. and what it had offered me.

Frank was such a great programmer that he had managed to land an internship with Microsoft while he was going to school—an internship that led him directly into a full-time position once he earned his degree. So, when school ended, they asked him to move closer to their offices at the PowerPoint division in Menlo Park, which is next to Palo Alto. I drove him there with a rented U-Haul trailer attached to my truck. The engine blew out on the way home, in Belmont, on the 101, which was a major unexpected headache at the time, and it turned into a major expense for me that summer. Thankfully it was an expense I could absorb without going totally broke, but it hurt. Big time. And those sorts of ongoing expenses and unexpected problems can be devastating when you have no family wealth or other financial safety net to rely on.

I was doing well by Student Painter standards. So well that the company presented me with an opportunity to move to Texas to start and own the business there. But I wasn't sure that was the right move for me. I was truly starting to wonder what it would take to start another business on my own, something that had higher earning potential than painting. I had no idea what that business might be.

My brother had not only started a great job but had also gotten married.

Sure, he was a few years older than me, but after graduating around the same time, it felt a little bit like I was falling behind. Here he was, settling into adulthood and starting his own family while I was still messing around with this business that was no Microsoft, and which now might take me away from my family, after wanting nothing more for so many years than to see our family back together.

I was a little unsettled, I think. Unsure of what I should do next. I suppose a lot of young adults feel that way after graduating from college. But I also knew myself. I wasn't going to sit around agonizing over what to do for very long. I needed to make up my mind what to do. And soon.

It's funny looking back on different periods in our lives. I think in retrospect we can recognize the feelings we had at a certain time—when there was a sense of unease, doubt, or discomfort in the choices we were being offered, coupled by dreams or yearnings for something to change, even if those yearnings weren't yet well defined. I know for me there's a pattern to them, and the pattern may be familiar: Often, those periods are followed by significant changes in our lives.

I know now to watch for those feelings, not in the past, but in the present—to recognize them as indicators that it's time to make a change.

It's during those times when we're feeling uneasy and unsure of what comes next that we need to be especially open to seeing what's right in front of our eyes—to look for doors that might be opening and that we need to be ready to walk through if we want to make dreams come true. To recognize those doors as life moments and not allow them to get wasted.

One of those life-moment doors presented itself just a month after graduation.

In July, my brother called and said, "So get this. I wanted to buy a Honda, and I went online to look for cars, and you know what's crazy? Honda does not even own a website."

"Okay," I said. "That all sounds interesting, but I have no idea what you're talking about. I've never been online."

"Seriously? Never? I'll hook you up. I'll be there tomorrow," he said.

My brother drove all the way to Walnut Creek (where I had settled after graduation) to bring me a new computer and to set me up on CompuServe, which was one of the very first internet service providers available to the average consumer.

"Now, you have the internet," he said. "And this is what it is."

He started entering addresses and doing searches and going around to different company websites and libraries, and I could hardly believe my eyes. It was like the whole world was at our fingertips.

"Oh my God. This is unbelievable!" I said. "I can have a house-painting website."

My brother said he could build a website for me, if that's what I wanted. But he didn't really seem to want to talk about that. Instead, he started going on and on about this experience he'd had trying to shop for a new Honda. Because of his line of work, he was way ahead of the online curve compared to most Americans. He was already used to looking up all sorts of information online for whatever he needed, and he found it ridiculous that he couldn't find any information about cars right there on his computer. No dealerships had websites. Honda and other major auto companies didn't have websites, either. And to him, it looked like nothing but a great big void in the marketplace.

Since no one else had done it yet, he said, "What if we start a website providing information about cars online?"

"Can we do that?" I asked.

"What's stopping us?" he answered. "The internet is wide open to anyone. It could be a big opportunity."

"Sounds amazing," I said. "I love cars. And I've been a victim of car dealers more than once. I love the idea of having someplace to get all the info I want about any car I'd want to buy."

"If we build this one site where people can go to get information on all kinds of cars, we could go around and get all the dealerships to join. We can build web pages for each of them, and then people could use our site to connect directly to those dealers. Maybe dealerships can pay us for that, like a sort of advertising fee."

"Maybe they could subscribe and pay a monthly fee for that service we give them," I said.

"Sure. Something like that."

There was no road map to follow. Something like this had never been done before. But the more we spoke about it, the more it seemed neither one of us could let go of the idea.

I made the decision right then and there to go into business with my brother. I had made enough money that summer to get me through a few months, especially since I didn't have any tuition to pay that fall, and Frank figured he could build our site around his full-time work at Microsoft. So the two of us decided officially to build this business together in November of 1994.

We came up with the name "AutoWeb," and we planned for it to become a sort of information and connection hub for car sellers and buyers.

My brother built a simple website during his free time, and I ran around to dealerships and started picking up brochures for every new car and truck on the market. We used the free information to populate the website, so consumers could look at the specs and colors and options from the comfort of their home or office.

We didn't have a logo, and we didn't have money to pay someone to design one for us, so I made a quick trade with a graphic designer customer of mine. I agreed to paint his garage in exchange for a logo. And in a couple of months, our site was up and running!

Now, all we had to do was get a few auto dealerships to hop on board and pay us a monthly fee for the exposure they would get on our website.

No problem, I thought. By this time, I believed in my sales capabilities. So I started driving around to car dealerships and dealership groups, meeting with managers, and pitching them on this great opportunity to "join America's electronic auto mall!"

The response from just about all of them was the same: "We have no idea what you're talking about."

"We're calling it AutoWeb. And it's like an auto mall, but it's on the internet."

The internet was still so new, nearly everyone responded the same way I did when Frank first called me about it: "We've never been online."

That's when I would break out my bulky laptop computer for a demo. The laptop had the type of screen that you couldn't see unless you were right in front of it, so I'd have them gather close for a show-and-tell. Most of them thought it was interesting. Some of them thought it was a waste of time. But then, almost across the board, they said the dreaded words, "Well, I don't know. Let me talk to some other people here and think about it."

For the life of me, I could not close a deal.

It wasn't for lack of trying. After a couple of months, I had collected a stack of 150 business cards from dealership and auto-group managers I had presented to, yet I hadn't sold anything to any one of them.

At that point, I think a lot of people might have given up—but I just wasn't ready to quit.

I loved this idea of creating something big online. It felt right to me. It felt like the internet was about to change the world, and I wanted to be a part of that.

I was also listening to self-development guru Wayne Dyer every day as I drove around to the dealerships. I was listening to motivational talks by Anthony Robbins and Zig Ziglar. I was busy reading all of Zig Ziglar's books, just motivating myself in every way I could think of. And on the day when my brother suggested quitting, I had just been reading about Colonel Sanders—the founder of Kentucky Fried Chicken.

"You know," I said to my brother, "Colonel Sanders got one thousand noes before he got a yes. I've had only a hundred and fifty noes. So I'm gonna keep going. If you think about it, I'm already a hundred and fifty noes closer to a yes. So this is not the time to give up."

It wasn't costing us much to keep going, other than gas money and our time, so I hit the road again and tried twice as hard. I started listening to Guns N' Roses and all kinds of loud music to get me pumped up before walking into the dealerships. I dropped into their offices with the computer ready to go, and started making these big presentations, where I basically did all the talking and they just sort of sat there stunned.

That didn't work, either.

Then one day, I heard from a young woman named Shiva, who was one of the managers I oversaw at Student Painters. She happened to be Persian, and she called me just to check in and see what I was up to, since she hadn't heard from me in a while.

"Well," I said, "I'm trying to start this business, trying to sell this product, and I'm not having any luck."

I gave her the pitch, and she found the opportunity really interesting.

"Do you mind me trying as a favor and as a friend?" she asked.

I graciously accepted her offer. "Great," she said. "I'll try. I'll go tomorrow!"

She lived in Oakland, and I hadn't been to the dealerships in her area yet, so it was perfect.

Just before noon the next day, she called me.

"There's this dealership who's interested to sign up," she said.

I was shocked.

"Really?"

"Yes, really!"

We hadn't set a firm price to join our site or anything at that point, which meant I had some quick work to do. But later that day, I drove to the Cochran & Celli dealership in Oakland and met with Todd Simi, the manager, who also happened to be the son of the owner.

Cochran & Celli had started with one Chevy dealership in 1906. They'd been around forever, which worried me. That was the problem with so many of the dealerships I'd been to: They'd all been around so long, and they were all so used to doing what they were doing, that they didn't feel the need to do anything new. They advertised in newspapers and on television and radio, and by direct mail—and they relied on the brands themselves to do much of the work. After all, if you were the only Chevy dealer in Oakland, and people were interested in buying Chevys, you automatically got to sell a lot of Chevys.

Todd was different, though. He was a younger guy. He knew about the internet. He saw its potential and he wanted to get ahead of his competitors.

"So you're interested?" I asked.

"Yeah, I'm interested," he said. "How much? I have eleven franchises."

Eleven? I thought.

I hadn't even thought of a reasonable price point for one.

I figured about $1,000 each could get them listed on AutoWeb for the year, but I wanted to aim a little higher so there was room for negotiation, so I said, "Fourteen thousand dollars."

I was judging numbers based on what was big to me and not to business owners. And my instinct told me that Todd was interested in doing something that could have big impact. I figured that was his bigger concern, and not whether he could spend a few thousand dollars less.

I was right. He didn't blink.

He said, "Okay. But I want to be exclusive for the next twelve months in Contra Costa and Alameda Counties."

That was clearly an opening for me to ask for more money, so I told him, "Okay, I'll offer you exclusivity for the next twelve months in these two counties for all of your franchises . . . if you pay me $28,000 cash up front."

"Okay," he said, and we shook hands. I thanked him, and I went off and wrote the contract up myself. I didn't have money to hire a lawyer, so I just did the best I could. And he signed it.

He paid us.

And I went out and bought myself a BMW.

I know that sounds a little frivolous and out of character for me (or maybe not, for those who know me well), but it felt like the perfect reward. We were in the car business now, and I wanted—dare I say, needed?—a nice, reliable car to drive around in. I think most salespeople will agree that projecting an image of success is an important part of being successful. And in California, in the '90s, a BMW projected just the right image. (They're also really nice cars, and fun to drive.)

AutoWeb was off and running.

I'm still not exactly sure what went right for us in that moment. Why did that sales pitch work when so many others had failed? Was it Shiva? Was she a better salesperson than me? Highly possible. Was it just the fact that Todd was from a younger generation and was really interested in modernizing the business? This was early 1995, so maybe we had been a little ahead of our time in the first few months. Maybe we needed the media to hype up the internet for a little while longer before we could break through. Timing is everything, in just about any business.

Whatever it was, it didn't really matter. What mattered is that we didn't give up, even when a pragmatist might have thought it was time to throw in the towel.

I kept going for the yeses without letting the noes deter me.

I was also humble enough to notice that I had a 0 percent close rate. That left me open to trying something new when an opportunity presented itself, by making an on-the-spot decision to bring Shiva into the mix rather than continuing to do the same failed thing again and again and carrying the weight of 100 percent of our sales efforts on my shoulders. After all, the only thing Shiva could possibly do was improve the close rate we had. And once she proved that there was one potential buyer for our product, we knew there would be many more. That first sale helped bring about the much-needed confidence, which often is all that's needed to open the door to more sales.

But that wasn't the case. In the weeks that followed, I hit walls at more and more dealerships. In the few where I saw some genuine interest met with a hesitation at the cost, I ended up signing them up for free.

I figured that populating the website with dealerships, even if for free, might entice others to join.

But then, in the spring of 1995, I went to Stevens Creek Boulevard in San Jose, the site of a well-known Auto-Row.

My first stop was the BMW dealership. The general manager was a very nice guy named Bill Radcliffe, but Bill had little patience for this modern internet stuff I was trying to explain to him.

"Look," he said, "I don't get these things. Go to Stevens Creek Honda, our sister dealership. Norm Turner is the GM of that store—he's a nice British guy, and he will spend time with you to get it."

I followed his instructions and told Norm that Bill sent me.

Bill wasn't kidding. Norm was the nicest guy and patient as can be.

Usually dealerships have a lot of hustle and bustle going on, but not this one—and not this man. Norm Turner had done something new at this Honda franchise. He changed the way he sold cars. He put one price on all the cars, with no negotiation. I thought it was a great idea. Half the reason people negotiate is not to get a lower price; they just don't want to pay more than the next guy. That was really cutting edge at the time. One-price selling was uncommon in the industry, and still is today. A lot of the tension on the sales floor has to do with salespeople going back and forth between the management and the customer, negotiating with both sides to reach a deal. Norm found a way to eliminate that headache!

I had a good feeling from the start.

He closed the door to his office and said, "I've got the time. Tell me."

So I gave him the whole pitch about how quickly the internet was growing, and how our platform could help deliver interested customers directly to his door. Anyone from his area who searched for Hondas on our website would be shown his page, complete with all of his contact info and the ability to submit a request online, which we would fax (yes, fax!) directly to his dealership.

He got it. Instantly.

But he wanted to make a deal.

"I'll sign up with you, but I will not pay up front," he said. "We'll try it out for three months, and if in those three months you help me sell three cars, just three cars, I'll not only sign up, I'll also bring you all of the dealerships on the Stevens Creek Auto Row."

I asked him how he could promise such a thing, when not all of the dealerships were owned by the same people.

"Because we have an association. We have our collective ad budget," he said.

I got it. Instantly.

"Okay," I said. "That sounds good."

We shook hands and I left—with a very good feeling that this deal would be the one that could change everything.

REFLECTIONS ON CHAPTER FOURTEEN

Do you have a decision-making style of your own? One that serves you well? If not, can you develop one by looking back over some of the big decisions you've made on your journey so far?

Think about some of your "life moments." How did you go about making the decisions, big or small, that changed the trajectory of your life in some positive way?

What would happen if you replicated that same style of decision making in more of your decisions going forward? If it worked for you once, chances are it will work for you again.

"There are four qualities which I love to see manifested in people: first, enthusiasm and courage; second, a face wreathed in smiles and a radiant countenance; third, that they see with their own eyes and not through the eyes of others; fourth, the ability to carry a task once begun, through to its end."

—Baha'u'llah

CHAPTER FIFTEEN

THINK BIGGER

I t was 1995.

While my brother and I had no idea just how revolutionary our idea was, or how big of a business it could become, we knew we were on to something from the start—and there was no question that we were ahead of the curve. We were entering a space where there was very little competition, and we were surrounded by companies all over Silicon Valley that were suddenly exploding. Pioneering companies that had been building infrastructure for the online experience were going public for massive valuations. Stock prices soared. It's like all of Wall Street and the world were looking at the internet and seeing nothing but a massive, uncharted future full of opportunities.

The internet was a small place back then. There were just a few thousand websites in existence. So keeping an eye out for any competitors or prospective competitors was easy. There was one company called Dealer-Net that was doing something similar to us. They were based in Seattle, had started small, and were purchased by a large automotive firm called Reynolds and Reynolds right about the same time I made the deal with Cochran & Celli. Reynolds and Reynolds had been around since 1866. They created the paperwork almost every dealership in the country uses for car sales, and they had already made a successful transition into sales software and other types of software that served as the backbone to dealerships everywhere. They were a thousand-pound gorilla, mainly because they already had a trusted presence at thousands of dealerships.

The fact that they were interested in acquiring something like Dealer-Net was a bellwether for our industry.

We heard that DealerNet sold to Reynolds and Reynolds for $2 million.

On one hand, hearing about that sale was exciting. Obviously, we were on to something big by creating a service in this space, and the idea of splitting $2 million with my brother sounded pretty great! But that sale also made us nervous. With access to the Reynolds and Reynolds reach and cash, DealerNet was surely planning to expand. We worried they could bury us.

Another competitor called Autobytel emerged in Southern California, too, and they would become our primary competitor over time. But there really wasn't anybody else in this space worth mentioning until Microsoft jumped in with CarPoint in mid-1996. Still, any way we looked at it, the clock was ticking. We needed to make our mark and grow quickly if we wanted to own this space.

My brother created a presence on our website for Stevens Creek Honda by June, and he started getting visitors to his pages on our website. A few of them filled out the form with their information, which we faxed over to the dealership—but we initially had no way of knowing if any of those potential customers actually followed through and showed up at Norm Turner's lot, or bought a car from him. So I went to see Norm a month later.

He smiled the moment I walked through the door.

"Payam," he said. "I sold the three cars already."

"From our customers?" I asked.

"Yes!" he said. "So I'm going to make good on my promise."

(Maybe I'm wrong, but a part of me had a sneaking suspicion that he hadn't sold any cars that he knew of at all. He was just a good guy who truly wanted to help us succeed.)

He asked me to come to the Stevens Creek Auto-Row Association meeting that August to make a presentation, and I'll never forget it—because I made that presentation on the very same day that Netscape went public: August 9, 1995.

Netscape was *the* web browser at the time. They quickly gained close to 90 percent of the limited number of web users who were online in that period, long before Safari or Chrome were around, and before Google existed as a search engine. People all over the world went flocking to Netscape, mostly because it was easy to use. Until then, the internet was really built for the techies. But with Netscape, without any tech training whatsoever, the average person could pull up that browser and connect to the World Wide Web—without having to subscribe to a service like AOL. And it just worked, which is such a big part of what consumers want most. They want things to be easy, and Netscape delivered. (I still don't understand computers and software the way my brother does, but from what I understand, the old coding for Netscape actually serves as the foundation of the Mozilla Firefox browser, which remains to this day one of the most stable and reliable browsers in existence.)

While I was busy making my presentation in San Jose, Netscape—which had only been founded a year earlier, and which wasn't even profitable—made its IPO.

It was initially priced at $14 a share, but demand was so high that it opened midmorning at $28 a share. By midafternoon, the stock skyrocketed to $74.75 before settling at $58.25 at the close.

That closing price meant Netscape was suddenly valued at more than $2 billion, and that $58.25 stock price would triple before the year was over, to more than $174 per share.

Netscape's launch set the stock market on fire. I've heard it described as a shot heard around the world, but it was really a shot heard by Wall Street investors, especially in the venture capitalist (VC) world. It seemed that everyone and anyone who wanted to make money was suddenly on the hunt to find "the next big thing" in internet IPOs.

It was also a shot that kept ringing in my ears and rattling my brain.

I knew what we were doing had the potential to change the automotive industry, at least in the way that cars were retailed. We were disrupting the automotive business.

A trillion-dollar marketplace.

I had visions of what AutoWeb could become. How big it could become. How my brother and I could be sitting on the next big internet IPO.

That vision, which was accompanied by the thought of making hundreds of millions of dollars from that vision, drove me forward like a locomotive.

But the first thing we had to do was get more dealerships on board.

At the Stevens Creek group presentation, there was one guy—the owner of Courtesy Chevrolet—who was adamantly against putting any of their advertising money into AutoWeb, or anywhere else on the web.

"No, no, no," he said. "This is wrong. There's no proof it works. We shouldn't be doing this. We're wasting our money."

But on August 9, the Association voted, and thanks in great part to Norm's personal testimony, the majority voted for it. The deal got done. The Association agreed to pay us approximately $56,000 for one year, half up front and the other half once the dealerships' pages were up.

With Stevens Creek on board, there was no way the rest of the dealerships in the region could ignore us.

This was huge.

There was just one issue. When I drew up the contract, the financial office for the Association came back and said: "You need to be incorporated in order for us to pay you."

"Okay, sure," I told them.

I had no clue how to get incorporated.

"Great. We're excited. We're gonna come to your office to deliver the check by hand on such and such date," they told me, and I said that would be fine, too, thinking, *Shoot. We don't have an office.*

I went back and told my brother, and we decided we had better call a lawyer. We found someone in the phone book, told him that we needed to incorporate, and went to see him.

"Who's the CEO?" this attorney asked. "And who's the CFO?"

My brother and I just looked at each other.

"Guys, I need to know, who are the officers?"

"Well," I said, "my brother is older, he's more like the CEO, so I guess I'm the CFO."

I could tell he thought we were a couple of nobodies who didn't know what we were doing.

"Well, let's start with this," he said, slowly, like he was talking to a couple of preschoolers. "What kind of corporation do you want? LLC? Or C? Or—"

"We want the kind that can go public," I said, with visions of IPOs dancing in my head.

"O-kay," this lawyer replied with a smirk. "That would be a C-corp."

"Yes!" I said. "Then that's what we want."

The lawyer put our paperwork through to the appropriate state offices, we paid him for his time, and we went looking for an office space. We found something for $600 a month, which was cheap enough for us to cover for a while. We didn't really have a need for an office at that juncture. I was on the road, selling. My brother worked from home. We didn't have any office-based employees. It was just a physical presence to make us look more legitimate, so when the folks from the Association came by with the check, they would hand us the money with a little more trust that we'd be around to deliver on our promises.

I went out and bought a U.S. map and a map of California, and I pinned those to the wall behind a couple of desks. I installed a phone, an answering machine, and (of course) a fax machine. I went to Best Buy, bought a couple of computers, put a screen saver on each of them, and put some pens and pencils on the tables. The guys from the Association came by, they delivered the check, and the next day I returned the computers. I know it sounds like we built a façade, but we really didn't need any of that costly stuff to deliver what we had promised. In 1995, that was difficult for some businesspeople to understand. So showing a physical presence just helped us to gain the perceived legitimacy we needed to get started.

Our office would sit empty for quite a while after that as we kept building our business the way we knew how. But we kept it. We had a feeling it would come in useful soon. After all, once we had that check in hand, we were poised and ready to grow.

Once the Stevens Creek dealerships came on board, and after the Netscape launch got absolutely everyone talking about the future of the internet, our sales job got a whole lot easier.

I ran the numbers, just as I had done at Student Painters, and I set a reasonable goal of landing one new dealership for every full day of cold calls.

By "cold calls," I don't actually mean making calls on a phone. I mean showing up unannounced at dealerships—just as I had done from the start. Making appointments was too long and tedious a process for me to put up with. It was too easy for people to say no on the phone or to cancel last-minute. So my sales tactic was to show up out of the blue and ask if I could have a few moments of the owner's or general manager's time.

It worked.

But doing this all by myself, dealership by dealership, one at a time, was too slow. We needed sales help, and I knew just where to find it: through the network of amazing salespeople I'd met during my days at Student Painters.

The first to join me in 1995 was John Truchard, the rookie manager I had hired to run our Napa operations—the all-American Texan who had a 50 percent close rate in his very first year on the job. John had become one of my closest friends, and in addition to being a great salesman, he was really a smart business guy. (Fast-forward to today: John is the owner and CEO of one of the biggest wine brands in the country, JaM Cellars, the makers of Butter chardonnay.) He was just about to graduate from university when we spoke, and when I told him what we were trying to do with AutoWeb, he jumped in with a resounding, "Yes!"

With the two of us making cold calls, I figured we could double our reach—and with John's now legendary close rate, we would triple our sales.

John and I connected the same way Shiva and I had. These two were great, wonderful friends who had the skills to help me when I needed help, and who trusted that whatever I was doing was something they would be happy to support. It was almost as if I had unknowingly planted seeds by connecting and working with such good people in the past, both through Student Painters and at school, and suddenly it was spring, and those relationships came sprouting up from underground just when I needed them most.

It reminded me how important relationships are—not only to find and work with good people, but to build and cultivate those relationships.

John came from a wealthy family and always had big dreams. His parents weren't ones for giving handouts, though. They taught him how to work hard for what he wanted, and he did. He worked all through school, and right around the time he joined me at AutoWeb, he bought himself a BMW.

"I'm gonna keep this car until I make my first million," he told me.

I loved his attitude.

The two of us got to work. We had no more BMWs to buy. No perks we wanted or cared about. We wanted to build this business into a major enterprise, so whatever up-front cash we collected from those dealerships would get spent on building the business.

It wasn't complicated. One day at a time—one new dealer for every day of sales.

That was the number we wanted to hit, building a company one brick at a time.

Toward the end of 1995, I stopped by to check on the empty office space, and I noticed a light flashing on the answering machine. There were a few calls from business services looking to sell us paper and office supplies and things, but one call stood out: "Hi, this is so-and-so, and I represent

202 CROSSING THE DESERT

a venture capitalist. We want to invest in your company, so please give us a call back at . . ."

I'll be honest, neither my brother nor I really knew what the term "venture capitalist" (or VC) meant. We had a growing vision for our business and dreams of hopping on the tech-market excitement in the stock market if we could keep growing the way we were, but we knew nothing about raising money from investors. We didn't know that we could give up some percentage of ownership in order to gain the capital we needed now to build the business faster and stronger. Neither one of us went to business school, and it simply wasn't common knowledge to two twentysomethings who only a few years prior had come to the U.S. as refugees.

Why would someone want to give us money? we wondered. What's the catch?

We cautiously called the man back, and he let us know that they had some big backing: Motorola, the clear leader in cell phone technology at the time, and clearly a company with some money to spend. So we agreed to meet with him at our office. My brother and I put on suits, we showed up, and since we didn't have a conference table, we just set up three chairs facing each other in a triangle for the meeting.

Most people didn't carry cell phones in those days, but this guy? Not only did he carry one, but the whole time he talked to us, his phone kept ringing; and every time, he picked it up, to the point where it was extremely annoying. And on these calls, he spoke in German. After a few of them, he finally hung up and said, "Okay, I'm going to introduce you to this other guy, Mark Ross, so you guys can continue the conversation. And Mark is really interested in investing in you guys."

So we set up another meeting, this time with Mark Ross, and we realized what was going on. Prior to this, Motorola had bought Mark's business, On Word Information, an early database/imaging company, and they were getting ready to shut it down. Before that could happen, Mark and his team bought On Word's assets back, and they were left with $150,000 cash that they wanted to invest, rather than disperse to their shareholders.

Mark, God bless him, drove us nuts. Over eight months he met with us, again and again, to ask every question imaginable and study our numbers and learn every in and out of what it was that we did and how we were gaining new clients every day (which we were).

Finally, he agreed to invest the $150,000 in AutoWeb at an $850,000 valuation.

We agreed—turning Mark into the first investor in August 1996, and our first outside board member of AutoWeb, which meant that Frank and I, who were the only board members before this, would have to hold real board meetings going forward.

One of Mark's buddies was his lawyer, and we agreed that he should do the legal work to close the deal. That attorney then charged us $36,000. For legal fees. On a $150,000 raise. It was crazy. My brother and I were floored. The only lawyer we had ever paid was the guy who did our incorporation for a few hundred bucks.

But that was nothing compared to the news that hit us next. The very same month that we closed that $150,000 deal, our primary competitor, Autobytel, announced that they had raised $10 million at a $100 million valuation.

Frank and I were crushed at first, thinking, *What did we do?*

Had we really just wasted eight months negotiating for pennies on the dollar compared to what we should have or could have been asking?

Suddenly, in this brand-new industry we had helped pioneer, we weren't the big dog anymore.

We weren't the guys ahead of the curve.

In terms of finances, we were the underdog.

And what does the underdog do? Does he roll over and give up?

Not in my world.

After everything we had been through, every obstacle we had pushed aside, climbed over, and crawled through on our journey so far, there was only one response we could possibly have to receiving that kind of news.

It was time to think bigger—and work harder.

CHAPTER SIXTEEN

BECOMING THE FATHER OF LEAD-GEN

We took our little infusion of cash from Mark Ross and went on a bit of a hiring spree. Since John and I both knew how to sell and how to manage a sales force, I decided we should cover the country with commission-only salespeople. That was by necessity: We didn't have enough money to pay salaries. It's important to learn as an entrepreneur to work with what you have rather than what you wish you had. Cash is the lifeblood of any business, and cash flow is driven by sales. So we put everything we had into it. We placed small sales teams in key regions around the country, specifically to build on the work that had been done almost exclusively by John and me until that moment.

We looked at a map, divided the country into four sections, and opened an office in each: the Northwest handled by our Bay Area office; the Southwest handled out of Huntington Beach (which, along with the rest of Southern California, is a huge car market); the Northeast, handled from Foxborough, Massachusetts, right outside of Boston; and the rest of the country handled from down South in Atlanta.

Finding great salespeople was easy. This was a new industry, a new thing was being invented, so great salespeople came to us.

There's a certain excitement that comes with innovation. For salespeople and those with an entrepreneurial mindset, it lights a fire in the belly that's rarely rivaled by anything else in life. And when talking about innovation, I mean things like this: We published invoice prices online for cars. I know that seems like no big deal today, but back then? No one had ever done it before. At first that made dealers angry. (Entrenched businesses in any field tend to dislike anything that breaks the status quo, right?) They felt like they were losing their edge when negotiating with customers. But it didn't take long before they realized that, whether or not consumers had more information on the pricing of cars, they still had to go to a dealership to make a deal. The consumers just wanted to make sure they were getting a fair deal. Plus, there was no way they could stop the flow of information. After all, this was quickly becoming known as the Information Age, and if we weren't the ones doing it, someone else surely would. In addition, our service was bringing them lots of new customers—customers who, for the first time, felt like they were finally gaining some bargaining power they never had before. There was excitement in the air!

The automotive industry is sexy, it's exciting, it's as American as anything. A car is usually the second-largest investment most people make, so anything that made consumers feel better about the purchasing process was a good thing.

Eventually, dealers embraced what we did because it drove more business their way.

It was more than just the excitement of innovation that at some point enticed all of our salespeople to move across the country to join us and live in the Bay Area, though. If they were just "employees," I think it would have been a much harder sell. But from the very beginning, we gave our employees shares of the company. It wasn't us and them. It was all of us. If our company did well, they would benefit from the rise, which made all of them a part of the growth, a part of the excitement, a part of the energy that drove AutoWeb forward. (And, given how so many internet companies were performing on the stock market, even a few shares could have been worth a lot.)

On the flip side, my brother and I felt great responsibility to each and every one of them to do everything we could to make AutoWeb a huge success. They mattered to us. We wanted them to be happy and fulfilled and enjoy the journey as much as we wanted to enjoy the journey. And that drove us to keep innovating and building on what we had begun.

Traffic to our site kept climbing. More and more people in the auto industry—and throughout Silicon Valley—knew who we were. Through hard work and nothing but grit and determination, we grew the business. But it wasn't long before we started running out of cash. The cash flow from sales wasn't enough. We needed more outside investment.

In December 1996, one of our smaller competitors, AutoScape, reached out to us and said they wanted to sell, and sell quickly. Unlike us or Autobytel, they were simply not designed to grow as a stand-alone business. But we knew what kind of reach they had. It was big enough that gaining their customers and clientele would instantly grow our business by 25 percent or so. That was valuable. So we made the decision very quickly and agreed to buy them for $150,000. We were hoping they would take that offer in shares of our growing company, but they said, "No. It has to be in cash."

This happened at the beginning of December, and we agreed to pay them by the end of the month.

We didn't tell them that we were running on fumes. I love big challenges, and nothing motivates me more than a deadline like this.

Faced with the challenge of covering payroll and bringing in enough new cash to pay for this $150,000 acquisition, John and I had no choice but to do what we did best: rally our sales force to go out and close as many sales as we could and asking all new clients to pay for one year up front.

Failure was not an option, and we wanted to give it our all. So the two of us basically went on a multi-week road trip, from one city to another, all over the country, hitting every major Auto-Row we could find. With our cash dwindling, we shared rooms at the Motel 6, sometimes forced to share a bed if the motel didn't have any double rooms available. It didn't bother either of us because we were on a mission.

We did whatever it took. But we did it: We closed enough cash-up-front deals to pay every bill and then some.

We purchased AutoScape at the end of 1996, and that immediate increase in traffic and market share brought us more attention, press, and income than we could have possibly earned if we'd tried to go after all of their dealerships one at a time.

That was transformative.

We were starting to appear bigger and more established, and we thought that showing such rapid growth after raising one-tenth of the money Autobytel raised would set us up well for some fundraising meetings. So, in 1997, with one hard-learned lesson in the world of venture capital under our belts, we started making presentations to VCs.

It wasn't easy. While the internet was hot, we were not. We were still seen as two newcomer refugees with thick accents. So, even though our company was based in Silicon Valley, after pitching a number of VCs, we ended up raising money from a little-known VC in Fort Lee, New Jersey: Geocapital Partners.

They invested $5 million into AutoWeb at a $25 million valuation.

The new cash infusion helped, but we were nowhere near where we wanted to be. I was twenty-six years old. I was determined to bring to life the vision we had for AutoWeb. To me, in that moment, there was only one way to do that: to build AutoWeb into a company that would meet its own potential. The game was ours to lose. Competition didn't bother me. In fact, our fierce competition with Autobytel motivated me and drove us to build a better company, a better solution for consumers and dealers.

Interestingly enough, the founder of Autobytel, a guy named Pete Ellis, felt the same way about us. I knew Pete. We met up from time to time. We both had a lot of fun being rivals. The real-world competition was fierce, but I think it was healthy.

We didn't look at the infusion of millions from Geocapital as something massive. It was just enough to allow us to grow more quickly on the way to going public. That capital allowed us to hire a CFO and a few other executives to start to run some of the more "businessy" sides of the business with that goal in mind, as my brother and I continued to do what we did best. It also brought some experienced, Wall Street–minded individuals into the mix and onto our board of directors.

As Autobytel started spending their giant infusion of cash (they had raised even more by this time) in an effort to knock us and any other competitors out of the ring, we started going to major industry shows around the country, where we could set up a booth and let dealerships come to us. That helped us become better known in the industry, especially in areas where we'd never been before. But we also needed to find a way to bring more potential car-buying customers to our site—and the solution for that was found in another Silicon Valley startup.

By the end of 1997, Yahoo had become a significant player in the online search space. I had seen its potential early on and had gotten to know some of the early people at Yahoo, just through proximity and shared interests in the Silicon Valley region. So I reached out to them.

"I want AutoWeb to become the go-to automotive site for your visitors," I said, "and we want all of your automotive traffic to be exposed to our brand. So if anyone comes to Yahoo that seems interested in purchasing a car, or to get a price on a car, they will be connected to us."

Because we saw Yahoo's potential early on, I made that call before any of our competitors. And that gave us a leg up. The Yahoo execs looked at their traffic tied to automobile-related searches, and ran some numbers, and they said, "Okay, yeah. We can do that."

"For how much?" I asked.

They responded with a quote in the range of $4.5 million for a year.

"Well, that's not gonna work," I said. "We can't afford that."

The $4.5 million would have been paid in installments, over time, so I decided to try a little negotiating, just like we did at car dealerships, but in reverse: "What if we pay you cash up front?" I asked.

Amazingly, they were willing to listen. I managed to bring them all the way down to $1.5 million. I know that still sounds like a lot of money, especially coming from a guy who was excited about the prospect of making $20k in a summer just a few years earlier, but for the traffic they would generate to our site? And the power those numbers would hold in the industry? Believe me, $1.5 million was a bargain.

They said yes!

There was just one problem: Once again, our cash supply was dwindling. It's amazing how quickly $5 million goes when you're trying to grow from nothing to something. Payroll, insurance, technology, advertising . . . we didn't have $1.5 million in cash left to give away all at once and still continue to cover our monthly losses.

A few days before signing, I told my contacts at Yahoo what was up: "Unfortunately," I said, "we don't have the cash."

But here's the lesson: Remember when I spoke about making decisions? About moving forward without letting fear or the unknown stop you? Moving forward with optimism? Without overly worrying? Trusting that you can almost always find a way to work things out later?

Here's how it comes into play: Just before we sat down to sign our deal, Yahoo also went through a brand-new round of funding. The company received a huge influx of cash to build their own business. So our $1.5 million in potential revenue was small potatoes to them at that point, and far less pressing a need.

"Oh, well, that's okay," they said. "Since we just raised a lot of money, it's fine. We want to be in business with you, so let's sign the deal and you can pay us later."

We put off the due date, signed the paperwork, and Yahoo went ahead and made good on the AutoWeb relationship immediately—tying every relevant car-related search to a high-placed AutoWeb result.

Our traffic tripled overnight.

Incidentally (as Yahoo would later give us credit for), we had just taught Yahoo how to do what became known as "portal" deals. They ended up selling hundreds of millions of dollars' worth of portal deals in the months and years that followed, which propelled them to their own IPO.

If we did not have a can-do attitude, if I had not pursued Yahoo with optimism, if I had allowed our temporary financial situation to prevent us from getting this deal done, we would never have created the optionality and the opportunity that was simply transformative to our company. Our deal with Yahoo was a life moment. If I had waited cautiously, letting worry or fear keep me from asking and negotiating when I did, we would have given up on an opportunity that would never repeat itself. But because we already had a deal in place before they themselves became flush with cash, all it took to close the deal was a slight modification of terms. Done. Easy.

Tripling our traffic overnight should have been reason to celebrate, but that's when I realized we had a problem: We were hitting a wall.

AutoWeb and Autobytel were both operating on a similar revenue model: We were both selling dealers on a subscription program, basically signing up car dealers to join our sites for something like $1,000 per month. If the dealers got customers from us, great. If not, too bad. It was $1,000 per month regardless of real-world results. So, every month, one party or the other was unhappy: Either the dealers would feel like they did not receive enough new business from us for what they paid, or we would feel like we sent them way too many customers for the $1,000 we got paid.

Our business model was flawed. And once we had Yahoo on board, the equation shifted drastically to the benefit of the dealerships. Our traffic tripled, which meant the dealerships reached three times as many customers, but our revenue from those dealers remained flat because they were on a subscription program that wasn't traffic dependent.

The business model that we (and Autobytel, and anyone else in this business) were operating on didn't provide us with the incentive to increase our traffic at all. And without increasing traffic, the dealerships themselves wouldn't see an increase in inquiries from new customers, which was the reason they had signed up with us. That's a lose-lose situation.

We needed to change the model.

We went to the drawing board, trying to figure out how we could modify things so that everyone in the equation could win; so dealerships would be happy, and we would be happy, too, as traffic increased.

I thought about the phrase that John F. Kennedy used to describe how a strong economy should benefit everyone: "A rising tide lifts all boats."

How could we change our model to accomplish that goal at AutoWeb? To bring more revenue to us as we brought more potential paying customers to the dealerships?

And then it hit me: What if the dealerships paid us for every lead we sent their way? What if their cost, and our revenue, was based on our performance instead of a flat monthly fee?

Forget about the people who were just browsing, who didn't follow through, or who failed to click or call or email the dealership. Those visitors weren't ultimately all that valuable to the dealerships. So what if we just focused on the value of the customers who actually filled out a form detailing what they wanted to buy, and who wanted to be connected with a dealer in their area to receive a price quote?

What are those customers worth?

How much would dealers be willing to pay for the leads we sent their way?

What if we charged them per lead, instead of charging them a flat monthly fee?

Perhaps this "lead-generation" would be a better option than the model we were currently following.

We were considering this idea right before we turned the calendar to January of 1998; right before the NADA—the National Automobile Dealers Association—convention, which is attended annually by almost every car dealer in the U.S. There's something like a $1 trillion spending opportunity at that one event. It's crazy.

I didn't want to miss the opportunity to start selling this new idea at NADA. So I went to the board and said, "We're going to change our model to cost-per-lead. No more subscriptions. We'll charge $29.95 a lead. So a dealer is not making a thousand-dollar decision or a two-thousand-dollar decision. They're making a thirty-dollar decision. 'Is a customer worth $30 to you? If it is, sign up. If not, don't sign up.'"

The board thought I was crazy. They thought it could cause all kinds of problems at this juncture, when we were getting ready to go out and raise more money.

I understood why they were nervous. We had a good thing going. Boards generally want to play it safe. In general, MBAs—which all VCs are—get very nervous about revenue models and pricing, and so on, especially when they are untested. But to me, this is not something that should be solved through spreadsheet work. You need to have real knowledge of the market. And we had it. We knew this idea would be huge.

They thought our model was enough, and they wanted to keep a good thing going. And my reasoning as a founder was this: How is it a good thing if our existing model isn't aligning our success with the success of our dealer customers?

Even if we signed up every dealership in the country on a subscription basis, and even if we were the only website dedicated to connecting customers and dealerships on the entire internet, our revenue would remain flat under the subscription model. Sooner or later we would hit a wall. We would wind up on the losing end while the dealerships flourished on the back of the services we offered, the infrastructure we built, and the continued growth of our consumer traffic.

I also believed in the power of advertising technology that was being developed at the time, and the power of performance-based marketing, which is what we were really inventing.

We came up with the $29.95 per customer figure because it was the average current value of our leads, when dividing total revenue per month by our total leads per month before the Yahoo deal. It felt right.

Plus, imagine how many more dealerships we could sign up if it wasn't going to cost them $1,000 per month up front! Why would any dealership turn us down? Generating customers at $29.95 a pop would seem like a bargain to them, for sure.

So, ultimately, I overcame the board's hesitation. I took their indecisiveness as an agreement (or at least something less than a red light). I did what I wanted to do.

I had no idea that we had just invented something that would wind up being used as a revenue model by businesses all across the internet, and all over the world.

We didn't set out to invent something. We were just trying to solve a math problem.

But I was about to make a name for myself as the father of "lead-gen"—a market that today generates tens of billions of dollars in revenue every year.

We set up a giant booth at NADA, and spent a ton of money to have race-car driver Bobby Rahal, the world-renowned Indy 500 champion, as our spokesperson at the booth.

We announced our new $29.95 lead-gen model, and I'm not kidding you, dealers that we previously had a hard time closing literally lined up at our booth to come on board. We were mobbed!

We made another change to the way we did business at the same time, one that I hoped would hook those dealers on the benefits of working with AutoWeb for good.

I noticed that Autobytel was trying to incentivize car dealers to sign up with them by offering exclusivity. Meaning that if a dealer in a certain city or region was first to sign up with them, they wouldn't allow any other dealerships who sold the same brand in that city or region to sign up with Autobytel. That was great for the dealers, but it made no sense for the company. By doing that, Autobytel was limiting their subscription revenue from every region to only a thousand bucks a month. Why would any company want to limit itself so massively in that way?

So again, we thought, *Let's try something different.*

Once a dealer said yes to paying $29.95 a lead, we put a contract in front of them, and in that contract, we asked them point blank to name four competing local dealers that they didn't want us to sign up. The only caveat was they had to be dealers selling the same brand, and within twenty-five miles of the one who was signing up. "You get to choose the four dealers you want to exclude from having any presence on AutoWeb," we told them.

They loved that. I can still hear the voices of those dealers in my head: "Are you telling me that I can tell you that Joe Schmo down the street can never sign up?"

"Yup, you can tell us not to sign up Joe."

Some of those dealers got giddy at the thought of it. Every one of them had rivalries with certain competitors that got under their skin. This wasn't exclusivity; it was exclusion. It made it personal. It appealed to them on an emotional level, while leaving us with the freedom to go get more dealers signed up. And since we were getting paid per lead now, one dealer or ten, it was the leads that would generate revenue for us, with the potential to earn more revenue than we could have ever brought in on the flat subscription model.

Just to break it down, let's say there are sixty-four Ford dealerships in the Chicago metro area. Autobytel would sign one and then promise to exclude all the others. We would sign one, let them pick the four they wanted to exclude, and then have fifty-nine more dealers left to sell to. If each one we picked up excluded four others (assuming no overlap), we'd still be generating income from ten times the number of dealers as Autobytel.

We signed up a few hundred dealers at NADA.

The folks over at Autobytel were . . . how can I put this kindly? Not happy.

Come to think of it, they weren't happy with us from day one.

The NADA convention was held in New Orleans that year, and when we arrived, there was a big sign hanging up on the outside wall of the parking garage across the street, using big, bold letters to advertise: "Autobytel is bigger than CarPoint and AutoWeb combined!"

I don't blame them for trying to make a splash. Things were really picking up in our industry. There was big money involved now. I mean, CarPoint was a Microsoft brand. Talk about deep pockets! But Autobytel's claim was false advertising—and I called them on it.

These were crazy days. The press was so interested in tech start-ups, a company like ours could call for a press conference, and press would show up. I mean microphones everywhere, people taking pictures everywhere—a press conference like you see when Tony Stark calls one in an Iron Man movie or something.

So I called for a press conference, and I said, "What Autobytel is doing is defamatory. It's false advertising. They're saying they're the biggest based on what? I'm fine giving you guys our numbers—the number of car dealerships, our traffic, whatever you want. We are transparent. You guys can look at everything we have. So, unless they can produce the same and prove that their statement is true, they need to take that sign down. Now."

The sign was removed the same day.

What did Autobytel do in order to come back from that blow?

They came after us for our innovation.

They called for a press conference themselves and said, "What AutoWeb is doing is against the law. You cannot charge per lead." Their claim was that by charging per lead, we were acting as a broker, "and you cannot be a broker in many states."

That statement turned out to be partially true, as someone from the state of Texas Department of Motor Vehicles came out to back them up. In Texas, the law was interpreted in such a way that the official believed charging dealers on a per-lead basis meant that you were, in fact, acting as a broker between buyers and sellers. While brokers are perfectly legal in most of the country, they were illegal in Texas. Of course, charging per lead is far from being a broker, but we had no interest in fighting a lawsuit against the government of Texas. But applying laws to companies on the internet would become a complicated task for lawmakers in the years ahead. Should Texas laws even apply to a California-based company? Should any state laws apply to companies operating online from other states? In the 1990s, no one could really answer those questions. They hadn't been adjudicated.

Just to be safe, we stopped making per-lead deals with dealerships in Texas—but that was it. None of the dealers we spoke to from other states were the least bit worried, and we were not about to let Autobytel's blustering stop us from acquiring new clients.

The bottom line is this: Changing to a lead-gen model transformed us.

It was another life moment, and I'm glad we took advantage of the opportunity.

The lead-gen model started working immediately, and revenue went through the roof—just as we predicted it would,

Even then, we were quickly running out of cash: Our payables were extended, and the deadline for the Yahoo payment was fast approaching. We had no choice but to go out into the VC world and seek another infusion of cash.

This time, we got a much better reception in Silicon Valley. We were growing so fast that they simply could no longer ignore us.

After a series of meetings, we received two term sheets: one from a pair of VCs who joined forces in the deal, one called Trinity and one called Benchmark; and one from Technology Crossover Ventures (or TCV). All three were big names in Silicon Valley. Getting money from any one of these guys meant you'd arrived. Benchmark in particular was like the up-and-coming, really sexy VC to raise money from. But at this juncture, to us, it was all about the numbers—which, I realize in retrospect, was a big mistake. (I'll share more on that in upcoming chapters.) We didn't focus on reputation or potential long-term relationships with these VCs. We wanted to drum up the highest valuation possible so we would experience the least level of dilution.

The Benchmark-Trinity combined offer put us at a lower valuation than TCV. So, as a result, in the middle of 1998, we went with TCV. We made our decision based on a few million dollars in valuation, not the best long-term potential, and that turned out to be shortsighted.

But this was also an important moment for my brother and me. A moment to celebrate. Because for the first time ever, the two of us made some real money for ourselves. As part of the $5 million deal we put together, he and I each sold some of our personal shares of AutoWeb, which allowed each of us to receive half-a-million dollars cash from the transaction.

For the first time ever, my brother and I had a sizable amount of money to put straight into our bank accounts. He bought a house. I bought a house. We took care of family, too.

The day before the deal with TCV closed, the two of us were basically broke, running on fumes, scraping by and giving every dollar back to the business we were trying to build; the next, we both had the ability to lift our whole family up.

Only in America, I thought.

Ten years after arriving in San Francisco. Four years after graduating from UC Davis.

I was grateful.

It wasn't time to rest on our laurels, though. As good as it felt to have some security and to share our success with our family, I knew we were nowhere near the finish line.

We used the cash infusion to expand like never before, expanding our workforce to better sell our service as well as manage, build, market, handle customer service, and more. I could already see that in the months ahead we would be short on cash again.

In late 1998, we would raise another $2 million from the *Toronto Star*, the largest newspaper in Canada. And I know that raising millions sounds impressive, but the fact is, we knew we would be back to running on fumes in a matter of months after that. I was tired of that cycle. I wanted to find a way to end it by becoming profitable. But I wasn't in charge. My brother was CEO, and the board of directors had some serious sway over nearly everything we did; a "necessary evil," I thought, if we ever wanted to achieve our tech-IPO dreams. But it frustrated me.

Three years after the Netscape pop on Wall Street, tech excitement had not slowed down one bit. Companies all around us were starting to go public for really big valuations. Our board saw that and started to whisper about making some changes.

Boards at almost every one of these tech startups were interested in seeing companies have older people running them. These days, they don't care that much. Young people and founders can remain as CEOs. But in the mid-'90s, that wasn't the case.

I didn't like what I was hearing. Neither did my brother. How could someone older and without a vision for what we were inventing and building understand how to navigate these uncharted waters better than

those of us who were creating the boat upon which all of us had set sail?
Old ways of thinking, caution, resistance to change—those were the last
things we needed.

It was time to make a change. A major change. I felt it.

My brother felt it, too.

CHAPTER SEVENTEEN

MAJOR LEAPS FORWARD

B ack when we hired a CFO in 1997, I had become the executive vice president. Not exactly a satisfying title for the cofounder of a company, but I didn't care much. My brother was the CEO, and we had a great partnership. (When we argued, it was still brotherly, and we'd be over it very quickly.) No matter what my title was, I was always the main sales and marketing guy at AutoWeb, and I loved it. I was happy in that role. Maybe Student Painters had taught me to love that side of the business; maybe my upbringing taught me some of that, too. Either way, our sales and marketing teams always answered to me, while my brother owned the technology side of things, which was what he really loved.

We knew our roles, and we made our partnership work.

Coincidentally enough, one day, in the middle of all of this sweeping change and growth, Frank came to me and said, "I don't want to be the CEO anymore."

I cannot say I was surprised. I could see that the responsibilities of the CEO role had weighed on him. It was one thing when it was just us, or just us and like ten employees, but now? He had just recently become a father, and the responsibility for sustaining nearly one hundred employees on top of caring for his young family sat firmly on his shoulders. More tiring than that was answering to the board. An unreasonable board that would take so much of our time that we had little left to actually run the business. They thought more board meetings and more spreadsheets and more reports would somehow auto-magically help us grow faster and become more valuable. They were not an easy bunch to work with, and frankly, they made life unnecessarily difficult for both of us. I left our monthly board meetings with a huge migraine, every time.

It was all just more weight than my brother was interested in carrying. Plus, he hadn't come to his conclusion in a vacuum.

"I think you know this already," he said, "but the board wants to hire a new CEO."

"Yes, I know."

"And look," he said, "I'd rather resign before I'm forced to do so. They want us to hire an older, more experienced guy to run the company."

"Did they already approach you about this?"

"Yes. But I told them, 'Look, if that's what needs to happen, fine. But between now and then, I want Payam to be the CEO.'"

"You said that?"

"Yes—and the board agreed."

"Wow, thank you for that," I said.

He knew I wanted that role. He also knew I would thrive in that role. But I worried about it being a temporary move; I was concerned about who might be brought in to replace me, and when; and most of all, I worried what this change in roles might do to us as brothers.

"If I do this," I said, "there are a bunch of decisions I'm gonna make that you might not like."

"That's fine," he said.

I think he was more ready to exit that role than I had realized. He showed zero interest in fighting my decision-making at all.

"You're the CEO," he said. "You make the decisions."

So I became the CEO.

And the first decision I made was a big one; a decision based on an idea I had, which the board had said no to from the moment I pitched the concept of changing to a lead-gen model. More importantly, it was an idea that my brother wasn't excited about, either.

As a business, we were losing $500,000 a month in the summer of 1998. We were bringing in about a million in revenue per month from selling leads, but we were losing half a million bucks. That's a big part of the reason why we had to keep raising money. To remedy this, and also to make AutoWeb a better experience for consumers, I wanted to give customers the opportunity to send leads to more than one dealership; to allow them to get multiple quotes on the vehicles they were interested in; essentially to get the dealerships to compete with one another for their business.

(Up to that point, when a customer would send the lead, it would go to the dealership that was closest to them, in terms of physical distance. One dealership, which generated a single lead-gen fee of $29.95 to us. That was it.)

My brother's response to my idea was, "If you do that, you're reducing the value of the lead for the dealership; because now that lead is going to multiple dealerships and that will automatically reduce the value of our leads."

So I said, "Well, we'll limit it to two. Let's say you cannot send to more than two, at least at the beginning." I noted that some consumers made a habit of going to more than one dealership to get multiple offers anyway. "So if we allow them to get what they're after from our platform, then we keep them within our platform."

Now, as CEO, the decision was mine and mine alone. So I launched my idea—and our revenue doubled overnight.

That was another life moment: It changed the trajectory of our company.

The company went from losing half a million dollars a month to making half a million dollars a month. And for the most part, the dealers didn't complain.

Of course, Autobytel complained: "You can't do that," they shouted into the wind of the business press world. "They have reduced the value of their leads. Dealers will leave—and will come to us!" (It was expected from a company still stuck with an outdated subscription model and an old-school name: Auto-by-Tel? As in "telephone"? What? We teased them with that back then.)

The dealers did not care. "It makes sense. Almost everyone wants more than one quote before they purchase," many of them told us. "It works for us."

Whatever brought them more leads with a reasonably close rate they saw as a good decision. It was up to them to close the deals, and the more customers they had, the more negotiating they could do. Once again, it was a win-win.

And so, we became profitable by the fall of 1998. Second to eBay, we were the only other profitable internet startup at that point in time. Everybody else in Silicon Valley was losing money.

We brought ourselves to profitability by "taking risks," people said. But again, I ask, what did we really risk? If any of the changes we made didn't work, we could have gone back to the subscription model, or something else.

Not taking risks would have been the biggest risk of all.

We had only raised $12 million, which was nothing compared to most of the other internet companies. That allowed us to be nimble.

When creating something new, everything is a risk—including the act of staying put in a lane you created, but which may not have been tested or questioned for some time. It's important to think forward. To think bigger. To act without unnecessary hesitation.

And we were not about to stop.

For example, as exciting as it was to build our sales force in four regions around the country, it was also a massive amount of work. At times it felt as if things were progressing too slowly. So, after a year and a half of using that regional sales model, I changed my mind about how to handle things.

What I started to realize is that while selling on the phone was less effective than in-person cold calls, it was also more productive. By working the phones, our close rate would potentially go down, but with enough salespeople and no time lost to traveling, we could make so many more sales calls that we'd more than make up for that lower close rate in sheer volume. Also, by selling on the phone we could easily and quickly focus on different pockets on the map where we had coverage gaps and needed to pick up more dealers.

We had eight salespeople in each of those far-flung offices when we decided we should bring everyone in-house, where we could not only work more productively, but we could also build a more unified culture for this growing company.

We rented a new office space that was big enough to handle the whole crew (our third move by then, having outgrown the original small office space quickly), but I wasn't sure how many of our existing salespeople would be willing to move to the Bay Area on short notice.

I shouldn't have worried. Without exception, they all got up and moved.

Everyone we'd hired wanted to be a part of the AutoWeb story.

Another fast decision. Another success.

At about the same time, we came up with an idea to expand the value and scope of AutoWeb's offerings yet again.

All we had to do to make it work was to go sell the idea to an entirely different industry.

My thought was, *We have all these people coming to us because they want to buy a car. Part of that process involves going to insurance companies to figure out how much it'll cost them to insure that car before they sign the paperwork, or soon after. Why should they need to look anywhere else for an insurance quote other than right here on AutoWeb?*

I started making calls to the big insurance companies. Allstate wouldn't even call me back. But one day, I managed to start a dialogue with a guy named Bob Reiner at State Farm.

He kind of liked the idea, and he was willing to talk to me, but he wasn't really moving it forward. So I went back to my old-school sales techniques: I surprised him by flying to State Farm's headquarters, in a beautiful setting in the middle of thousands of acres of corn fields in Bloomington, Illinois, to see him in person.

Those who know me know that when I really want to sell something, I don't give up. So I literally went there every month. I took a red-eye from San Francisco to Chicago, followed by a small-plane hop to Bloomington, which made every trip a two-day thing. Not easy. But, like I said, I don't give up. Frankly, after a few visits, I saw that he was getting tired of me. But he also told me, "You know? I'm kind of impressed, because we get calls from Silicon Valley and some of your competitors, and these people don't come to Bloomington. They all wanna sell on the phone."

At that point, I was pretty sure he was starting to warm up.

Finally, on my next trip out, he said, "Okay, we'll sign up."

I was expecting his next question to be about how much we were going to charge per lead, but instead he said something I had never heard before: "We have a buying office, so you have to go to them. They do the negotiations. I'll let them know it's a yes if we can get the right price, and they'll take it from there."

"Okay, great!" I said, but I was thinking, *Oh no. These guys have a buying office? These guys are trained negotiators.*

I went to that office feeling nervous, and the first thing the guy asked me was, "How much per lead?" I started thinking: *Our core product is selling leads to car dealers, so if I can get even five bucks a lead, it's gravy. But let me start at $15 and see what happens.*

"Fifteen dollars a lead," I said.

"Is there any room to negotiate?" he asked.

I'd learned a lot about sales by then, so I said, "No, not really."

And he said, "Okay."

Frankly, I felt a little bit bad. I just sold this guy on triple the price I wanted to get! But I also wanted to bring this new influx of revenue in as fast as I could, which I figured would reduce our need to raise more money from VCs. So I thought on my feet.

"But," I said.

The dreaded "But." I'm sure he thought I was about to hit him with some extra fee on top of the lead-gen fee, or something. Instead, I said, "But there is a way you can get a better deal, if you pay cash up front for a year."

"Oh," he said. "Let's talk about that."

"Based on our math, you guys will receive $3 million worth of leads in a year, so how about $2.5 million cash up front? You get a half-a-million-dollar discount."

"Done," he said. (State Farm certainly wasn't hurting for cash.)

I left Bloomington with $2.5 million.

It was the single biggest sale of my life.

Again, this is only five years or so after putting in countless hours trying to make $20k in a whole year with Student Painters. People ask me how I made that leap, from thousands of dollars to millions of dollars, and the only answer I have is, "It's just numbers."

Sure, we're adding some zeros, but it's all just numbers, and I love numbers!

It's not as big of a leap as people make it out to be. It's just not. People are closing multimillion-dollar deals every hour of every day. So why not me? (Why not you?)

A sale is a sale, and the techniques are the same.

It all goes back to what Zig Ziglar calls "need satisfaction selling."

And at the end of the day, unless you can believe it, unless you can think it, you're not gonna get it. It goes back to putting my fist through the board in Karate class; or even further, to believing that I could make it to the U.S. and make it in America; or even further, to believing that I could make it through the desert and out of Iran.

You've got to have the confidence that it can happen if you're ever going to make it happen.

Also, some people get all caught up in the idea that pricing something is such a difficult thing, like it's some sort of science with formulas to follow and long explanations that have to be made. It's not. Price just depends on how much somebody feels there's value in something for them. And often you don't know what that value is until you throw out a number. Ultimately, until both sides test the relationship for a period of time, no one knows the right price.

Only after you throw out a number will you find out: "Am I completely off the chart or not?" And you have to keep in mind that the price point you're after is about the cost to you, as well as value to your buyer. If I had sold leads to State Farm for five bucks apiece, I would've been happy; but at five bucks I could not have built the company into what it became. I never could have made our service as good as I was able to make it with the better cash flow of a $15 price point.

Cash flow, if invested properly, makes the service provider a better service provider for its customers, and a better company for its employees, the community, and shareholders. So there is nothing wrong with doing everything possible to maximize cash flow!

At five bucks, it was gravy on top of the auto-dealership leads we were already selling. But at $15? It was yet another game changer. It set a new benchmark. It allowed us to think bigger and build a better company.

The State Farm deal put AutoWeb at the forefront yet again, with yet another innovation that would disrupt another aspect of the trillion-dollar automotive marketplace. That was a given. What wasn't a given was what happened next, and it just goes to show: You never know what kind of attention a game-changing relationship might bring.

Two months after we made that deal, I got a call from State Farm Bank. I didn't even know State Farm had a bank. They said, "Hi. So, we finance cars, too, and we love this deal we've signed up for on the insurance side. We would also like to get customers on AutoWeb to come finance their cars with us."

"Wow. Great! I love that idea, and consumers will, too. One-stop shopping . . . for everything!"

I negotiated a deal to get that going for $1.2 million cash up front. But that was only the beginning.

A few weeks later, in November of the same year, the chief marketing officer of State Farm, along with the CEO of State Farm Bank, and

Bob Reiner, and a couple of others came calling for a completely different reason.

"We want to come out to California and meet with you," they said. "We're going to bring some folks from J.P. Morgan along with us—because we would like to buy your company."

It's amazing how fast it all happened.

If I hadn't focused so hard on selling our product to Bob Reiner, if I hadn't gone the extra mile—literally—to fly out there and see him in person, multiple times, and if I had not charged them $15 per lead, which created more value for our product, would any of this have happened?

We set a meeting date, and I immediately thought, *I need help.*

As much as I had learned, as far as we had come, I wasn't prepared to take on a negotiation to sell the entire company. Especially with the VCs and board members breathing down my neck, getting stars in their eyes over how many hundreds of millions we might be able to sell AutoWeb for after the tremendous growth we'd seen in 1998 alone.

We needed to let the State Farm and J.P. Morgan teams know they were dealing with a serious company. So I thought, *Who's the biggest dealmaker in the U.S.? Who's the heavyweight? The power hitter? The top dog in the dealmaking world right now?*

The name that rose to the top was none other than George Boutros.

George had served as managing director of Deutsche Bank in Palo Alto until June of 1998, when he made a big move to Credit Suisse. He'd earned a reputation as a brutal negotiator, in the old, 1980s-style *Wall Street* (the movie) notion of "Greed, for lack of a better word, is good." From what I had read in the press, he often went into mergers-and-acquisitions meetings with a browbeating, briefcase-slamming style that tended to push buyers into making higher offers than anyone would have thought possible, and sellers into selling for far less than they ever imagined, depending on which side of the table he was on. He was already a legend in his late thirties, having brokered multiple billion-dollar-plus deals for Silicon Valley startups and major players alike. His boss at Credit Suisse, Frank Quattrone, was once quoted in *WIRED* magazine saying, "[George Boutros] is to M&A what Tiger Woods is to golf."

We reached out to George through one of our board members, and he agreed to come to the meeting. I told him I didn't think we would need any briefcase slamming. Just having him in the room was all we needed.

I was right.

After meeting with us at our new offices (which were just across the freeway from Intel), State Farm Bank and J.P. Morgan were even more impressed than they were before. A few days later, they made us their offer. It was huge. The kind of offer that would set us up for the rest of our lives.

They probably never expected us to make a higher counteroffer.

There were people within our own company and especially on our board who couldn't imagine we'd make a counteroffer, either. We had one VC who wanted to take it, and another who didn't, and to my brother and me, it just didn't feel like enough; not when we had seen how crazy the valuations had grown for companies all around us that weren't even profitable; and not when our primary competitor in this industry had refused to innovate. (Autobytel was sticking with its extremely limiting subscription-and-exclusivity model.)

So, we made a counter: We asked them for a quarter-of-a-billion dollars.

They took a few days to talk amongst themselves, and they told us that they just couldn't get there.

"Thank you very much," I said. And we walked away.

There were people all around us who thought we were nuts to turn that offer down, and that included a couple of VCs and board members who had invested in us early on.

But to me, the fact that this bank, this individual entity, would come to us with so large an offer sent a very clear message.

Our path forward was clear.

It was time to take AutoWeb public.

CHAPTER EIGHTEEN

EVERYTHING WE THOUGHT WE WANTED

I want to step back here, just for a moment, to tell you about two major life events that happened while all of this was going on.

First of all, in 1994, I officially became a citizen of the U.S.

I walked into an INS office (that's the United Immigration and Naturalization Service), where I was grilled by an official who asked me all sorts of questions about the various branches of our government; he asked me who the Speaker of the House was at the time, and how many people sat on the Supreme Court, and who the chief justice was. He asked who our senators were from the state of California, and to name some state capitals, and a few things about American history—all of which I knew well. Along the way, he was clearly trying to discern whether I could speak and understand English well, too, which I could. And when it was over, he invited me to join a swearing-in ceremony later that month at a stadium in Fresno, where I went by myself and stood alongside a thousand or so other immigrants, all of whom were being welcomed as citizens into this country. All together. All at once.

The swearing-in ceremony was an emotional one for me. When I crossed the Emptiness Desert on my way to Pakistan, as far as I knew, I had given up my Iranian citizenship. And up until that ceremony, I really felt almost homeless.

I have always viewed myself as a citizen of the world. I do not believe this planet was supposed to be divided up by borders. But the fact remains that I wanted to know that there was a country where I belonged, and there was a government that viewed protecting me as a fundamental responsibility. Until that day, if I were to have traveled outside of the U.S. and found myself in any sort of trouble, what country's embassy would I have called? Iran's? Yeah, right! The U.S.'s? Perhaps, but I wasn't a citizen.

Before that swearing-in ceremony, traveling outside of the U.S. would not have been easy for me—without a passport, going through customs, carrying nothing but temporary travel documents. The fact is, I didn't have the money or desire to travel abroad at that point anyway. But still, I hoped to travel. I wanted to travel. And once I was sworn in, I knew for the first time that I could. And that was a tremendous, overwhelming feeling for me.

Yes, having a green card for those first six years gave me many of the rights that citizens have. But I was different. I was an "alien." That's a very difficult designation to live with. For example, when I turned eighteen, I did not earn the right to vote, and yet, I had to register with the selective service, for the draft, just like every other eighteen-year-old male in this country. I wondered sometimes what it would feel like if the U.S. went to war with Iran and I was called up to serve. What a strange experience that would have been. Can you imagine standing in my shoes in that situation?

As I left the stadium, the enormity of that moment set in: I now held the same rights, obligations, and opportunities as every other U.S. citizen. That could never be taken from me.

That was a great feeling. I had a country. I had an embassy to call. I had a vote.

The other major life event that happened during this period was that I got married. Surprise, right? It was to me, too.

I was on a Southwest Airlines flight from Orange County to San Jose, and I sat next to a young woman who was reading *TIME* magazine. That by itself was a bit of an exciting thing for me because she wasn't reading *People* or *Star* or something like that, but a real news magazine. So I chatted with her. She was Persian, which was not a big surprise because in that part of Southern California there are lots of Persians. But we chatted, we hit it off, and less than a year later, we got married.

We did so despite some hesitations that were expressed by some rather important people in my life. People who repeatedly asked me, "Are you sure this is a good idea?"

Perhaps I should have listened to them, but I was young and determined. I wanted to move forward, so I did.

Right away, on our wedding day, there were red flags.

One, I don't drink alcohol. I don't serve alcohol. Not only is it against my religion, but also, as someone who cares about healthy living, I find it to be a rather unhealthy choice. Not to mention it's the number-one contributor to violence against women. Anyhow, for the wedding, per agreement with my bride, we were not going to serve alcoholic drinks. Out of respect for my values, she had agreed to that. As it turns out, our agreement wasn't good enough for my soon-to-be mother-in-law. Without asking, she set up a bar and served alcohol right outside the door of the reception. To me, that felt disrespectful.

Then, my wife's uncle (her mom's brother) refused to shake my hand because I was Baha'i. He thought that I was "unclean."

He was unhappy that his niece had married an infidel.

The woman I married was Muslim. She wasn't a practicing Muslim, but nonetheless, her family insisted on having someone come in to read Islamic vows during the ceremony. That was another surprise. I didn't understand it. You're either a Muslim or you're not. Why did her family want to have things both ways? Because remember: Muslims don't drink, either. So why insist on Islamic vows, but then open a bar outside of the reception hall against your daughter's husband's wishes? And also, about her uncle: Why would he choose to live in a country full of people that he considered to be infidels and unclean?

The marriage would not last. I'll come back to how it ended a bit later, because the timing of our split would come during a major turning point in my life.

Part of my journey in life has been learning lessons from my failures, but also learning to move on and not dwell on them. No one's life should be defined by their failures. The failures in my personal life were necessary steps and part of my destiny, and that's okay. I just choose to focus on other things when I look back at my life—and when looking back at this period, it was a period of development and accumulation of life lessons that would be helpful later on.

It's difficult to describe how much excitement I felt as we took the steps to launch our IPO, starting with filing the S-1 paperwork with the Securities and Exchange Commission (SEC) in January of 1999.

We had successfully undergone a required audit of our company, prepared the financials, and so much more. The paperwork was nearly completed and everything was just about ready to go, except for one thing: The board had yet to hire a new CEO that fit their desired profile.

There was one guy they really liked, who my brother and I liked as well: a former president at FedEx who didn't necessarily have the ideal background, but whom we all thought had the skills and energy to carry AutoWeb forward through the IPO and beyond. He came across as a genuinely nice guy. But while he was very interested, we couldn't get him. And the reason we couldn't get him was a surprising one.

Remember when I mentioned that we'd had an offer from two big VCs called Benchmark and Trinity? An offer that we'd turned down in order to take a funding round through TCV? Well, the cofounder of Benchmark also owned a head-hunting firm, and the board had hired this firm to help find our new CEO. It turned out that Benchmark itself had decided to hire the CEO we really wanted, the former FedEx guy, to work for one of their portfolio companies. And when an executive at Benchmark inquired why he was intervening and refusing to let AutoWeb hire the guy—even when we represented a more aligned opportunity for him—he apparently responded by saying, "AutoWeb effed us once. I'm not gonna let them eff us twice by hiring this CEO, too."

One would think the fact that we hired his head-hunting firm should have been a sign that we had nothing against him. We didn't take their investment simply because they offered us a lower valuation than TCV. But I guess, to him, it was much more personal than that.

So we couldn't get the CEO we wanted, and with the S-1 paperwork nearly completed, suddenly the board became desperate.

"We've got to hire somebody now," they insisted.

I did not agree. I tried to convince them, "Don't rush it, because if we do, we're going to make a mistake, and we'll pay a heavy price."

I wanted to remain CEO. I was happy in the role, and I had quickly proven myself. I was growing the company. I made it profitable. But they really felt that I was too young. I was twenty-seven. And that wasn't the only reason I did not fit the mold. So, the board moved forward in their desperate search and decided they wanted to hire a man that my brother and I did not feel was the right fit. At all. He had run a small company with a couple million bucks in revenue and sold it to AOL for something in the range of $20 million. He hadn't built something that was profitable or that held nearly as much promise for continuing to disrupt a major market the size of the auto industry. He just wasn't the right guy for the job. But my brother and I didn't have the votes. So the board hired him just a few days before we filed for our IPO.

With just one day left to go before filing, the CEO of a major company in the automotive space invited me and our new CEO to dinner at a Silicon Valley hot spot. He didn't know we were about to file, and his visit was totally unexpected, but at dinner he said, "I'm here to buy you guys."

"How much?" I asked him.

"I'll pay you $100 million," he said.

His timing was more than a little off.

"We turned down a bigger offer just recently," we told him.

We didn't mention that we were filing to go public the next day, but we also failed to show any interest in negotiating. We just said, "No thank you."

Even though that offer was smaller than the State Farm offer, it assured me that interest in AutoWeb was strong. We were doing the right thing. We were convinced that Wall Street was gonna love us!

There was just one problem. (Again with the problems.)

As the filing day approached, we discovered that Autobytel had filed its own IPO. We didn't want Autobytel to go public ahead of us and set the mood of the market, good or bad. We wanted AutoWeb to set the mood. We wanted the splash of being the first IPO in this brand-new industry, which would have a serious long-term impact on how we were viewed as the main trendsetter in the field.

And here's where the importance of listening to others and working as a team comes into play. (It's also an example of how a "problem" can easily turn into an "opportunity.")

One of the people in the room when we were trying to figure out what to do was a recently hired finance guy, a great guy named Thomas Stone, and he threw out an idea: "Look," he said, "everybody, including Autobytel, filed as a technology company. So . . . why not file as an automotive company?"

It was genius.

The technology desk at the Securities and Exchange Commission was overwhelmed. They were taking a long time to respond to every S-1 that came in. We had already been warned about that. But the automotive desk? There was nobody going public in the automotive industry in those days. "They're way more likely to respond immediately," Thomas said, which meant they could pave the way for our offering much faster.

Thankfully, everyone agreed.

We filed, and Thomas was right: The automotive desk had no IPOs on their desk. The technology desk was still overwhelmed. So our S-1 sailed through before Autobytel's S-1 was even looked at.

We were on the road to set our IPO date before them, which meant we had just leapfrogged over them.

The next day, I came into the office and our new CEO said, "Look, you've done a good job. But I really don't need you. I need to establish myself as the leader here, so why don't you take some time off? Take a month off."

As you can imagine, I found that suggestion pretty insulting. In my heart, I knew that he had no clue how to run this business. We had invented what had quickly become a new business model, one that even today powers tens of billions of dollars in revenue for the automotive industry. But he thought I, the inventor, was no longer necessary.

At the same time, I was fed up with fighting an uphill battle in the offices of the company I cofounded. Not to mention, I was tired. I had been going nonstop for nearly five years. I needed a break. I had never taken a vacation. Not one, ever since I'd taken a ten-day road trip with three friends before heading to UC Davis in 1991. So I took his offer. I took the rest of January and the first part of February off. I didn't check in. I didn't call. I just walked away and gave this new CEO the space he wanted to find his footing.

Unfortunately, as my brother and I predicted, while I was away, the CEO made some terrible decisions. I think it was February 10, less than one month after I left, when he and the CFO together called me up and said, "Please, come back. The numbers are down."

"How down?"

"Way down," he said. I could hear the sound of defeat in his voice.

I knew that any hint that numbers were falling in the middle of an IPO would be an absolute disaster. So I went back—and saw that our numbers weren't just down. It was a disaster!

I knew our business. I knew what worked and what didn't. I made some quick decisions, reversed a couple of his, the numbers came up, and before the month was out, we were back on track.

Disaster averted.

In the early hours of March 21, 1999—the shared day of the Persian and Baha'i New Year—my brother and I flew to New York City.

We spent the afternoon of the 22nd at Geocapital, in New Jersey, where we set our initial share price.

We dined at the finest steak house in Manhattan.

And on the morning of March 23, 1999, joined by our new CEO, we stood with the Credit Suisse team on their trading floor, and later on the floor of the Nasdaq Stock Exchange, and watched our dream come true.

The market went crazy. It wasn't Netscape crazy, but AutoWeb became the most-traded stock in a single day in the history of the Nasdaq. And by the time my brother and I headed to the airport that afternoon, AutoWeb was worth $1.2 billion—which meant that Frank and I were personally worth more than $200 million, each.

The next morning, I fielded the call from Credit Suisse letting me know that I now had access to a $4 million personal line of credit.

I made my way into the office, thinking this was the start of everything I ever wanted—only to be met by the CEO who, once again, through his actions, made it clear to me that he didn't really want me around. So I left—this time on a weeklong vacation to Barcelona. It was my first trip out of the country since I'd been granted citizenship; the first big trip I'd ever taken with some money in my pocket and a very big reason to celebrate.

I didn't think much could go wrong in a week, especially since our new CEO had watched how easy it was for me to come in and fix the numbers just a few weeks earlier. I let go of my frustration. I assumed it would just take time and patience for all of us to figure out how to get along together, to expand on the culture and dynamic my brother and I had created, and to work with this man to build the company into the industry game changer and behemoth of a business we all believed it could be.

I think getting away was a healthy thing to do regardless, because honestly, it was a lot to take in all at once. How was I supposed to fathom the idea of having access to so much capital? The fact that it happened so quickly made it more akin to winning the lottery than truly earning that kind of money. When I stopped to think about it, the whole thing had come fairly easily compared to anything else in my life. We went public without much in the way of obstacles, tests, or difficulties. My brother and I spoke on the plane ride home from New York about how we might find it difficult to motivate ourselves to get up and go to work every day. I mean, why work when you've made tens of millions of dollars, right? Then again, we built this business in Silicon Valley. We were already feeling the pressure to keep growing, and fast. AutoWeb was now worth $1.2 billion, so we were both thinking, *How can we get it to $2 billion and beyond?*

Looking back on it now, I'm a little embarrassed that those were the thoughts that invaded our minds. I wish I had the wisdom I like to think I have today—how that would have allowed me to control the outcome and use that IPO as a foundation for building a company that could have served a huge market, that could have benefited both consumers and the industry, and maybe even made the world ever so slightly better through good intentions and a desire to use business as a force for good.

But there were so many forces against us.

I was young. I had unknowingly become a pawn in a version of capitalism that leaves us all empty, in so many ways. A version of capitalism that, today, I want nothing to do with.

Back then? I still had a lot of growing to do.

In truth, I had no plans at all for what to do with my personal stake. I didn't really know how to preserve it, or spend it, or even how to give it away. I had no plan to buy a fancy house, or a Ferrari, or a nice watch. No plans of any kind.

If I made a couple hundred million dollars in a single day now, I would know what I want to do. I have a life plan in place. But back then? I was about to be named one of the "Top 30 Under 30" wealthiest people in the country, and it all just felt a little surreal.

I would soon come to realize it was time to grow up—and maybe to step out on my own.

REFLECTIONS ON CHAPTERS FIFTEEN THROUGH EIGHTEEN

I'd like you to write down some of the business ideas you've had over the years. You don't have to be an entrepreneur to have had ideas. We all have them! An invention that would make some aspect of your life (or the life of others) easier. A product that you wish existed. A service you wish you could buy. A specialty shop. An online service. An experience that you believe others would pay for. Let your imagination and memory run wild here.

Now, ask yourself: What stopped you from turning any one of those ideas into a reality?

Having read the story of AutoWeb's founding, is it possible that one of your ideas can come to fruition today if you put in the hard work to make it happen?

If it's money that's holding you back, is it possible that your idea is worthy of attracting investors? If not Wall Street investors and VCs, then smaller investors who might believe in your product or service as much as you do, who have the funds to match your drive and enthusiasm? How do you know if you never try?

Make a list of what you believe is wrong with our Wall Street–driven world and how it treats companies, founders, and employees. We'll come back to that list a little later on.

CHAPTER NINETEEN

WHEN THE BUBBLE BURSTS

truly enjoyed building AutoWeb. I loved our employees. I loved the culture we were building. I loved the dealers who believed in us. I loved the partnership I had built with my brother. I loved that we had been able to make an attempt at elevating our whole family and bringing some financial security to our lives along the way—my brother and I, who had both overcome so much and come so far, through sheer will, on the backs of his tech skills and my sales and marketing skills. I especially loved that AutoWeb was ours—an original idea, built on our interests, our innovations, our relationships, our integrity, our instincts, our hard work, our willingness and desire to share our growth with our employees, and our attempts to do right by all of them, by our clients, and by consumers. I was grateful for the amazing people we met along the way, who supported us and who helped us not only financially but in tackling so many things we could never have tackled on our own: Mark Ross, Norm Turner, our employees, even our competitors. We were so fortunate and so blessed in so many ways. It took this incredible combination of teamwork, skill, vision, timing, and circumstance to bring this company so far, so fast. And that's not counting the number of stars that aligned in the 1990s in Silicon Valley, on Wall Street, in the press, in the economy, and more.

If Frank hadn't signed me up for CompuServe in the summer of 1994, would any of this have happened? If I hadn't walked into the student employment office and discovered Student Painters and learned about sales and marketing outside of the classroom, would any of AutoWeb's growth have played out the way it did? Going all the way back, if my parents didn't raise me the way they did, to stand up for what we believed in and never quit; if I hadn't felt forced into escaping from my own country; or if the U.S. hadn't been willing to welcome Baha'i refugees under Reagan—I mean, come on! It's amazing how many stars had aligned to bring us to this point. I'm so grateful for the people who came before us and sacrificed so much to create a country that made all of this possible. I'm grateful to George Washington, Abraham Lincoln, Rosa Parks, Martin Luther King Jr., and so many others. They all sacrificed in different ways to bring about a better country—a country that, while not perfect, at least makes an attempt to bring about a just society, and a society with opportunities for all—including refugees.

No company is created by chance through timing and the alignment of stars alone. And no company is built by the founders alone. Companies are built on the foundation established by those who came before us, hard work, and principles—whether those principles are well thought out and intentional, or put into practice without much intentionality at all.

Today, looking back, I can admit that the principles I wanted to apply to the building of AutoWeb were not clearly defined at the time. I was in my twenties. I was still very much a work in progress. But the beliefs I held in my heart, which aligned with the teachings of the Baha'i Faith, were built on ideals of unity, honesty, and love. And while I didn't talk about such things at work or print out a list of my guiding principles to hang by the coffeepot in the office, I tried to live up to my own beliefs in my role as a founder and as a CEO: Whether it was treating customers and clients well, making sure our employees were taken care of, or being honest with our board members—the idea of being true to myself, even when things were "just business," was important to me. It was something we just did. We believed that the principles we followed in life were just as important to the long-term success of building a business as they were to being a good person.

And yet, I would soon come to learn that a few of our board members weren't in this for the long term. They didn't get involved in order to build a successful company that would stand the test of time. They weren't in it for much more than the potential short-term gains. To them, and to the bosses that some of them answered to, our company was not much more than a pawn in a game that I didn't yet fully understand. A game that was established and defined by the likes of Milton Friedman, whom *The Economist* once described as "the most influential economist of the second half of the 20th century."

A game that was driven by money and greed, and little regard for much more.

In the middle of the exciting journey, my eyes would be opened to all of it. And in the aftermath of what happened next, my belief in my guiding principles, and my dedication to bringing them forward to the work I did in the business world, would only grow stronger.

After spending time in the beautiful city of Barcelona, flying first class, and passing through customs with my American passport in hand as an American citizen, I returned to our offices feeling excited about where we would take AutoWeb next.

I couldn't understand why some of our employees seemed to be smiling through odd expressions and raised eyebrows when I walked through the door.

I made my way back to my office, and that's when I saw it: Our new CEO had divided my office in two. He had a wall built right down the middle of it. He gave one side to his new lieutenant, someone he had just hired, and left me with half the space I had before. It wasn't a very big office to begin with. So now? My furniture barely fit in the room.

I popped my head in to see him.

"Hey! Welcome back," he said. "Good trip?"

"Yeah. Some welcome," I said.

"Oh, that, yeah. Had to be done. Needed the space. Hope you don't mind," he said.

"You couldn't talk to me about it first?"

I don't remember what his excuse was, but it was very clear that this guy had no idea how to work with a founder. This wasn't going to get fixed with time and patience. Any guy who would do something so callous in the course of a single week had no interest in treating me as an equal, a partner, a peer, or anything close. For some reason he felt the need to defend his title around me, and I really didn't want to be around someone like that. Not only did it rub me the wrong way, but his attitude and actions ran afoul of all of the principles I had devoted myself to as we built this company.

Truly, what was he thinking? He knew our employees were loyal to me. He did this while they all watched and saw what was going on. Did he think they would approve? Did he think that would engender good feelings about their own futures at AutoWeb? The only thing it did was create a feeling of unease that rolled across the entire staff. Then again, he told me that he liked tension in the company. He thought a competitive atmosphere, particularly within the management team, would incentivize people to try harder—as if an always present tension would bring out the best in them. *Really?* I thought. I had always found that a sense of love and togetherness brought out the best in people.

Our approaches could not have been any more opposite.

I didn't need an office. I would have worked from a cubicle if that's what was called for. I was frugal. I didn't need much. Everyone who worked for us knew the sacrifices we'd made along the way. This was about the message. I found it toxic, and I had a very bad feeling that our culture would never be the same again. Our company would never be the same. I felt it. The loss. And I found myself mourning that loss.

I squeezed between the wall and the edge of my desk, and I stuck around and stuck it out for a few weeks, but I finally told him, "Look, I cannot 'work for you' as 'your vice president.'"

I told the board the same. I would stay on as a board member only. I removed myself from the daily activities of the company.

A couple of months passed, and the situation turned into a real disaster. We had turned AutoWeb into a profit maker just a few months earlier, and he managed to turn it into a money loser in a massive way by ignoring what I'd done and instead burning through the cash we'd raised in our IPO at a rapid pace—in the name of trying to build a brand.

"This isn't the type of company you build a brand for," I tried to explain to him. "People buy a car once every so many years. This isn't fashion, or groceries. If you build a brand through advertising and billboards and cute marketing ideas, they'll forget about it by the time they're supposed to come back, five years later. You build this brand through usage, by being in front of people who are interested in buying a car, at the exact time when they're doing their research. You build a brand through customer service and building a loyal base. You also make money at the same time, so you're not just building a brand in thin air and hoping they'll come back and buy something at some point in the future."

I heard him and the CFO afterwards saying that I had "the founder's disease"—an inaccurate, derogative, and biased term many Silicon Valley VCs use to brush aside the very founders of the companies they've invested in, deriding them as "too close" to their own companies to be able to see clearly. Meanwhile, they wasted tens of millions of dollars chasing their flawed ideas.

At board meetings, I reiterated that we'd made a mistake. At one meeting in particular, I'll just say it: I tried to get him fired. That's the reality of it. I told the board, straight up, "You have made the wrong decision. The business is dying. I'd be happy to step in as the interim CEO until you hire somebody else if that's all you'll let me do. But what's happening here will kill this business."

Finally, the board agreed that he needed to be fired. But one of the board members pointed out, "If we fire him, the stock price is gonna take a dive."

That got everybody in a tizzy.

We had a CFO who, for the most part, was liked, and whom every-one agreed would be a better CEO than the one we had, so the board came up with this "brilliant" idea: "What if we don't fire him, and we tell the CFO, 'You're not the CEO, but as the CFO, you have a greatly expanded role. So almost everybody reports to you. In other words, you run the company but you're not the CEO.'" The board managed to confuse everyone.

Did the board do anything illegal? Technically, no. But unethical? I think so. And that lack of transparency and truthfulness rubbed both Frank and me the wrong way. Neither one of us believed that greed, as a primary force, would help us build a company. But we were learning, quickly, that we were in the minority. It seemed a great number of VCs and bankers, including some on our board, were primarily interested in keeping a stock price high just long enough for them to dump it and move on. There was no concern about what would happen after that.

During the summer of 1999, my brother was the chair of our board, and one day he stood up and said, "I can no longer be a part of this." He grabbed a napkin, wrote his resignation on it, handed it to our outside counsel from Fenwick & West (who was sitting right there at the table), and he said, "I'm outta here."

He walked out and never, ever returned to that building.

The funny thing is, by making that spontaneous decision, Frank made out better than I did. Because he was no longer on the inside, he was free to sell his shares.

I was more stubborn. I didn't want to let AutoWeb go. I continued to serve on the board for another four months, until I attended one board meeting where the CEO and the CFO tried to tell the board that the lead-gen business wasn't sustainable. "It's just not going to continue," they said. "At max, all across the web, it has maybe a year left. So we have to think of a different business model."

Twenty-five years later, I can tell you that the lead-gen model as a form of performance-based marketing is still thriving all across the web. I have no idea where they were getting their information, or if they were just pulling it out of thin air, but they were wrong. Anyone can see that now. But then? Well, I saw it then, too. These guys just didn't know the industry. It was not their fault that they had no vison for the industry; they were put in the wrong roles by a board driven by the wrong things. Their primary goal was not to establish a company to massively influence automotive retailing as we knew it. Our company needed the vison of a founder, as do almost all startups.

"So, as a result of having to change models, we have a new plan to go buy this company, and that company," they said.

They were trying to use this bold new plan of theirs to obscure the actual headline of the meeting: AutoWeb was going to miss its numbers. Just months after our massive IPO, our company was going to miss its quarterly numbers.

A wave of disappointment washed over the room. We decided to take a break. The CFO left rather quickly, but I managed to stop the CEO.

"Just so I'm clear on this," I said, "what is the street expectation from us for this quarter?"

And he said, "I don't know."

"Excuse me?" I said.

"I don't know," he said again.

"Seriously?" I said. "You're the CEO. You don't even know what the street is expecting? What is your North Star, then? What is it you're managing toward if you don't know?"

He shook his head and looked away like he always did, and that was my last straw.

I was in shock. We had gone public, but we were not acting like a public company. Executives had joined us for a big payday, but they were not there to put in the hard work. It was depressing to see the company we had worked so hard to build being treated so badly, and so recklessly.

I had no influence, and I was watching a train wreck. I had to remove myself from such a heartbreaking and painful experience.

When the meeting reconvened, I said, "I'm done. I can no longer be a part of this."

I left the boardroom, and I resigned from the board.

I had to walk away in order to heal.

I didn't allow myself to get down about any of it, though. I was young, healthy, and wealthy in spades (or so I thought).

So what did I decide to do?

I decided to go build another company, from scratch—only this time, using all of the knowledge and Silicon Valley startup experience I had gained during my AutoWeb journey.

By around October 1999, once Frank and I had both left AutoWeb, we thought about starting another business together, a business very similar to today's Dropbox. We even incorporated and went about doing all the things necessary to get it off the ground. Ultimately, though, we decided not to go down that path, because we each had other ideas that we wanted to bring to fruition.

I was still more of a consumer-oriented guy, while my brother was more of a technology guy. So he decided to build a SaaS (software as a service) business focused on the low-code/no-code market; and I went down the path of building PurpleTie.

The basic idea behind PurpleTie came to me—and I wish it hadn't come to me—after listening to Wayne Huizenga, the founder of Waste Management, AutoNation, and Blockbuster Video. During his speeches at automotive conferences, he told the story of how Blockbuster took a loose, unstructured, industry—the mom-and-pop videocassette rental shops that had popped up in towns all over America in the 1980s—and turned it into a large, integrated industry that ultimately changed the consumer experience for the better.

Once they got started, he'd said, Blockbuster opened up one store every eight hours for eight years straight.

I loved the idea of turning a long-overlooked, mom-and-pop industry into something better. I was determined to go after an industry that had personally frustrated me for years: the dry-cleaning industry. There were more than one hundred thousand dry-cleaning locations in the country, most of them independently owned, hardly any of them chains. Which made it seem like an industry ready for major disruption.

We've all had the typical dry-cleaning experiences, right? I started talking about it with friends and family: "Lost clothes, botched cleaning jobs, lousy service, major inconvenience, failure to deliver what's promised. That spot you pointed out when you dropped the clothes off? Still there. Poor pressing, broken or missing buttons, toxic cleaning agents that stink up your closet for days and may or may not give you cancer—and did I mention how expensive it is?"

Anyone I spoke to seemed to nod in agreement, to all of it.

"Well, what if we could offer something better?" I asked.

What if, I thought, we could change the industry forever, and massively improve every consumer's experience? What if we could do this by giving customers online-ordering options (remember, this was 1999), with free pickup and delivery from their home or their office? What if we could track every garment and guarantee to never lose an item again, and, of course, guarantee on-time delivery? What if we had one centralized hub in every major metropolitan area that used environmentally sustainable and responsible cleaning agents? What if we gave businesses a special deal on uniform cleaning and saved their employees even more money on dry cleaning? What if this was a branded service? What if you could buy suits from major department stores that would come with lifetime cleaning included from our trusted brand? Even further, what if this theoretical company also tracked each garment by brand? That way, the company could advise its customers about the expected life of their garments and reorder that piece of clothing from a major clothing supplier after its life span was up. What an opportunity for clothing manufacturers, and retailers, too! They could identify loyal customers by brand, market directly to them every time they got their freshly cleaned clothes back, and even offer them deals as their garments began to wear out. The best part? Every one of those opportunities for interaction between customers and brands was a potential revenue stream for us.

The more I thought about it, the more I liked it. It looked like a very doable model to me. So I started PurpleTie in 1999 and officially launched the company in 2000.

I started making the rounds to VCs, and my pitch was outrageous—basically, "I need $400 million to build this business."

One of the first major VCs I met with was Tod Francis at Trinity Ventures. The same guy who was in partnership with Benchmark had offered me a term sheet that I had passed on back when AutoWeb raised $5 million from TCV. After Todd heard my pitch, he said, "I don't believe in the concept, but here's the odd thing—you'll get the money."

He was right. I made the rounds in Silicon Valley, and while I never raised anywhere close to $400 million, the startup capital began to flow in. The money was available, and most people I met with (besides Todd) were enthusiastic about the business model. Now we just had to deliver—literally and figuratively. I signed a long-term lease, which I personally guaranteed (using my own name, and my own credit), on a one-hundred-thousand-square-foot warehouse facility in Manteca, about an hour from San Francisco. Then we went about getting approval from the city council, and major water-use approvals from various agencies. (I know it's called dry cleaning, but it uses lots of water!) We had to build a massive infrastructure, not only in our plant but with our pickup and delivery service. We'd also committed to building something environmentally friendly, which wasn't simple or cheap, but it was all part of the plan. I was devoted to solving many of the major problems that existed in the dry-cleaning industry, which would go a long way toward helping our planet while we did it.

After we got the permits and the equipment and the space, we made the front page of the Manteca newspaper: "PurpleTie coming to Manteca!" The promise of thousands of jobs was something many politicians were happy to try to get credit for.

On the delivery side, we hired great people out of UPS, including the guy who ran their Southern California division. We hired experienced operations people. We bought a large fleet of trucks, and I personally guaranteed their leases. We put together a spoke and hub model, designing our pickup and delivery routes for maximum efficiency. We hired design and implementation companies to help us think through the complexities of what we were trying to accomplish. We built a factory, our own mini-UPS, the dry-cleaning service itself, a customer service infrastructure, and online platforms, all with lots and lots of innovations.

We hired experts in fabric, since we had to know how to properly clean and care for every type of fabric imaginable, as well as experts in running every facet of the business. We added shoeshine and bulk laundry services to our offerings. We added a radio frequency microchip to every garment, which made each piece of clothing easy to track with total accuracy. We knew how many times each garment had been washed, where in the warehouse each garment was at any moment, and this allowed us to automate the sorting of each order back together. We invented hangers that stopped clothes from getting crushed together during delivery, avoiding flattened collars and disfigured creases. We filed for patents along the way.

We began the process of making deals with Nordstrom and other high-end retailers, too: "You buy a suit, you get lifetime cleaning from PurpleTie!" I had lots of ideas that I couldn't wait to implement, along with the many ideas from the pent-up creativity of people who had worked in the dry-cleaning industry and wanted to reform it. We delivered first-class service from day one. We followed through on every promise. And PurpleTie quickly developed a name for itself in the Bay Area.

Even our trucks were a sight to see: My team was adamant about cleanliness, so those sparkling white trucks with the PurpleTie logo got washed every day. In the Bay Area, where the streets are crammed with delivery trucks covered in grime and graffiti, even that tiny detail set us apart. Our trucks got heads turning everywhere.

Best of all? After ratcheting up through all of that innovation, after overcoming a million little hurdles along the way, after going the extra mile to make sure every aspect of the business was the best it could be, the numbers still worked. This wasn't some unproven tech idea with growth on paper built on crazy valuations. This was a click-and-mortar, wheels-on-the-ground business that could do everything it promised with great margins, hovering at around 67 percent. So our profitability projections looked terrific from day one. And since research showed that most dry-cleaning customers rarely switched service providers (even when they were unhappy), I could assure investors that every customer we acquired would provide annuity revenue—for years.

I felt like a pioneer. I put my head down and threw everything I had into building that company. At about this time, I had moved onto the twentieth floor of a high-rise in San Francisco, and once we started rolling out the service, I'd get up in the morning and look out the window from my perch in the sky, admiring my sparkling fleet of white delivery trucks crossing the Bay Bridge on their way into the city. What a feeling!

PurpleTie was off and running.

And then, we turned the calendar into 2001—when the late-'90s tech bubble, finally, burst.

Looking back on it now, it's easy to discern what happened. In a fit of frenetic exuberance, Silicon Valley had gone about making a whole host of irrational investments that were no longer paying off. The herd mentality of Wall Street and the VC world, which of course had driven all those irrational investments into the stratosphere, turned against tech investments. As a result, the stock market crashed. That crash, which lasted for a total of two-and-a-half years, saw $5 trillion in market value evaporate like water on a hot sidewalk.

Investors' exuberance for anything based in or around Silicon Valley quickly turned to fear. Which meant that, in the first quarter of 2001, there was no longer any money to be found. I desperately tried to get more capital, but it was just impossible.

To make things even more difficult, AutoWeb's value had tanked, which meant my personal source of funds had dried up, too. (The reason I hadn't already sold my ownership is that doing so as the founder could have caused further collapse in the stock price and created bad blood with those at the company I was still friends with. Having said that, if I'd had a mentor and received proper advice, selling would have been the right decision. I was naïve.)

In short order, PurpleTie was out of money—and there was no more money to be found.

I made the tough call to shut PurpleTie down in early 2001. Most dot-coms, when they went belly-up, just turned off the lights and took their computers home. But in PurpleTie's case, I had real assets to worry about. There were the employees whose jobs were about to disappear, and the garments we had to return to our customers. And even though it was expensive, we kept people on the job until the job was done; and we made sure that every single PurpleTie customer got their clothes back.

Once the orders were returned, we had to get rid of the dry-cleaning machines, the trucks, and the long-term lease on the facility in Manteca, which was peppered with expensive equipment still ready and waiting to be installed.

I had given my personal guarantee. For all of it.

On the final day, everybody left the company except for me and the fleet manager. He handed me a duffel bag full of keys to the fleet of trucks that were parked in the big yard. They were my responsibility now. Everyone else was gone.

I could have walked away at that point, and several people had advised me to do just that. Other executives in other bankrupt companies did, and they likely took a much smaller financial loss dealing with the inevitable lawsuits. But that's not who I was. I felt that I had to honor my commitments.

I worked with a company in Sonoma, California, to liquidate the trucks, and for every truck I sold, I had to write a personal check to get out of the lease, because the sales price wasn't enough to cover what we owed.

When all was said and done, I lost more money than any other Purple-Tie investor.

For nearly two years I had dedicated every waking minute to building PurpleTie. It was all I thought about, morning 'til midnight. I truly thought we were about to disrupt an entire industry. That our business would leave a positive mark on the world.

I thought the money I made with AutoWeb had come relatively easy, so I rushed right out thinking that I could do it all over again, even faster and smarter the second time around. But like a child actor, I learned the hard way that early success doesn't mean you'll necessarily continue to be successful later on.

Once the final truck was sold, after I bought $50,000 worth of dirt to fill the hole we had dug for a boiler in our factory, after I paid $500,000 to get out of our lease, after I locked up the facility and said goodbye to the millions of dollars of personal money I had invested, I said goodbye to PurpleTie for the last time, and I took a walk. I was maybe a quarter of a mile away from our headquarters when I stopped, turned, and looked back at the building.

I contemplated all the hard work and energy that went into creating it. I remembered the terrific people who'd helped realize my vision of a new kind of service-industry company. I felt frustrated and hurt that such a good concept couldn't make it in the real world, especially due to circumstances that were mostly beyond my control but still fully my responsibility.

As I stood there, reflecting, I suddenly had an epiphany. From that distance, the great, big building we had leased looked small—and I suddenly saw that the company we had built was small, too. In the grand scheme of things, PurpleTie wouldn't be all that missed. This thing that had seemed so big and important to me for the last two years was gone, and I realized that very few people even knew or cared. From that macro perspective, it really wasn't something to be all that upset over.

I detached myself from taking the failure so personally, and I was sure that holding on to that macro perspective would help me grow in countless ways in the coming years.

Even then, the loss I felt over what had gone wrong at AutoWeb still stung—perhaps because that part of my journey wasn't over.

REFLECTIONS ON CHAPTER NINETEEN

Are you able to detach yourself from the personal and business losses in your life? To see them from a distance, and not get lost in the pain of the immediacy of failures?

Would gaining the ability to detach, even a little bit, allow you some freedom? Allow you to move on? Allow you to hurt less over the losses in your life?

Have you ever tried to build a business that failed? If so, what did you learn from that experience? Were you able to apply it to whatever you did next? And if not, was the fear of failure the thing that held you back from starting a business in the first place? Or going to school? Or taking a new job?

Make a list of all of the major things you've failed at in the past. Really! It's important. Because as you think about all of those failures, I want you to think about where you are today. What you learned from those failures. What you gained by participating in whatever it was you failed at. What you know now that you didn't know then. Failures are part of the journey, and the more we embrace them and learn from them, the more we can detach from them and realize they weren't all bad. In fact, they may have been our best teachers.

CHAPTER TWENTY

AFTERMATH

In early 2001, the tech bubble was bursting all over. The whole industry sank like a torpedo aimed straight down at the bottom of the ocean, and AutoWeb was a company with no vision, no real leadership, out of cash, and out of options.

I attempted to come back, to try to rescue things. More than once. I even tried to buy the company back once the share price had fallen so low that I could have picked it up for a song. But VCs, especially in Silicon Valley, have a thing about letting founders back in: They just don't want it to happen. They're perfectly fine making decisions against their own interest, as long as they don't have to admit any mistakes. That includes almost never letting a founder come back. Why? I honestly think it's nothing more than stubbornness, believing that by allowing a founder to come back they have announced defeat. I think a level of humility would actually make them more effective in their roles (after founders) as primary drivers in shaping the future of business. They often don't know how to build companies themselves or how to rescue companies when they flounder, and they simply don't want to be "shown up" by the founders. (Is it obvious that I've lost the fondness I once held for the VC world? Don't get me wrong, there are many great

VCs and it's a necessary industry, but most are driven by fundamentally flawed drivers and values.)

Personal pettiness in these situations is supposed to be overridden by the fact that public companies have more mature boards of directors—independent boards full of members who are supposed to make unbiased decisions in the best interest of the companies they run. But that idea, which sounds so good on paper, isn't real. It's total BS. There is hardly an example to be found of a board that backed a founder who was previously forced out when the chips were down post his or her departure. If you can find one, it's usually a case of some extraordinary pressure from powerful people or other powerful forces that forced the board's hand. Or they were just so desperate that they simply had no options left, like Apple in the late 1990s, when they allowed Steve Jobs to come back. But in nearly all cases, the board members, as a rule, believe that the future is with the money, with the VCs. So why would they back the founders?

Instead, the founders are the lonely ones that the boards let drown.

Less than two years after our IPO, AutoWeb had fallen so far that it basically had no choice but to merge with its old nemesis, its lesser competitor, Autobytel (which because of their own founder/board drama wasn't in a much better situation). And when the merger happened, Autobytel was the acquirer. They had never been profitable. They had stuck to models that didn't offer anywhere near the growth potential or innovation that AutoWeb had in its DNA—but at the time of the merger, AutoWeb's share price had fallen to just eighteen cents a share.

Our VCs, as it turned out, were more like house flippers in a cheap neighborhood. "How can we make some money and move on?" They didn't want to be long-term homeowners. They didn't even want to be landlords. They were in it to flip it, and that was it. So their primary focus was on maximization of stock price. All VCs want that, of course. They're all about the short-term gain. But ours in particular (especially at that time) were all about the stock price. To them, nothing else mattered.

I believe what was done by the AutoWeb board was simply bad business. Was it illegal? No. But to me, it was unethical. And it wasn't until much later that I would learn that our astronomical IPO share-price surge may have been driven by something unethical, too, which was orchestrated by Credit Suisse.

In typical Wall Street fashion, as Americans have learned the hard way in every stock market crash since, there's a big difference between unethical and illegal, which is why so few people in the banking world ever go to jail, even when it's determined that their behavior sits at the very center of the ripple effects that cause national and international economic crises.

The operation that Frank Quattrone led at Credit Suisse was so astounding that somebody wrote a book about it, called *The Prince of Silicon Valley*, and in it, my brother and I are named as two of Frank Quattrone's friends. The truth is, we've never met Frank. We've never been friends. The book got it wrong. What it got right is that Frank ran Credit Suisse's capital markets at the time that AutoWeb went public. And what the SEC charged was that Credit Suisse was guilty of doing this thing called "laddering" with their IPOs, which we were not aware of.

Let's say (hypothetically) that somebody had committed to buy two hundred thousand shares at $14 a share at IPO. The bankers would say to them, "Okay, we'll give you that, as long as you also commit to buy another one hundred thousand shares in open markets at $20 a share." So, this way, the stock was guaranteed to go up.

Why was that important? Because every IPO has this thing called "the shoe" associated with it. The shoe is made up of additional shares, usually 10 percent of the total offering, that the bankers are allowed to sell in the month following the IPO—but they buy them at the starting price of the IPO, at $14 per share in our case. So, when the stock is trading at, let's say, $45, which was the case with ours at the end of the first day, that's $31 more per share than the $14 they paid. When they flipped the shoe, they instantly made $15.5 million (in addition to all of their fees).

So, by laddering the deals, Credit Suisse was guaranteed to double or triple their earnings for every IPO out of the gate, not including what they would make from the trades that followed.

And that, my friends, is why certain people like to say the system is rigged. Because it's true.

The Credit Suisse team apparently did that with many, many internet IPOs that they took out, which landed them in a class-action lawsuit that included AutoWeb.

At the end, Frank Quattrone was acquitted. There was a settlement. As far as I know, the insurance companies paid the settlement, and Credit Suisse walked away mostly unscathed. There was a lot of unethical stuff like that going on that we were just completely unaware of—and in this case, what we didn't know hurt us. It hurt our employees. It hurt everyone.

And for what? Greed. That's all it was. Nothing more. Just the greed of a few powerful men who measure their net worth by dollars alone.

Thanks to men like that, and the system as it stands, at the age of twenty-eight, I made more than $200 million—and two years later, more than 94 percent of it was lost. (By the way, that 94 percent financial loss I went through didn't include the sums I'd personally spent trying to get PurpleTie off the ground and then shutting it down.)

The $1.2 billion AutoWeb valuation was not real and was clearly too high; just as the $0.18 per share price wasn't real and was far too low for a company that would go on to sustain itself under various leadership and ownership to this day.

The ride on Wall Street didn't benefit us, the people who created the company.

It only benefited them.

Our company would have been much better off being valued at its worth—I would say $400 million at IPO—and over the years, it would have earned its way to a higher valuation. Instead, the out-of-the-gate $1.2 billion valuation satisfied Wall Street, but set up the company for failure. How can you go up from a valuation that is already unsupportable? It's a fundamental question we should all be asking, and one for which we should be seeking answers before the next major market crash.

Thankfully, I never went out and bought a mansion or a fleet of Lamborghinis with any of that IPO money, so I was fine. I still had money in the bank—a lot of money compared to what I'd made in all the years before 1999.

I was grateful for what I had learned. I was grateful for the experience.

I made it. I lost it. I learned along the way.

It was all part of an extraordinary journey that still made me shake my head with gratitude and joy every morning when I woke up.

It was humbling, though, to have so much wealth and to realize that I never really had it. My wealth was on paper, just like the so-called "wealth" of so many millionaires and billionaires.

I found comfort in one of the lessons I'd learned from the writings of Baha'u'llah: "The world is but a show, vain and empty, a mere nothing, bearing the semblance of reality. Set not your affections upon it . . . Verily I say, the world is like the vapour in a desert, which the thirsty dreameth to be water and striveth after it with all his might, until when he cometh unto it, he findeth it to be mere illusion."

So the tangible parts of both PurpleTie and AutoWeb were left in shambles.

While AutoWeb didn't close its doors, many of our employees, the men and women we'd hired and given shares to with the full intention of getting them the best deal possible when we took AutoWeb public, had either moved on or been let go.

So what did I have to show for all of our work? All of their work? All of our innovation? All of our effort? I had made some money, yes. But what was the real value in any of it?

That was a question I would grapple with in the years ahead.

I have learned some of my most valuable lessons from failures. It's a harsh way to learn anything, but in some respects, failure can teach us a lot more about ourselves than success. In fact, I highly recommend failure—not as a goal to aspire to, but as something we should never fear. Failure tests our inner character and contributes to our spiritual growth much more than any other life experience.

In 2001, the failures in my life just kept coming.

As PurpleTie went through its demise, my marriage eroded also. I don't feel it's appropriate to get into the personal details in this book, but I will say that the red flags I witnessed at our wedding were precursors to what would later emerge as the most fundamental problem of all: The two of us did not share the same values at our core. It's not just that we came from different faith backgrounds, although that was a part of it. It was about the essence of who we are as humans and why we are on this planet, which I believe need to be 100 percent in alignment in order for a marriage to work. We went through a very difficult, emotional period as I was dealing with PurpleTie, and that struggle spotlighted the core of every problem we had. Our relationship was untenable. It was time to go our separate ways.

When I told my brother that I had made up my mind to get a divorce, he said, "I'm proud of you. That is not an easy decision. It is a very challenging, difficult one, but you did it, and you're gonna be better off as a result of it."

I wasn't looking for affirmation from my brother, but it felt good to have it. Those words allowed me to detach a bit from the sorrow of what was happening; to see it from a distance.

Filing for divorce was one of the hardest decisions I'd ever had to make, and yet, as I've said, making such a decision isn't the worst thing a person can do. To me, indecisiveness is the worst thing. We went through our divorce proceedings amicably. Not happily, of course, but with enough dignity and grace to not make any attempt to destroy each other in a court of law, as so often happens in the white-hot anger of a couple's split. We both left with enough money in our pockets to live and to start our lives over. Why would I want anything less than that for the woman I was once married to?

We didn't have children, which I suppose made it easier. We could go our separate ways and move on without having the constant contact and potential friction of shared parenting between us. And when it was over, I was able to stand tall and feel confident that I had done the right thing.

So there I was, in my early thirties, starting over in just about every way a person can start over. For some, experiencing so many failures at once could have brought them to their knees. But this is why it is so important to embrace our difficult journeys in life: For me, a person who had known what it's like to nearly die of heat exhaustion and thirst—having truly been brought to my knees while crossing a mountain in the Pakistani desert—reaching this point in my personal and professional life was hardly crushing by comparison. On the contrary, as I distanced myself from the emotional pain and put it all into perspective, there was something refreshing and exciting about reaching this point in my life journey. I felt as if I had already taken a drink from the proverbial oasis. Now, all I had to do was to gather my strength, stand up, and continue to walk. The bus would be waiting for me right around the corner.

I decided to take some time off. To gather my strength.

But I would not rest for long.

I had my whole life in front of me, and I knew that the opportunities were endless—all I had to do was open my eyes and take advantage of them.

America rewards hard work, and one of the rewards is the ability to earn more opportunities. For the most part, there are no predetermined classes in the U.S. designed to keep us down. People from any background have the opportunity to build a successful life in this country, and it shocks me that not everyone really understands what a gift that is. Many people seem oblivious to the opportunities that exist here, and even worse, a growing number of Americans seem to believe conspiracy theories or imaginary ideas that make them think that their road to success is blocked, especially when it comes to blaming big business for their inability or unwillingness to go after their own dreams.

Please understand that I do believe portions of our society have many more roadblocks than others because of racism, sexism, nationalism, and more. But just because they (which includes me) face more roadblocks does not mean the road is fully blocked. The remarkable and uplifting thing about life in the U.S. is that there is always an opening. The roads are never entirely closed. I wish, collectively, that we would focus on that, that we would focus on the opportunities rather than focusing so much on the power of those who have put the roadblocks in front of us. I think that focusing on the roadblocks only gives them more power.

Again, I want to be clear, this does not mean that any of us should stop working for justice and equality, but I would rather see us do all of those things while also doing our best to get ahead and gain our own influence—so we can build a society and country and world defined by better values and ideals.

In my own experience, immigrants are often quicker to recognize the high level of opportunity in the U.S. because of the stark contrast between the U.S. and their home countries. They often become enormously successful as a result. Studies show that immigrants are more likely than U.S.-born citizens to become entrepreneurs: The Kauffman Foundation's index of entrepreneurial activity is nearly 40 percent higher for immigrants than for natives, and that is clearly the case in Silicon Valley.

In the tech industry, immigrant entrepreneurs or their children founded such now-iconic American companies as Apple, eBay, Google, Sun Microsystems, Yahoo, YouTube, and Tesla—and many, many more. I've met a huge number of successful and mega-successful immigrant entrepreneurs—people who fled their countries of origin to come to America, where they now have the freedom to build concepts and companies that never could have flourished elsewhere.

And maybe it's no coincidence that many of them are Persians who've fled similar atrocities and persecutions to those I faced as a boy.

It was now entirely up to me to move forward with my eyes open and to make use of the knowledge I had gained along the way.

Living through the burst of the tech bubble could have been nothing but depressing. Every morning I woke up, poured myself a cup of coffee, and scanned a website called "F**kedCompany.com," which listed all of the companies that had gone out of business the day before or were just about to close. I refused to wallow in the self-pity of negativity, though. What good can possibly come from repeating a mantra of, "Aw, man, the world sucks. Everything's falling apart. The dream is over!"

No.

In every failure, there is opportunity—even when the failure isn't yours.

I spent those mornings on the web looking for opportunities.

During the bubble, investors were buying up companies with "extravagant exuberance." After the bubble popped, people went around dropping everything, at extravagant discounts, including assets and whole companies that still had significant value—at least in my opinion. The bargains were as extreme at the bottom as the inflated valuations were when the market was at its apogee.

One day, I saw that a company called iMotors.com had gone out of business. I knew iMotors well. They weren't a direct competitor with AutoWeb, but they were in a similar marketplace. They dealt in used cars, buying them from auctions, refurbishing them, and selling them to consumers online.

I knew one of the investors who had poured over $100 million into iMotors: Tod Francis at Trinity Ventures—the same guy who declined to invest in PurpleTie, but who had made me an offer at AutoWeb.

I emailed him, and he put me in touch with iMotors' founder. I told him I wanted to buy the company's soft assets—basically the brand and the domain, which were still generating a bunch of consumer traffic, along with the hundreds of billboards they had put up around the country while trying to build that brand.

We were in the thick of an economic bust. I figured no one was spending the time or capital to take down those billboards any time soon, which meant that they would sit there, advertising this brand to millions of passersby, every day, for free.

He sold me those assets for $60,000.

So, overnight, for very little money, I gained ownership of a website with a large online presence, and a whole bunch of physical real estate advertising the brand. The only thing I needed to figure out was what business I could operate to monetize the consumer traffic that was showing up on the website at no cost to me.

The first step was easy: I was getting web traffic to iMotors.com, and that traffic was valuable. So I redirected that traffic and sold it to none other than Autobytel—the company that AutoWeb had recently merged with.

A company called CarClub went out of business, so I bought their assets, too, and did the same thing. Then an online home-improvement site went down, and I bought their assets. And that's when I started to see how this could really become something.

Optimism is a powerful force.

Here I was, in 2001, in the middle of the dot-com bust, in the year that would be remembered for the September 11 terrorist attacks that brought down the Twin Towers in New York City, getting ready to start another business.

I enjoyed what we had built at AutoWeb—a bridge between consumers and car dealers and carmakers, which gave all parties exactly what they wanted and needed. (Consumers received information that was useful in their decision-making process, plus an introduction to local dealers; the dealers got direct leads on new customers.)

Now? I wanted to build a company that did the same thing but went across verticals and helped people with all sorts of life's big purchases: buying a car, buying a home, making home improvement decisions, and so on. So that's the business I started to build in 2001. I placed it all under the umbrella of a new name in 2003: Reply.com—a domain name I was able to purchase for $10,000. And what I built was a performance-based marketing platform for a significant portion of the market that was, in a sense, ignored by the large players—essentially category-agnostic, locally targeted marketing and advertising, connecting consumers to whatever they were looking for, and making money through lead-generation along the way.

Reply grew to significant revenue, quickly. As a company, we went to VCs, raised money, bought another company, raised more money . . . and after a little while, it started to feel like I was riding a train I had watched derail twice before.

I knew that wasn't what I wanted to do.

I knew there had to be another way to build this company—to incorporate every value I wanted to infuse into my business and life.

I found myself asking questions about how I could change the business model to have a greater impact on the world—to build a business that was guided toward a North Star that was much more meaningful than just money and that existed for more than the shortsighted cycle of producing quarterly results aimed at pleasing investors at any cost.

In 2002, in the middle of all of this enterprise-building, my brother asked me to attend a Baha'i business conference in Reston, Virginia.

"I'm too busy," I said.

He kept asking.

"I really don't want to go," I told him.

For some reason, Frank wouldn't let it go.

Looking back on it now, I think he saw more clearly than I did that for all of the hard work I was doing to build yet another company in the wake of my divorce, I was more than a little lost in terms of my personal well-being.

Finally, Frank insisted that I meet him at the conference, and he handed me a business-class ticket with my name on it.

So I went.

As soon as I arrived, one of the organizers asked if I'd be willing to give a presentation to about 250 attendees. He wanted me to speak about being an entrepreneur, and especially about the process of taking a company public.

I would have preferred to talk about anything else. I felt like I was starting a new chapter in my life. I wanted to accomplish something important, something big, something that made a difference in the world. I didn't want to let myself get caught up again in the rush to gain Wall Street riches, let alone to stand up and tell other people how to do it.

But I took a breath.

I was at a Baha'i conference.

A short presentation is the least I can do, I thought. So, reluctantly, I agreed.

I gave my talk on the second evening of the conference. I filled my speech with honesty and caution—and of course there were lots of people who were dreaming about the possibility of one day launching their own IPOs after hearing what I had to say. The temptations of the potential riches of the IPO world are so huge, they seem to block out the red flags of dealing with a system that is not aligned with most of our cherished values, as well as the limitations and expectations that process carries with it. But who was I to discourage anyone from taking their own journey into the Wall Street den?

There was a lot of interest in what I had to say, and after the speech, I held a small workshop. About fifteen people attended. We had a great session. A few people even stayed after that to talk to me, one-on-one, including a fashionable young woman who caught my eye—and not just for her looks. I noticed during the group discussion that she was sharp, and I really wanted to speak with her one-on-one, but too many people with too many questions kept taking up my time. I found myself getting anxious and worried that the one person I really wanted to speak with might simply give up and leave.

She didn't. She waited. Patiently.

When we finally got a chance to talk, I learned that this remarkable and very attractive woman had a career and a life story that was strikingly similar to mine.

Gouya grew up in Tehran, where her father was a successful businessman and her mother worked for an airline. In the prelude to the Revolution, she and her mother and grandmother were out shopping in a quiet, commercial neighborhood, when suddenly shooting broke out. Everyone on the street panicked and ran, darting into whatever door they could find, even if they had no idea who lived there.

Tehran's streets descended into chaos after that. Protests and shootings became commonplace, as the Shah's government imposed martial law. Her parents, who were born into Baha'i families, could see immediately what the new Revolutionary government had in mind for the

Iranian Baha'i community—persecution and slow destruction. Living in the thick of the turmoil as it unfolded, Gouya's mother finally told her father, "We're leaving." Her father, naturally, wanted to finish some things first—to close a few deals, to find a way to get his savings out of the country. But Gouya's mom said, "No," and the family left with nothing more than what they carried in a few suitcases.

Gouya was eight years old.

When she came to America, Gouya developed the same entrepreneurial drive that I did. After graduating from the Art Institute of Seattle, at the age of twenty-one, she founded and successfully ran a number of fashion and footwear companies. I knew nothing about fashion, and I was shocked to learn she had become a formidable force in the shoe industry, and her Gouya M. fashion footwear brand (which was often private-labeled) sold in places like Aldo and Nordstrom. She was in her early thirties now, the same age as I was, and I could have stayed up all night just listening to her stories.

I almost did.

The two of us talked nonstop from 10 PM until 3 AM

When I left her, I was overjoyed. I could tell that something important had happened. Somehow, by the end of that evening, I knew that I was going to marry her—not that I was ready to make that kind of a decision so soon after my divorce, but regardless, my decision was made.

In the weeks and months that followed, Gouya and I began to build a relationship, and I could not believe my good fortune. This woman—assertive, opinionated, and confident—won my heart and won my mind. She thought in much the same way I thought, but she evaluated things from her own unique set of concepts and experiences, which added a surprising richness to everything we discussed.

Nine months after we met, we got married, and my world—which had been so wholly focused on business—became focused on something so much greater: love.

I have Frank to thank for that. He couldn't have known that I would meet the love of my life at that conference in Virginia, but somehow he knew that I needed to go. He knew that I needed to be there and to shake up the routines I had established for myself in the nonstop world of entrepreneurship. He knew that I needed to step out of my comfort zone—which wasn't all that comforting—and maybe take a brand-new journey.

As a result of that one trip and the connection we carried with us afterwards, Gouya became more than my wife. She became my alter ego, and my soulmate. She is my equal partner in life, and the unity we aspire to build in our family and in our work comes directly from that deep sense of equality.

In that love, through my own desire and through our partnership in marriage, I was able to take a deeper dive into the teachings of my Faith. Our Faith. And in those teachings, I started to find answers to many of the questions that had nagged at me.

While the spiritual teachings of the Baha'i Faith don't have specific answers for how to run a business, they do provide us with a framework that can help us with all aspects of life, personal and professional. It was in those teachings where I started to find a sense of direction that would lead me toward a destination I had yet to define.

I started to find the strength to trust the longing I felt in my heart—this unfed desire to build a company differently, and to make my life's work about more than making money, more than simply acting as another startup entrepreneur in a system that left me feeling let down and unfulfilled. I started to believe that what I felt was not only something I should consider embracing, but it was clearly the fundamental journey I was meant to take. Perhaps even a journey we were all meant to take.

Strangely enough, I soon realized it was a journey I was already on.

REFLECTIONS ON CHAPTER TWENTY

When you're down, when you're struggling, when things go wrong, when your whole world seems to be collapsing—where do you turn for help and healing? Where do you turn for guidance?

Have you ever found yourself at what felt like the bottom? If so, where do you find yourself now? (I'm guessing it's not down there.) How did you get back on your feet? How did you turn things around? Can you find solace in your past ability to rise up after a fall? After all, if you did it once, chances are you can do it again. And shouldn't that fact make you just a little bit fearless when it comes to tackling whatever journey is ahead?

What is the purpose behind what you do for work? Is there a purpose besides making money? Perhaps it's as simple as wanting to support yourself and your family, to give your loved ones the best life you can. Or perhaps it's something else that's meaningful to you. Does working toward that purpose drive you? Excite you? Make you feel fulfilled? And if not, what would?

Really think about it: What would make you feel excited to get up and go to work every day?

PART III
THE WAY FORWARD

"Only by improving spiritually as well as materially can we
make any real progress, and become perfect beings."
—Abdu'l-Baha

CHAPTER TWENTY-ONE

FAITH

Nothing, and I mean nothing, is more important in life than purpose and love.

Purpose because it is the underlying, emanating force that causes us to gain fulfillment from our journey beyond the mechanics of simply living.

And love because it is the one unifying force that gives us energy, which serves as our motivation to be a source of good, and which elevates our journey to a spiritual experience.

I was reminded of this message and felt it more deeply in my marriage with Gouya—especially through our dedication and alignment to live a life congruent with the teachings of the Baha'i Faith.

Of course, no message ever resonates more deeply in our hearts than when we feel it and experience it firsthand, and such messages often come to us through life's unexpected turns, in moments that take us by surprise.

I would feel the full force of this again and again during the early 2000s and 2010s—in the middle of growing Reply.com toward yet another "successful" IPO.

If it isn't obvious from the passages I dedicated to him in the early chapters of this book, my cousin Sean was very dear me. In Tehran, he played the role of a second big brother. He was the one who took me to his father's studio at the U.S. Embassy and gave me a taste of America for the very first time. Our correspondence after he moved to the U.S. was a huge inspiration and beacon of hope for me, as he put me in touch with the potential of a life full of freedom and, of course, the opportunity to make money from American music, too. It was Sean who sent me tape reels from cassette tapes that he'd purchased in the U.S., and who later sent Frank and me money to get by during our long wait in Pakistan, and who picked us up at the airport when we finally landed in San Francisco. Sean, whose parents took us into their home. Sean, who got me my first job at Pizza Palace. Sean, who was more than just a family member to me; who had remained one of my closest, dearest, and most trusted friends ever since I had come to the U.S.

In 2003, around the same time I married Gouya, Sean moved to Arizona with his wife and young daughter. I was happy for him, and I wanted to return the many, many favors he had done for me over the years. So I talked to him about opening a call center for Reply.com near Scottsdale, where he lived. The company needed a satellite office in a less-expensive state than California, and I had every confidence that Sean could build and manage one really well.

As an adult, Sean had become hyper-responsible. He had always been a capable, highly intelligent person, someone with a great deal of natural talent. I felt awed, for example, when I would see him pick up a new musical instrument and quickly master it. He had an unusual ability to just figure things out, and he rarely failed at anything he tried.

Sean joined Reply in 2004, and we successfully worked together for three years. I stayed in close touch with him, and he did a terrific job. But in 2007, America's economic downturn began, and Reply was forced to cut costs. We had no choice but to close the office he had set up in

Scottsdale. I offered to keep Sean on board—he was an asset to the business, and I wanted him to stay—but he made the decision to move on.

At the same time, even though I didn't know all the details, Sean's marriage began to break apart. During the process, he told me he was hurt in many ways, and before long he was prevented from seeing his children based on unsubstantiated and false accusations. One thing I knew for sure about Sean is that he was a sensitive soul. He felt things more profoundly than others, which meant that he hurt more, too.

After leaving Reply, Sean ended up working with my brother at his SaaS company for about a year. During his divorce, he moved back to Modesto, where it all began, and I thought to myself, *That is a mistake.* While Modesto is a wonderful city and had been good to all of us, I worried it represented a figurative, if not literal, step backwards in his life that wouldn't be good for my cousin.

My worry was warranted. It wasn't long before he began to question himself. In middle age now, he started to feel that his life had taken a wrong turn. He talked to me about the emotional toll of divorce, and about the massive legal bills from his lawyer and his wife's lawyer, and that he was responsible to pay for both. I knew he wasn't making very much money, and although he could have asked for financial help, he didn't. All of this was compounded by the fact that his wife tried to keep him from seeing his kids—an action that very clearly broke his heart.

Things were so bad, he said, he didn't even want to talk about it—and I respected his wish. I stopped asking.

On January 18, 2009, I was startled awake at 3 AM. I jumped out of bed, sweating and thinking about death—not my own death, just death in general. I told Gouya I had no idea why this was happening, but that I knew that something, somewhere, was terribly wrong.

Later that day, I learned that Sean had taken his own life that night.

My brother, sister, and I drove to Modesto to see my aunt, Sean's mom. Then Frank and I went to Sean's house—where his laptop was still open and music was still playing through the speakers. We spent about an hour there, in reverence and in prayer, and it felt as if Sean was there with us. His presence was strong. I thought about what those rooms and walls had witnessed just a few hours earlier; about what happened behind that garage door while people were casually driving by.

It took ten days for the coroner to finish the autopsy. On the day of the burial, I went to the morgue. No one else was in the room when I arrived. The workers brought the body in, and then left.

I had seen dead people before, but never someone who had taken their own life. Never someone this close to me.

It was indescribable.

Frank arrived and joined me in that room a few minutes later. We stood over the body that once belonged to Sean, and we prayed. Baha'is do not condone suicide. We do not take lives, our own included. But we do believe in God's mercy. We believe that every death, no matter the cause, is another birth. It is an experience that is a part of the soul's ongoing journey.

> "O Son of Man! Thou art My dominion and My dominion perisheth not; wherefore fearest thou thy perishing? Thou art My light and My light shall never be extinguished; why dost thou dread extinction? Thou art My glory and My glory fadeth not; thou art My robe and My robe shall never be outworn. Abide then in thy love for Me, that thou mayest find Me in the realm of glory."
> —Baha'u'llah, *The Hidden Words*

We cleansed and wrapped Sean's body according to Baha'i laws, and then we put a ring on his finger that was engraved with the words "I came forth from God and return unto Him, detached from all save Him, holding fast to His name, the Merciful, the Compassionate."

We placed his body in a wooden casket and left it open, so that close family members could see him one last time.

After the last family member came through, we closed the casket and joined Sean's friends at a cemetery in Modesto. Frank and I served as two of the pallbearers. My father said the Baha'i prayer for the dead and the casket was lowered into the ground.

Sean's young children, the ones he had been prevented from seeing, as well his older daughter from an earlier marriage, watched. And cried.

After all he had been through, all he had overcome—after all he had given to others in his life and the extraordinary gifts he brought to the world, nothing could overcome the heartbreak Sean felt over the love that had been taken from him.

Sean had left me a voicemail on January 16—two days before he died. A voicemail that I hadn't responded to. We all tend to leave voicemails unanswered at times, don't we? And I could not have known or even imagined that I would never see him or hear from him again—but I will forever feel guilty for not having been more responsive.

Sean had always been there for me, but I had not been as accessible as I should have been for him in his final days.

If I had been there, if I had picked up my phone, if I had listened to the message and called him back, could I have changed things? That's a question that will never get answered.

I promised myself I would never make that mistake again.

I promised myself that when someone I loved called, I would listen.

I promised myself that I would listen to all of the messages my heart needed to hear.

And over the course of the next few years, I would do my best—perhaps more than I ever had in my adult life—to put love, purpose, faith, and family at the forefront of everything I did.

Not just at home. But in everything.

As we turned the corner into the 2010s, my life had changed drastically, and my interests had, too. My wife and I were making a humble attempt to dedicate more time to our spiritual pursuits. We also had a family of our own now: two little girls, Sophia and Ella. They opened my eyes to every promise that this life offered, this time from a whole new perspective as a father, knowing just how profound the opportunities of freedom and overall absence of oppression and religious persecution would be for these two kids, simply because they were born as U.S. citizens.

What a gift that was.

Seeing the world through their eyes made me think even harder about what I hoped the future would look like for them, and I was struck by how little my business life had changed.

Reply had become sizable, generating tens of millions of dollars in revenue.

We were profitable.

I was the largest shareholder in a company I had once again built from scratch.

But Reply now had a large board populated by what I felt were too many VCs. The former CFO of Apple was on my board, the former CFO of Yahoo was on my board, and a group of VCs who were attempting to push for some of the too-familiar kinds of things I had already experienced at AutoWeb.

And I looked around, and I realized that I just didn't care.

I did my best to carry on for the sake of the company and all those involved and invested in it. While I had made attempts to elevate our business, I still struggled with the idea that my business life was so separate from the rest of my life—my spiritual life, the life of service that I wanted to lead and had been taught to lead through the examples of my Faith, and the examples of my parents.

As we approached 2014, I kept asking myself, *Why are we still doing business like it's the 1980s?* While long-term growth is a necessary part of any business and any endeavor, why are Wall Street and the VC world so attached to the idea of growth at all costs? It seems so old-fashioned. So outdated. So empty. So repetitive. So wrong.

I wondered how we could do better. *Why can't our companies contribute to the betterment of the world?*

The American Dream, that optimistic view of the future and what it can bring, is a powerful source of hope. But had capitalism lost its way? Somewhere along the line, it seemed as if the greed of a small few had eaten the core of the Dream itself, leaving only scraps and peels for the masses.

To add to that, I had a hard time imagining how any of this would ever get fixed when the political unrest and divisiveness in Washington and elsewhere seemed to be growing at such an unstoppable pace. The problems in front of us seemed too big to tackle. Economic inequality was growing. The middle class was suffering and almost disappearing by some measures. And here I was, leading a company that was feeding into the very system that I now felt was failing us all.

I was fed up with practicing capitalism as we know it.

I had lost interest in doing things the same way they had been done in the past.

I had spent my thirties building this company, and I did not want to spend my forties repeating myself in any way.

I was tired of VCs pushing for the same, archaic, one-size-fits-all models—especially the sort of unnatural growth that VCs insist upon, which so often leaves a trail of carnage behind for the employees, the partners, and more. Growth is not everything. I simply and fundamentally have come to believe that companies, and for that matter countries, should not always pursue economic growth, but instead they should pursue what's right for the well-being of the people they serve; what will bring about more sustainability, more joy; and what is more in line with a long-term strategy, which "growth" often is not.

I no longer wanted to be a part of a growth-at-any-cost system, a system that values nothing but share price.

So, in 2014, I went to our board, and I told them I was planning to resign.

I suggested (and they agreed) to make our CMO the CEO, and I promised to stay on as the chair of the board. But I told them, "I'm not going to show up to board meetings for a while."

In some ways, I did that simply to clear the way: "I don't want the new CEO to feel like, as the founder, I'm not allowing him to operate the business," I said. And that was true. But the deeper reality is that I needed a break. I needed some time away. I wanted to see what it was like to spend time with my family without the pressures of the business hanging over me.

Was that a drastic move? Yes. But it was a move that I felt I had to make. And once I made the decision, I didn't second-guess myself. I did not hesitate to move forward—even though I had little idea what destination lay ahead.

On July 16, I said goodbye to my team at Reply, and later that very same day Gouya and I loaded the kids into the car and took off on a road trip of open-ended duration.

The four of us spent a few weeks driving up and down the West Coast. We first headed south to San Diego, but then we were reminded that we loved soccer, and there was a friendly match between two European teams coming up in Portland, Oregon, so we turned back and drove all the way north to Portland to attend the game. We breathed the fresh air and marveled at the size of the trees in Redwood National Park along the way. We dined at all sorts of fun roadside restaurants and grabbed snacks from twenty-four-hour convenience stores, just as all good American road-trippers should. When we saw a shop or a park or a tourist attraction that looked interesting, we stopped and checked it out. Why not? We had no agenda, no schedule, no place to be.

When the sun set over the ocean, we watched it go down together. And every second of that drive was touched by a sense of wonder and excitement as we explored the unknown in this great land of ours, and sang songs, and told stories, and laughed together—never knowing what fun new adventure might be waiting for us around the next bend, or just over the next hill.

In August, Gouya and I attended the Association for Baha'i Studies conference in Irvine, California, where we went to many workshops and listened to a speech by Layli Miller. Layli is the founder of the Tahirih Justice Center, a nonprofit organization that serves women fleeing gender-based violence, including girls fleeing forced marriages or the horrors of female genital mutilation or beatings at the hands of fathers or husbands. Perhaps the most surprising statistic I heard that day was that 70 percent of the Center's clients were fleeing violence that occurred right here on U.S. soil.

As a Baha'i, I believe in the total equality of men and women. The stories she told broke my heart. Gouya and I both wanted to support the cause. But there was more: Layli is the daughter of Lawrence M. Miller, a renowned business consultant who has advised such companies as 3M, Corning, Merck, and Chick-fil-A on how to restructure and reinvigorate their organizations. He was also the author of a book I had recently read, called *Spiritual Enterprise*. In that book, he argues that spiritual principles are just as important to apply to business organizations (and even national economies) as economic principles, and that there should be no conflict between material pursuits and spiritual pursuits—a concept that resonated with me, deeply.

As I sat there watching and listening to his daughter speak, I remember thinking, *You know what? I'm jealous. For leaders of nonprofits, their life of service and their professional life are one and the same.*

Gouya and I spoke about it. "They don't have to go home and say, 'Well, if I have time, maybe I will go offer some service this weekend.' What greater joy is there than thinking, 'You know what? I'm offering service to people all the time'?"

I couldn't stop thinking about it: *Why is it that for-profits stand for greed, and nonprofits stand for the betterment of the world? Why can't we blur the lines between the two?*

We had seen the growth of social-impact companies in the 1990s and 2000s, but while I cared for most of the causes they stood for, I did not like their business models. Their pitch to investors and consumers alike was, "We are for social impact, so don't expect us to be financially successful." Great. So, then why not be a nonprofit so you don't have that challenge? I mean, don't stand in no-man's-land. Don't place yourself in a socially conscious purgatory. Pick one side or the other.

But that's when my imagination started to envision something different. Something better. Something richer and fuller. What was stopping us from building a profitable company that did good in the world as part of its DNA? Why did it have to be one or the other? Profit vs. nonprofit. Greed vs. good. Those are old ways of thinking, and the divisions are entirely made up. They don't need to exist. Why can't we redefine capitalism itself to eliminate the us-vs.-them mentality of winners and losers to create a more unifying capitalism? Truly, what is stopping us from creating companies that thrive, and that benefit all the players: the shareholders, the employees, the communities we work in, the environment—all of it?

At this point in the history of humanity, why can't we evolve capitalism into spiritual capitalism—one that believes in the inherent nobility of humans and one that measures success by much greater metrics than money alone?

Greed is the only thing stopping that from happening, I thought. Nothing more.

That's where my heart was, and that's what I was thinking in November, four months after I'd left, when the board at Reply.com called me. I was actually in Shanghai at the time. I had joined my wife on an exploratory trip to China to look at a few business opportunities, but more importantly to learn and open our minds and eyes to opportunities beyond the U.S. I was having lunch with a few Chinese businesspeople when my phone rang. I picked it up, and the lead board member told me they were running out of cash. The solution they proposed? They wanted to raise more money.

As a reminder, Reply was comfortably profitable before I left.

They started to explain a bit about what was going on, and I said, "You know what? The problems of this company won't be solved by raising cash. The problems are a problem with strategy. So I'm not in favor of raising money. Not at all."

They believed (and I agreed) that a change in leadership might be in order, but they also said the timing wasn't right to make a change in leadership. Raising cash was the right answer, they once again tried to insist. But the board could not proceed without my approval, and I told them again that my stance was firm.

We were deadlocked.

A couple of weeks later, the CEO and CFO of Reply, along with our lead board member, met with the company's major lender to try to buy themselves some time. The company had busted all of the covenants associated with the loan requirements by then and was standing in about $16 million of debt. One of those bankers texted me in the middle of the meeting to say: "Payam, this meeting is not going well. You've got to come back. If you don't come back, we may have no choice but to shut down this business and liquidate the assets."

I didn't want to see that happen.

"Well, I am willing to come back if the board asks me to," I said.

The board reached out the next day and asked me to return. I told them exactly where I stood: "I'm only coming back for three months," I said, "to help sell the company and move on. I have decided that I don't want to be a part of this anymore."

What I wanted to do was to start a business that aligned with my beliefs, my values, and my vision of building something better. I wanted to take a new approach. And yet, I did not want to impose my way of thinking on the investors of Reply.com. This was a journey I was excited about, but not one that they had signed on for. I didn't want to force them to be any part of that, and I also didn't want them to try and talk me out of it. More importantly, I wanted to do it with no financial partners.

I wanted a fresh start.

So the board and I agreed that I would come back to sell the company; to try to do right by our employees and our partners.

It was painful. The company I had left in their hands had gone down by more than half in less than half a year. It fell from making half-a-million dollars a month to showing half-a-million a month in losses.

The company barely had any cash left. I had no choice but to take drastic action.

The day I returned, the first thing I did was ask the CEO to leave.

I then brought my top ten people into the room, those who would be my executives, and said, "We need to rebuild this thing. Are you with me? If you're not, tell me now, because we have to reduce costs across the board, and if you are not going to stay then I know that I should give that seat to the next person. We don't have the money to sustain the current cost structure, and if we don't take action, then everybody will lose their job."

With the exception of one of them, they all said, "We're committed."

The next day, the ten of us put our heads together and made a bunch of decisions that would turn the company profitable overnight.

For some reason, people find that unbelievable. They think it's impossible or that it must take some sort of "genius mind" to make such a thing happen. It doesn't. It's just like pricing: It's not nearly as complicated as people make it out to be.

Gordon Bethune, the retired former CEO of Continental Airlines, lays it out pretty clearly. I saw him speak at a J.D. Power Conference during my AutoWeb days when the following question was asked: "Gordon, how did you make Continental Airlines profitable so quickly?" (It was nearly bankrupt when he took over.) And he replied, "It was easy. We had profitable routes, and we had money-losing routes. I shut down the money-losing routes, and we got profitable overnight."

As long as a company has revenue, it's just not that complicated. If it doesn't have revenue, as so many tech startups do not, I cannot help you. It still surprises me that Wall Street investors make money off of companies that show "growth" while losing millions of dollars every month. Why are we measuring growth instead of profits? Still? After all these years, all these bankruptcies, all these market crashes?

Don't get me wrong. I know it takes investment to build a business, and at times you have to lose money before you become profitable. What I don't understand is the perpetual money-losing strategy for the sake of growth that many employ. And we know why: because most billionaires have become billionaires not because of the cash flow they have generated, but rather because of the stock price they have constructed through all kinds of games played in our capitalist society. Imagine for a moment if you could only become a billionaire if you had generated a billion or more in free cash flow. We probably would have only a handful of billionaires.

Once again: To me, that is one of the greatest failings of a rigged system that only benefits the few. A broken system that needs to change. A system that rarely rewards the building of great businesses, but rather rewards the building of a stock, whether through promise of continual growth, or maybe even manipulation. I don't want to generalize and I should not, but too often this is the recipe followed.

Anyway, the Bethune method is exactly what we used to get Reply's profits back on track. We had to let go of all emotional attachment to various pieces of the business. When you're at the point of making cuts or facing bankruptcy—assuming you want to keep the business alive—there is no room to say, "We have to hold on to this part of the business that's not making money because I like it," or, "It was my idea," or this, that, or the other thing. We got rid of whatever wasn't making money; we held on to stuff that was making money. And we were profitable again.

Does it hurt to make those cuts? To tell some people they no longer have a job? Of course it does, and I am vehemently opposed to companies that use layoffs as a cost-saving measure just to meet their quarterly numbers for the benefit of investors and to manage their stock price. That is cruel, it is shortsighted, and in many cases, it is inhumane. The investors are not the only stakeholders in these companies. The employees are, too.

In this case, our company was in a true make-or-break financial situation, which meant the worst was unavoidable. Unless we gained control of our own destiny, and fast, we were toast. So we made the cuts and moved forward.

Part of what I did, though, was that I cut costs enough to not only turn the company profitable, but also to double the salaries of the core team who agreed to stay and help me rebuild. I think the mistake many CEOs make is that when the times are tough, they only cut. I believe in overdoing the cuts so those who are left behind will have the motivation and the drive to turn the business into a major success.

Concurrently, we hired a bank to help us sell the business—but the only potential buyers who stepped forward were bottom-feeders.

During one call with a potential buyer, I found myself getting impatient. The way he was talking about the business, and the way he was valuing the business—or not valuing the business—just bugged me. So I stopped listening.

In my mind, I started thinking, No. *There's no way I'm letting any of these bottom-feeders buy Reply.*

Instead, I thought: *Maybe I should buy this business myself.*

If I truly want to run a business according to my Baha'i-inspired principles, why should I start from scratch? Why not start with this business I already know so well? Why not make Reply.com my platform?

When the phone call ended, I emailed the board: "I have to recuse myself from any further sales-related discussions," I said, "because I'm going to make an offer."

I offered twice as much as any other offer we'd fielded so far. An offer I thought was a fair price.

The lender, the one that was threatening to shut us down, financed me. They financed me 100 percent. Why? Because they believed in my ability to get them all of their money back. Plain and simple. They had seen how I operated, and they trusted me.

Trust, as I've said before, is priceless.

So are our relationships.

A guy named Steve Kuo made that happen for me. He stood up for me at the bank and made sure that deal happened.

So I bought Reply back from our investors and made it a single-shareholder entity.

I now had the freedom to build it the way I wanted to build it—and from that day forward, I vowed I would never raise a dime from a VC ever again.

I'm proud to say, many years later, I have followed through on that promise.

I realize I walked into this from a place of privilege, and most entrepreneurs don't have the luxury to make a similar pledge when they're starting out. But my pledge also meant that I would purposefully go against the grain in the way capitalism (as it currently stands) works. I had to be okay with slower growth and more of a focus on sustainability than building for Wall Street. My playbook was not one designed to maximize the size of the company, nor the stock price. (At least not based on the conventional wisdom.)

I firmly believed that applying spiritual principles to my business would cause my company to become a stronger company for the long term, and I did not want to have to convince any investors to believe in my new approach to building and running a business. I wanted to pave my own way, which meant that I was willing to take that risk, personally, and thankfully my wife was supportive of me risking everything, if necessary, in order to succeed.

So I personally guaranteed the loan.

I bought Reply, a money-losing company. If it had not gone well for me, it would have been a major blow.

But I believed in my abilities, and I believed in my team.

Thankfully, Gouya believed in me, too.

I had been in performance-based online marketing since before it existed. My brother and I invented it. We invented online lead-generation. If there was one business I knew well, it was this business. So I felt very comfortable that we could continue to fix whatever problems we had, and then build Reply in a brand-new way that would finally make sense to me—mind, heart, and soul.

REFLECTIONS ON CHAPTER TWENTY-ONE

Are you as responsive as you would like to be to the people you care about? Do you acknowledge that the people you love could be here today, and gone tomorrow, and therefore deserve your attention and responsiveness? Is there someone in your life that you would be devastated to lose if you got the call tomorrow saying they were gone? Is there any reason you can't reach out to them right now?

Have you experienced a midlife crisis yet? Or a mid-twenties crisis? Or any type of existential moment when you question what you're doing with your life? If so, how did you get through it? What did you change? How did you cope with the uncertainties and doubts? And if not, what are you currently doing that you think could potentially become a crisis for you at some point down the line? Are there things you could do now to make your work and relationships more fulfilling before a crisis arises? Are there workshops you could attend, speeches you could listen to, or trips you could take that might help you to better set your compass for the course you want your life to take going forward?

CHAPTER TWENTY-TWO

IT'S NEVER "JUST BUSINESS"

While business debt is not always a bad thing, at that time, given how fragile Reply was, it felt important to me to get rid of the debt as quickly as I could.

I was grateful to have the support of the bank, of course. Their support is what made the deal possible. But I wanted to be free of it.

I had made a good deal: The loan was set up in a way that allowed a big portion of the debt to be forgiven if I made a balloon payment early on.

So, in the middle of rebuilding Reply, accomplishing this was my new challenge.

The question was simple: "How can I repay a large portion of this as quickly as possible?" So I looked around. I took an inventory of what we owned, just like I did when I was a boy. And just like I did with the baseball cap my mother had purchased for me way back then, I happened upon a potential buyer for one of our most valuable assets: our brand, Reply.com.

I knew of a company called "Reply.eu."

They were a public company with significant business.

I looked up the CEO. Tatiana was her name, and she was based in Milan, Italy.

I found her on LinkedIn, and I messaged her.

"Tatiana, would you be interested in purchasing the Reply.com name?"

She replied almost immediately: "Yes."

So I said, "Make me an offer." And I let her know: "Your offer has to be seven figures."

"Okay," she said. "Absolutely. Let's get it done."

She sent that message from Italy at the beginning of August. Then, as Italians often do, she promptly disappeared for a monthlong holiday. I didn't hear from her for so long, I was afraid she was backing out. But when she finally returned, she made good on her promise.

I had purchased the Reply.com domain name in the early 2000s for $10,000.

I sold it in 2015 for seven figures.

That sale allowed me to pay down a big portion of our debt. But what now? How could we exist without our name?

Simple: I changed our company name to Buyerlink, a name that was actually more fitting and descriptive of the business we were in. Because of the way our business operated—as a business-to-business platform and not a consumer brand—we didn't take a hit when we made that change.

I actually think it allowed us a clean departure from our tumultuous past.

At that point, I was free to get started on the uncharted journey ahead: integrating my desire to serve and live in alignment with my spiritual values with the work that our company was doing.

First, I decided to create a new tribe of business executives. There were about fifty people left in the company, with nine of them representing great capacity for leadership. Instead of shuffling around the corner offices as so many companies do, I did not keep any of the previous executives and rather made most of those nine into VPs. None of them had been executives before. I promoted people who were on their way up rather than established in corner offices. I didn't want them to come with preconceived ideas of how executives should operate. I wanted them to approach people with love and care.

Each of the nine new leaders were given a right to participate in our success, meaning that if the business were ever sold, they would each receive a distribution from the proceeds. It was a promise I made, and perhaps there are lots of other leaders who make similar promises, using stock options—which may or may not ever be worth anything, as anyone who has ever received them as part of a compensation package can attest. But when I sold the Reply.com name, which was, technically, one of the assets of the business, that meant that each of those nine employees owned a piece of it. So, even though the proceeds from that sale would be used to pay down debt, each of the nine was owed a small percentage of that sale. So, after the deal closed, each of the nine received a check for the amount they were owed.

One of those executives, a great guy named David, who only recently left the company, actually got tears in his eyes when I handed him the check.

"What's up?" I asked him.

"You know," he said, "it's just really great to see the ideals we've talked about"—he wiped the tears away, and smiled—"to see the ideals we've talked about be put into action."

That moment with David served as an affirmation of the importance of follow-through every step of the way as we were building this new culture.

Chris Rock has a comedy routine in which he talks about how some men brag about "having a job and taking care of their families." I'm paraphrasing here, but Chris's response to that sentiment is something like, "You're supposed to take care of your family. That's nothing to brag about. That's, like, the bare minimum!"

To me, running a business is kind of like that: Taking care of our family of employees should be the bare minimum. It was nothing to brag about. It is just a matter of doing what we should be doing. And it's not something we can fake. We will be tested every step of the way, and

every financial decision and its moral dimensions and its inevitable consequences will have to be considered.

I encouraged our entire management team to read the book *Spiritual Enterprise* by Lawrence M. Miller. Then we talked about it. The
book emphasized the noble origins of every person. Every person. And we
decided, together, to honor the nobility of every person who worked for
the company, at every level.

We provided profit sharing to all employees, and we worked to create
a culture of respect.

One of the ways we did that was to attempt to eliminate workplace
gossip by creating a channel through which employees could submit
anonymous comments and questions, which were read and addressed at
our weekly all-hands meetings—encouraging open and honest communi-
cation from the bottom up.

We also made it clear that we were not in this business to win at any
cost. We made it clear to everyone at Buyerlink that our success would not
depend on someone else's demise.

But I didn't want anyone to have to guess what we were all about. I
didn't want anyone to feel confused about what our culture might be built
upon. So, together, we spoke about the principles that were most important to us and were in line with the spiritual beliefs that were the animating
force behind everything we did. Principles that had guided us. Principles
that we felt were missing from the business landscape, and which we
believed could set our business apart—to make it an example that, if we
did well, might serve as a model for others to follow.

Perhaps what surprised me most in all the discussions we had was
that no one objected. To any of them. So we memorialized them into
a culture manual and made it key to onboarding. It would serve as the
founding document to which we would hold each other accountable; a
set of rules and values, which we would put into action every day, in the
workplace and beyond.

The principles we espoused aligned not only with how we wanted to
conduct ourselves in the business world, but as conscientious adults and
human beings. And while we have expanded upon them and allowed the

definitions to grow as needed, they remain at the core of everything we do to this day. And they are: Unity, Intention, Independence, Love, Truthfulness, and Justice.

1. Unity

Every entrepreneur, business pioneer, or tech innovator must be comfortable with getting things done in groups. Accomplishments almost always come from teams, not lone individuals. We may have a great idea, or a new way of manufacturing something, or a breakthrough creative concept—but the people we gather around us will help us bring it to reality. No one accomplishes anything entirely on their own, so unity of intent and purpose is absolutely necessary. Entrepreneurs have to know how to build and sustain unity. I firmly believe that unity is an essential ingredient for success in any aspect of life.

2. Intention

Why am I interested in starting a business? Why would we invest in one thing vs. another? Why do we market in a certain way? The point is we need to check our intention every step of the way. Are we being self-serving? Are we driven by greed? Are we motivated by power? If so, how can we change that so our intention is better aligned with the other values and principles we're aiming to live up to? For instance, when it comes to a current example that our society is beginning to wrestle with more and more: I've always said, AI doesn't worry me; it's the intention of the innovator that does.

3. Independence

Baha'is believe in the independent investigation of truth—that each person has the duty and the responsibility to determine what's true and what's not. That's also one of the cardinal qualities of every good entrepreneur: an independent mind. This means much more than the old "think outside the box" cliché. Instead, it means fostering creativity, the courage to depart from the crowd, and the ability to truly think for ourselves. Independence also calls upon our willingness to question the status quo.

4. Love

I believe that humans are essentially spiritual beings, and that there is no greater power than the power of love. The entrepreneur or businessperson who loses sight of that fact runs the risk of departing from reality. When we recognize and love the noble essence of every human, we acknowledge their highest aspirations and their most profound goals. If we really love our employees and our customers, we'll treat them as the noble beings they are. We will elevate them, and elevate us. After all, we are all spiritual beings having a physical experience, but maybe this life can also be (and probably is) a spiritual experience, and that's where we need to live. By the way, this love should not be limited to those I work with but also my clients, my community, and even my competitors.

5. Truthfulness

Just about everyone in business will talk about the benefits of integrity, truthfulness, and honesty. But surprisingly, these virtues stand out like a beacon when we encounter them, because they're rare. Ask yourself this question: What would you be willing to say or do to close a major deal? What if that deal involved an enormous profit for you or your company? Would you shade the truth a little or even lie to get that deal signed? Many people would—but I believe we should not ever go down that road, because it's always a dead end. A lack of integrity will only cause grief in the end—lawsuits, broken partnerships, and financial ruin. Why trade a short-term advantage for long-term grief? I believe that "truthfulness is the foundation of all human virtues," meaning: Only if we have acquired this foundational virtue can we also be generous, loving, kind, just, compassionate, and so on.

6. Justice

No entrepreneur or businessperson wants to be unfair (I hope)—but few business environments truly offer level playing fields. Unfairness seems built into business life in many ways: huge disparities between the lowest wage-earners and the executives; a big gap between compensation and job responsibilities for women and men; greed-driven approaches with little regard for impact on environment and communities in which we live and work. Fairness and equality, at every level of a business, will always pay off, and they should not be something left for another day. Every day of our journey has to be one we are proud to live and lead—as this day may be the last day. Our employees will be happier, our business partners will respect us, our quarterly results will thrive. Doing the right thing may seem expensive at first, but the fact is, it actually makes a business more profitable in the long run. At the end of the day, it improves our bottom line, but most importantly, it offers us the opportunity to live a fulfilling life, a life where our professional engagement is designed to be of service to others. That is what will fulfill us.

It should come as no surprise that several of these convictions reflect some of the teachings of the Baha'i Faith, or that they were drawn directly from the lessons of my own life experience, as I've shared with you in this book so far. And while I do not claim to be an ideal model of putting these principles into action, I do believe that my humble pursuit of these principles, striving to live up to them and do my best to achieve them in our business pursuits and in life in general, has contributed greatly to every positive thing I've accomplished so far.

By doing our best to adhere to these principles in the examples we set through hiring, through sales, and through the dealmaking we had done so far, they were fast becoming an integrated part of our company culture—and we were already successful because of them, simply because we were putting this new example of how to run a business into the world.

One major way in which we tried to set a new example early on was to set aside a percentage of our profits to give back to the community around us—to causes that mattered to us, and more.

The idea wasn't to "give 1 percent back" as many Silicon Valley companies do to attain some sort of feel-good PR value. The idea was to give so much that it hurt—to make giving a top priority. To give so much that it was a relevant figure—one that would cause us to rethink investments elsewhere.

Within months, it was clear that by focusing on even a handful of timeless, spiritual principles—which none of us had ever experienced in a workplace before then—we had already built a much better company. Not only a company that was profitable, and growing, but one that was more fulfilling—where each of us felt happier working, which quickly attracted great employees and retained customers. Remarkably, hardly anyone we encountered during this transition showed any resistance to the ideas we were putting forth. Instead, the most common reaction was something like, "Wow. If they had fostered this sort of culture at the last place I worked, maybe I wouldn't have quit!"

As a private company, free from any outside investors who often were in it for what I believed were the wrong reasons, Buyerlink was profitable. But more importantly, we were quickly growing into a self-sustaining, highly fulfilling company, supporting a wide array of employees, clients, and offices around the world with the humanitarian values of service and giving at its core.

And Buyerlink was just the beginning.

If I wanted to prove to myself (and the world) that a new form of capitalism was possible, I knew that we needed to give the world an even better example. We needed to build something that was more relevant and that would create a platform with much more expanded reach.

So, in 2015, just as all of our new ideas for the company were getting on their feet, I created a parent company that would allow us to expand into other areas. With a parent company we could grow and invest in other businesses and be an active incubator and ecosystem through which we could test our ideas while helping other forward-thinking entrepreneurs launch their own journeys.

I thought about one of the core principles of the Baha'i Faith—Unity—the ultimate spiritual vision of a peaceful connection between all people on this planet, beyond the arbitrary concepts of borders and the divisiveness of politics or religious dogma.

And in that spirit, I named our company One Planet Group.

After everything I had witnessed through my experiences in the business world so far, this would be the laboratory in which we would try to answer the many questions I found myself asking:

Could we set a humble yet robust example of pairing good business with good intentions?

Could we measure success in more than dollars, but by how we spend our resources on helping and serving others, by how many lives we touch in a positive way, and by how we better our communities and the world around us?

My inspiration for creating this laboratory of a business model clearly came from my Faith, but I never wanted to impose my religion on anyone. Instead, I asked our employees and managers if we could try to meet the challenge of bringing certain timeless spiritual principles to the business. And at first, these ideas seemed radical—because they are the opposite of what we usually talk about when we're talking about "business goals." But the truth is, these are the very principles that lead us to a spiritually satisfying life. To happiness. To fulfillment. And shouldn't such principles that we seek in our lives be applied to our work as well? If not, how can we ever be expected to lead coherent lives?

Values and principles shouldn't be turned on or off the moment we walk through one door or another, should they?

Perhaps the most "radical" idea we brought to the table was this: The first thing that One Planet will deliver is love. Outrageous, right? I don't think so.

If we want to make our world a better place, then as business leaders, we've got to love our people. We've got to love our clients. We've got to love our partners and our vendors, too. Because, without that, the whole thing falls apart. Our humanity gets lost.

This means that we should even love our competition.

We tell this to our employees all the time: If our success relies on someone else's demise then maybe we should get out of that business.

If our product is superior, if people truly prefer whatever it is we're selling and that naturally affects a competitor, we don't want to deny the consumer of that choice. But we never want to think about Company A, B, or C and say, "We want to beat them." Never. That is simply not the way we operate.

We are competing against ourselves, and never someone else—which basically means that we're taking the aspect of war out of the workplace and replacing it instead with a spirit of "let's work for the benefit of all."

We can always be better at what we do, and there is no question that focusing on what the competition is doing can quickly cause us to lose our bearings. That's a scary path to go down. There's no end to it. There will always be someone out there doing things differently than we are, and maybe doing things better than we are. We see the results of that outward-facing pressure on social media all the time, as people fill themselves with anxiety and worry because someone else is getting more "likes" than they are. It's not healthy. But we also see it in the hoarding of wealth amongst the super-rich, especially in recent decades. I mean, how much is enough? Do we value anything other than more, more, more and take, take, take? Where is the value of balance and mutual benefit? Why is it so difficult in our society to embrace the idea that a rising tide should lift all boats? Doing so wouldn't make the wealthy become anything less than they are. It would just mean that the poor and middle class can rise, too, as we all benefit from the riches of this planet.

There will always be somebody wealthier. Someone prettier. Someone stronger. Someone smarter. Someone more innovative. Always. So, if all we're doing is competing with each other, then we're bound to be unhappy. And I don't think it's hard to argue that, statistically speaking, we are unhappy. Workers are unhappy. Leaders are unhappy. Even billionaires are unhappy! Because we're unhappy with the status quo. And one of the driving reasons for that unhappiness is because we feel there isn't enough purpose to what we do.

Doing things the way we've always done them is no longer working for the vast majority of people on this planet.

So, at One Planet Group, we decided: We don't think the world needs another "successful" business built on the outdated, unfulfilling, old measures of growth and competition. There are already plenty of those. What we want is to build our success on broader, more inclusive terms.

The very definition of "success" must change if we want to build ourselves a better system, and a better world. We cannot continue to measure "success" by dollars and cents and quarterly results alone. Shareholder value is one measure of success, but how can it continue to be the only measure when we see the overall poor results of that system in action? The destruction of the planet, employee instability, worsening mental health crises all across the world, price-gouging under the guise of "inflation" that brings the vast majority of middle-class, hardworking families to the breaking point every month—let alone the poor. The VC-driven startup world doesn't even support the businesses themselves in many cases, let alone the founders and innovators who should be driving our economy forward. So, if the shareholders are the only ones benefiting, I argue that's not a "success" at all.

Even those who are making the vast majority of the money aren't happy. There are countless stories of "successful" business leaders who flame out in their forties and fifties—who quit and try to find fulfillment elsewhere, working for charities, building homes in Africa, teaching, starting over in the countryside somewhere. Why? Because making money and maximizing shareholder value are not fulfilling reasons to live and work. They do not bring happiness. The entire idea of building businesses solely for the sake of getting rich isn't only an empty endeavor; it's an archaic way of thinking.

If we want to find true success, we have to modernize.

If we want to find true success, we must think bigger. We must think of all of the stakeholders in the lives of our businesses: the employees, the communities around us, the planet on which we live, the customers, the vendors, our competitors, all of it. We have the means to consider all of those factors in our business endeavors, so why not get started? Not tomorrow. Today!

In spiritual teachings of all sorts, there are timeless tales that tell us how to live more fulfilling lives. And one universal message that crosses the boundaries of nearly all religions is this: When we focus more on the happiness of others than on the happiness of ourselves, we become the happiest version of ourselves.

Our attempts to put these dreams into action during our first couple of years of One Planet's existence happened to align with the release of what I saw as a foundational message from the only internationally, grassroots, completely democratically elected body on Earth. A body solely focused on building a better world.

On March 1, 2017, the Universal House of Justice, which is the supreme governing body of the Baha'i Faith, released a statement about our economic lives. There are plenty of teachings to be found about our economic lives in the words and writings of Baha'u'llah and 'Abdu'l-Baha. Things like profit sharing are advocated for in Baha'i teachings. Eliminating the extremes of wealth and poverty is at the core of the teachings. The Faith teaches us that wealth should be earned by an individual's hard work and not through inheritance, and that wealth is only praiseworthy if it's spent for philanthropic purposes. But these teachings are scattered across many texts. There isn't one book or one paper that sums it all up, saying, "This is how we should manage our economic lives," or, "This is how the world's economies should run." So this document, which is in the form of a letter from the Universal House of Justice to the Baha'is of the world, consolidates many Baha'i ideals on these subjects in just a few pages. And that would become the blueprint for me and One Planet Group going forward.

I have shared the entire document for you to read in Appendix B at the end of this book, and I hope you find it as powerful as I do. Then, and now, it helped inspire me to keep thinking about business in a new way: Why not apply the overriding principle of happiness to business? Why not use our businesses to make the world a better place to contribute to our collective betterment?

What we're attempting to show at One Planet is that applying these principles to business is not an act of diminishing returns. We're not "giving up" on things that make good business sense. What we're attempting to do is to show that a winning business, one that does all of these things, is not only possible, but in fact offers us a better way to build a great organization. An organization elevated to not just deliver financial success, but one that delivers a great journey to its employees and leaves the world what I like to call "ever so slightly" a better place.

REFLECTIONS ON CHAPTER TWENTY-TWO

Have you ever taken an inventory of your personal or company assets? Have you ever considered whether you might have something to sell that could be very valuable to someone else, and from which the profits could be put to better use in your household or business than the asset that's just sitting there collecting dust, or not serving you in any meaningful way? Why not sell?

If you were asked (and I'm asking right now), could you make a list of the core principles that guide you as an adult, in life and in business? Do you have a set of principles that apply to one part of your life, but not another? And if so, does that make sense? If you're putting on different cloaks of morality, spirituality, guidelines, or actions when you move from one part of your life to another—from home to work, or school, or church—does that cause you any discord? What do you think it would feel like to bring a cohesiveness to all aspects of your life and work?

Are there principles that we've applied at One Planet Group that you would like to see put into action in your own business or your own place of work? What's stopping you?

CHAPTER TWENTY-THREE

LEADING FROM THE HEART

When a business is founded upon love, the rest of its core principles will follow.

For example, at One Planet Group we believe in building our business on honesty. Absolute honesty. Baha'is believe that truthfulness is the foundation of all human virtues. Without truthfulness, you cannot acquire any other virtue.

Think about it: Can a liar have integrity? Can a liar be generous? Can a liar be a unifier?

So how does that translate in the business world?

Let's say we're facing a lawsuit, and perhaps we have done something wrong, broken a rule or a law, or whatever it may be. Hopefully we never do that, but if we do, we would prefer to lose if the only way to win would require us to lie. Truly. A loss would be less painful in the long run. So, in sales, marketing, payroll, taxes, interoffice discussions, the rule is simple: We will not lie under any circumstance. We will not even appear to be lying.

I know that seems almost impossible in the business world as we know it. Think about how this applies to sales alone: If I only have one potential buyer for something that I'm trying to sell, and that buyer is ready to make an offer, I'm not going to lie to make it look like we have multiple offers waiting in the wings. I'm just going to negotiate based on the merits of the business. Might that cost us in terms of getting a lower price? Yes, if we are not great at properly communicating the value of our service. But no, not at all, if we are. (I invite you back to the example I shared of selling AutoWeb's services to State Farm for a reminder of what I mean.) Still, the fact is, if truthfulness does cost us in terms of getting a lower price, I truly believe that our integrity and honesty will reward us tenfold—and it has.

Today, a variety of businesses, both large and small, across a wide range of industries, coexist under the One Planet umbrella:

- Buyerlink is a major player in the performance-based marketing space and has expanded its reach through many sub-companies.
- We own California.com, a website dedicated to the great state of California.
- We run One Planet Media, a full-service production company that focuses on producing content that matters. The largest subsidiary of the group is a forward-thinking TV and film company called WestWind Pictures, which had a huge hit in Canada with a show called *Little Mosque on the Prairie.* We produce TV series, documentaries, and feature films, all with the hope of bringing about positive influence on the world around us, while doing so in a commercially viable manner.
- And, while I was writing this book, we repurchased AutoWeb. After all these years, I bought back my old company and took it private. The purchase included all the brands and services that it owned, including Autobytel, Usedcars.com, and Car.com. Talk about a full-circle moment. After all these years, I am finally able to grow the company my brother and I founded with the values I wanted to infuse it with from the start.

One Planet Group has also invested directly in companies that are changing the world through education, health care, mobility, and more. We've committed to making a minimum of 60 percent of our investments in companies run by women and/or people of color—and as of the writing of this book, 79 percent of our investments meet that standard. This is while in recent years only about 2.3 percent of VC funding has gone to women entrepreneurs.

We've had great success investing in businesses led by women entrepreneurs and executives, from SoulPancake to Gro Intelligence to one of my favorites, The RealReal. I originally invested in The RealReal before launching One Planet and did so as an individual investor. You may have heard of them. They're a high-end designer resale/consignment concept that gives new life to designer clothing, jewelry, bags, and shoes that might otherwise be relegated to a corner of a closet or a landfill somewhere. It's recycling at its best: good for the planet, and it solves a real problem.

Coincidentally enough, the founder of the company, Julie Wainwright, became the oldest woman funded in Silicon Valley when she launched The RealReal in her fifties.

As a rule of thumb, Hollywood and Silicon Valley alike could both benefit from paying more attention to women and women in leadership roles. It's no exaggeration to say that the companies we've invested in that are led by women have outpaced just about all of our other investments. Clearly this is not to say that men cannot be great leaders. The fact remains that the business world stubbornly ignores—to their own detriment—many entrepreneurs and leaders who actually have proven to be better at building and running companies.

A full list of our investment portfolio can be found at our website (oneplanetgroup.com), and if you have a chance to check it out, I'm sure you'll recognize some of the other companies, too. I know you will be hearing a lot more from many of them in the future.

Yet, here is what really sets the recipients of our investments apart: Every one of them has signed a document agreeing to commit a portion of their resources, revenues, know-how, products, and/or time for the betterment of the world. And they do so out of a love for humanity. That isn't an obligation that would necessarily hold up in court, contractually speaking. Instead, it is a pledge that answers to the higher power of love and personal commitment. A pledge that comes from the heart. And the types of founders we work with, the types of companies we work with, are ones we believe take these commitments seriously. They may not adhere to any particular religion. All that matters is that the people who make up these companies believe in the growing notion that, as businesses, what we give should be more important than what we take.

While the businesses we're in are diverse, the beauty of our company is that they all exist—and thrive—under the same umbrella. So, while we invest in and partner with a wide variety of companies, One Planet attempts to influence and set the tone and the example.

This brings us back to the value of unity, not divisiveness, to which the no-gossip rule applies across everything we do.

We started the tradition of reading anonymous questions from staff every week at our global all-hands meeting right after Buyerlink began, and we've continued to implement that tradition at One Planet.

Gossip—saying negative things about an individual in their absence—is a cultural thing outside of the workplace, too. It causes all kinds of problems within organizations and communities, and I believe we have to put a stop to it. So the best way to do that is to lead by example. Here at One Planet, we just don't do it. We don't talk negatively about anyone. It's against our culture—even when telling the truth. This does not mean that we are perfect and never make a mistake. Of course not. However, we make humble but robust efforts to adhere to the principle because we all know the negative ramifications of not doing so.

Talking negatively about others in and of itself does not make things better—especially when this talk is happening loosely and without purpose within the walls of a business and behind people's backs.

Every Monday, during our all-hands videoconference meeting, when all employees from over ten countries are present, we read the anonymous questions and comments submitted during the past week. We read them aloud, and we read them all. Even if they're embarrassing. Sometimes they touch on subjects that can be very sensitive, but we always read them—because our view is that, as painful as some of these comments and questions may be, by not reading them, it doesn't mean they go away. It does not matter if it's about the quality of our service, or if someone is questioning why or how I bought myself an expensive car when we were all supposed to be in this together. (That's a true story.) Or why we act "archaic" by expecting our employees to work from an office. If someone is thinking about something so much that they're inspired to write it down, then clearly they want to talk to somebody about it. In our view, it's better to get it out on the table now and talk openly rather than let people whisper. The fact is, usually when one person is thinking something, there are others who are also grappling with the same question or concern.

The ins and outs of all of these sorts of discussions are included in the One Planet Culture Manual, which evolved and expanded and was refined over time. And when new hires come aboard, we have study circle–type gatherings in which they read the culture manual together. They discuss it. They're introduced to our culture and the way we do business—because it's important.

As we grew the business, it was important to me that we approach everything with thought and meaning. Even the small stuff. For instance, I never wanted to produce a company T-shirt just for the sake of having a company T-shirt. They would have to share an important message.

I didn't want to have a logo just for the sake of having a logo. Our logo had to communicate a message. And if you look at our logo, the blue dot is, of course, the planet. And the number "1"—as a way to represent unity—connects the two words "one" and "planet." So I hope the "One Planet" message brings love and unity to the business world and beyond.

Which brings me to one of the truly unique and much-loved aspects of our business: Days of Service.

I don't work on Baha'i Holy Days, and I didn't want my companies to work on those days, either. But I don't want to impose my Faith on my employees. So we came up with this concept that balances the two desires: There are up to nine Baha'i Holy Days per year. If they fall on business days, those days are off for all of our employees as paid holidays (in addition to the standard paid holidays). But on those particular days, they're asked to offer service to the community rather than coming in to work. They can choose what kind of service. It could be that they just go visit a lonely elderly member of the community. It could be they volunteer at their kid's school. Anything. There's only one thing we lovingly ask them to refrain from doing on those days, and that is to serve a political party, because by nature, political parties are divisive, and we want to be unifying—at least on those days. At the end, though, this is an honor system. The employees get paid whether or not they actually offer any form of service on those days. Service to humanity cannot be forced and needs to come from heart.

As a company, we've also continued to embrace the idea of "sacrificial giving" to nonprofit causes, which started when we launched Buyerlink. As I already mentioned, this isn't a "1 percent to nonprofits" PR move. What it means to us is that we give so much it hurts. It's a priority. If it doesn't hurt, if it doesn't cause us to change our financial decisions about other aspects of the business, it means we did not give enough.

Since One Planet's founding, we've given away about 20 percent of our profits, either directly through the individual businesses or the parent company.

I know that seems overwhelming and untenable to most companies that operate on the principles of capitalism as we know it, but it's an important part of who we are. We have to continue to do that. Why? Because if we look at the world as an interconnected ecosystem, then our well-being is very much tied to the well-being of the whole. Therefore, it is my spiritual responsibility to contribute to that well-being in a meaningful way.

And that brings me back to the Faith in which I was raised, as witnessed through the many sacrifices of my parents, and the many tens of thousands of Baha'is who sacrificed so much before us: Ultimately, we believe that our true happiness and joy is not going to come from our financial and material success. It's going to come out of our service to others. So, unless we are not interested in living a life of purpose and joy, what choice do we have, truly, but to strive to bring our work lives, our personal lives, and our lives of service together as we travel the road that leads us to that end?

When trying to explain the reasoning behind this, I often turn to words attributed to Abdu'l-Baha, as recalled in unpublished notes by a pilgrim on August 5, 1910: "But if you are so angry, so depressed and so sore that your spirit cannot find deliverance and peace even in prayer, then quickly go and give some pleasure to someone lowly or sorrowful, or to a guilty or innocent sufferer! Sacrifice yourself, your talent, your time, your rest to another, to one who has to bear a heavier load than you—and your unhappy mood will dissolve."

I encourage people to try it for themselves, even in the smallest degree. When you're feeling absolutely miserable—you just had a fight with your wife, you got fired from your job, something smaller, whatever it is—just hold the door open for someone who's coming into the building. Through even that small act, you're doing something for someone else, and for that moment, you will be lifted out of whatever that pain is, whatever that thing is that you're going through. Even in that one small gesture, there's a momentary connection and a relief from the agony and the pain you're going through.

So imagine what happens to your happiness when you act in service to others in a larger, more lasting, more meaningful way.

Days of Service is one way we do that at One Planet. And the other is by holding what we call Holidays with a Purpose.

That idea sprang from the minds of some of our employees who thought, *What if rather than planning a typical, expensive holiday party, we do something outwardly? Why not hold an event that's meant to do something good, and invite our friends, families, and others to join us?*

So we came up with the concept of turning our holiday events, these gatherings of our employees, their significant others, our vendors, our partners, our friends in business, and more, into action-oriented days when we all join together in supporting a specific cause. We show up as one for a project, a cause that we care about, and one for which we believe our impact can be meaningful. And then? We encourage everyone who attends to become a part of that cause by making a donation. Whatever they give, One Planet matches.

We give our employees a very easy way to give, too, which doesn't directly affect their pocketbook: We allow them to cash in their vacation days as donations. For example, let's say I have fifteen vacation days and I'm getting paid $300 a day. That means I can cash in two of those vacation days and contribute $600 to the cause. And the company matches that. So their donation becomes $1,200 of real money that they get to give to our collective chosen cause.

That has become a great way for us to act as one family.

As a company, we have also decided to commit our resources primarily to two causes: the issues of racism in America and equality between women and men, globally.

Equality between the sexes is a core belief of the Baha'i Faith. Eliminating all forms of prejudice and bringing about social justice is also a core belief, and racism is perhaps America's most challenging issue—a deep force of division that has plagued the U.S. since its very founding. I believe that the moment we choose to look the other way and not do our part to address these issues, we become an accomplice, supporting the perpetuation of a system that has caused untold pain and injury for centuries—not only to the oppressed groups, but to our country and to humanity as a whole.

We have to start with us. And for me, the issue resonates on such a deeply personal level. I know what it means to get beat up and mistreated based on prejudice. A Black kid growing up in the U.S. is mistreated based on prejudice from the day they're born. I won't lay out the arguments to make the case for that in these pages. It is what it is, and there is no way for any intelligent person to argue that's not how it is. The difference between what I faced and what a Black child faces, though, is that being Black is by far more challenging in the U.S. than it was to be Baha'i in Iran—because as a Baha'i in Iran, I could move to another town, and they wouldn't immediately know I was a Baha'i. It was my choice, or my parents' choice, to make it known. But as a Black person? Wherever you go, you're Black.

Supporting these causes isn't just about donating money or volunteering. It's about looking in the mirror and making changes in the workplace, to show the rest of the world that it is not only possible, but profitable, and good for our soul too, to be the change we want to see in the world.

I'm also proud to say that fully half of our employees are women. In Silicon Valley, most companies—including Google, Facebook, and Apple—have workforces that are fewer than 30 percent women, and the vast majority of those are young, single women in their twenties. Why does that matter? Because, to me, if you want to serve humanity, you have to look like humanity.

We cannot change the world through beautiful slogans alone. We have to show change through action. At One Planet Group, we stand for equality, and stand up for equality, because it matters. In general, Silicon Valley hasn't been a very welcoming place to women, especially older women, and especially moms. The hours, the type of camaraderie that exists in the workplace—it just isn't conducive for mothers and for many fathers. So our female employees aren't made up entirely of fresh-out-of-college grads. They represent a wide spectrum of ages and backgrounds, and many of them are moms, just as many of our employees are dads, which is more reflective of the world around us—and isn't that what a workplace should be? I mention both moms and dads because they both require a level of flexibility to be there for their families and kids, and we make an attempt to offer that flexibility however we can.

It's not an affirmative action type approach. It's just a matter of fundamentally believing that we are stronger when our organizations are balanced and look like humanity. And if we want to build organizations that believe in a 50/50 approach to women and men in the workplace, if we really find that important, then I suggest we should start by promoting women to more leadership roles.

As a company, we also try to get our employees involved in the causes we care about, which allows them, hopefully, to be of service to others.

But it is never forced. Not on anyone. It doesn't have to be. The people we hire and the people we work with find joy and meaning in doing business this way every day. As do I.

Yet, while service is not forced, acts of racism and sexism are not tolerated. Acting equitably to people of all colors and appreciating the equality of the sexes are not things that should be left up to people to decide. They should sit at the core of what we do, and how we act, every day. And that is what we try to show by example, in the way we run meetings, the way we make promotions, and by how we reach out to the public where we can. For instance, as a company, we decided to support the building of the Legacy Museum and the National Memorial for Peace and Justice monument in Montgomery, Alabama, led by Bryan Stevenson and the Equal Justice Initiative. I know there is a feeling of joy amongst our employees, knowing that the work they do helped contribute to a place that memorializes the struggles and heroes of our country's fight for justice in the past, while simultaneously educating the public on these matters as a means to better our collective future.

My Faith teaches me that work offered in the spirit of service is the highest form of worship. And I believe that. You don't have to go to a church to pray to worship God. You can do that if you so choose and there is nothing wrong with it. But it's probably much more effective to do what Jesus did: serving our fellow humans.

Being of service to others is a form of worship, and all of our work can be "worship" if it's offered in that spirit.

Just a few short years after making the bold move to buy Buyerlink back from our investors, and after founding One Planet, I felt that I was finally on course to live the life that I wanted to live, by working the way I wanted to live: in a humble posture of service to others, and in service to our world—simply by showing up and living my Faith through my work.

I was reminded of just how far I had come on this journey toward the end of the 2010s.

I was traveling with my wife, and while we were waiting to board a flight at Charles de Gaulle Airport in Paris, I looked up and saw a group of children carrying IOM bags—just like the bag I had carried on my long flights and through so many airports when I finally made my way to the U.S. from Pakistan.

The emotion of seeing those refugees making their way through the airport washed over me in a way that I could not contain. They looked so helpless, yet so full of hope, just as I was all those years ago.

That was me. I was them.

It was an emotional experience.

People have asked me, "As a businessman, why do you talk about religion so much?" And while I have many answers for that question, one of them should be obvious to anyone who knows my story. I escaped religious persecution in Iran. I'm deeply grateful to this country, not only because it allowed me to come here, but because it also offers me freedom of speech. I appreciate that freedom of speech, and I intend to use it. I also have the freedom here to practice whatever religion I want to practice, and I intend to take advantage of that freedom as well. I mean, why escape Iran and come to the U.S. if I don't want to exercise these rights?

I also believe that we have an obligation to share potential solutions with each other and not keep them to ourselves. If somebody has cancer and you know a cure, don't you have an obligation to share that cure? And (hopefully) a burning desire to want to share it? I personally believe that the unifying message of the Baha'i Faith can be the answer to many of the ills of today's age. So I want to share that. I don't want to force it on anyone, but I want to share the message, and I don't see anything wrong with that.

From my perspective, everyone has a right to share what they want to share. If you're Mormon, Catholic, Jewish, Hindu, Muslim, or Atheist, you deserve a platform upon which you can stand and tell me what book you read that you want me to also read; that helped form your way of thinking or way of living. I want to hear from you. So why not make space in our work and our lives to appreciate each other's belief systems? Again, not to force anyone, but instead just to share, listen, and hopefully learn from one another.

Listening to others is a big part of approaching the changes we're trying to exemplify at One Planet with humility. I never want to sound like we've got things all figured out. We don't. We continue to make mistakes and hopefully learn from them. But rather, as an organization, what we want to show the world is that we think this is the direction we ought to go, and we're doing our best.

Which begs the question: How's it going?

As of the writing of this book, in the years since I bought Reply back from our investors and turned it into Buyerlink, the company has grown sevenfold. It is one of the most profitable companies in its industry.

Buyerlink, by itself, is now worth a few hundred million dollars.

I think that says it all, doesn't it? A company that was on the verge of being liquidated—this company that investors and VCs were ready to discard because they had concluded it was nearly worthless—is doing very well by any measure.

AutoWeb, within one month of acquisition, finally became profitable.

But we cannot measure success in dollars alone. So, in those other terms, how are we doing?

Buyerlink and the rest of One Planet Group's businesses have grown to the tune of hundreds of millions of dollars in value while simultaneously changing the face of a Silicon Valley–based workforce and giving away a significant percent of our profits each year to causes that matter to all of us. This, while spreading a positive message throughout the business world that says, "Yes, we can do this, and no, we don't have to keep repeating the ways of the past!"

The answers to all of the burning questions I had after trying to make sense of the failures of AutoWeb and PurpleTie are "yes." Yes, we can build a business in a new and better way. Yes, we can measure success in more than just dollars.

In Silicon Valley, where the average longevity of employees is about two years, our employee average in our Bay Area offices is closer to ten years—because so many of our team members have stayed on through all of these transitions. And what does that longevity represent? The happiness and fulfillment our employees feel. And, to me, there is no way to underestimate the importance of that one success. Especially since we aren't the highest-paying company in the region, and we can't afford to offer all of the best benefits, either—which also spotlights the relative security and longevity of the business we're building. Some of the highest-paying, most massive companies in Silicon Valley are enticing, of course. The salaries and benefits they offer are so enticing that many of us smaller companies feel like the biggest monopoly they represent is the monopoly of hiring everyone they can find, and therefore draining the market of talent. What gets overlooked in their over-the-top hiring practices, though, is that these companies are after one thing: a maximization of shareholder value. That means that whenever cutting the workforce achieves that goal better than hiring does, they won't hesitate to pull the trigger. When they lay off tens of thousands of people just because there's a downturn in a particular quarter, those big salaries and over-the-top benefits aren't worth very much. Real human jobs are cut without full consideration of the real human consequences.

What I don't want to do is to put ourselves in a position that we overdo anything. Because we're not competing with Facebook. We're not competing with Apple. We want to do what we can do in a sustainable way. Which means that often we're not offering the "best" of everything. But you know what? I think we're offering something you can count on. And clearly, for us to hold on to employees for the long term means they're finding something here that is more fulfilling than a higher paycheck alone can bring.

That, to me, is a huge measure of success. As is the fact that the Better Business Bureau named One Planet Group the most ethical company in the Bay Area.

To have all of that, and to be profitable, while growing and expanding into new areas with every passing year without raising a dime from VCs—all while answering to a higher calling in everything we do—is that "successful"?

I'll let you draw your own conclusion.

But for me, every day I wake up and I ask myself: If we've been able to achieve all of this inside of a decade, why would any of us want to go back to the old ways of doing business—ever?

REFLECTIONS ON CHAPTER TWENTY-THREE

Are you an honest person? How do you think your honesty (or lack thereof) affects your life on a daily basis? At work? At home? In your family?

Do your words and actions align? At work? At home?

If there are certain causes you care about in the world, are you actively trying to do something to help those causes? To make the world a better place? Even if it's just in one small way, is there a step you could take, a donation you could make, information you could share with others, a rally you could attend? Some time you could give as a way to stand up for what you believe in?

Does your company or your place of work offer ways to help the causes that matter to you? Company matching? Corporate giving? Could you offer (or encourage your employer to offer) time off for Days of Service? Outside of work, could you find a way to rally friends or family to give their time to Days of Service on other holidays, or instead of traditional family gatherings filled with expensive decorations or gifts that might not seem as fulfilling as they once did?

What can you do—as an entrepreneur, an employer, a CEO, a manager, an employee, a volunteer, a leader, a colleague, a peer, or a parent—to change things for the better in your organization or family? How can you step up to serve humanity—to become the example of the changes you'd like to see in the world?

CHAPTER TWENTY-FOUR

TAKING FLIGHT

I do not ever want to be put in the position of having to flee my country again. I would never wish that upon anyone.

Did I learn from the hardships I endured in Iran? Yes. Did facing religious persecution and government oppression make me a more resilient person? Yes. Did overcoming those challenges and escaping through the desert allow me to see the opportunities and freedom that exist in the U.S. with more clarity once I arrived here? Absolutely. Did all of my early life's journeys make the daily challenges of life and business seem smaller? Of course.

But is it necessary for a person to endure so much in order to gain insight and clarity along the way? Some of it, I think. Tests and difficulties are required ingredients for growth. But frankly, too much difficulty may leave too many scars behind. I firmly believe it is possible to embrace and learn from the journeys of our lives and the lives of others without enduring massive trauma.

I also believe it is possible to challenge ourselves in new ways and to take new journeys that bring us growth and new understanding of the world around us whenever we choose. These self-induced challenges can in a small way jolt our system and offer further clarity as the noise in our heads quiets down.

For example, in 2013, as I was trying to figure out what more I wanted out of life, before I left Reply and took our family on our epic road trip up and down the Pacific coast, I summited Mount Kilimanjaro with Frank, John Truchard, and another dear friend.

I am a firm believer that every now and then it can be a good thing to put ourselves through a difficult and memory-worthy experience—to rip ourselves out of our everyday routines in some physical or mental way. (Climbing to a height of over 19,300 feet without carrying oxygen is certainly one extreme way to accomplish that!)

It truly was the experience of a lifetime: to fly to Arusha, Tanzania; climb to the roof of Africa over six days; and then summit the last day in the beautiful moonlight. By the end of the long climb up and back, when we finally reached our base camp, I collapsed. I don't think I had ever been so tired—not even after climbing into the back of a Toyota pickup in the desert heat in Pakistan after scaling mountains all through the night. (Granted, I was quite a bit younger then.)

But that was the point. That's exactly what I wanted to experience. Jolting my body and experiencing something fundamentally different felt like a six-day-long meditation. Nature truly offers us the best opportunities to reset, experience the grandeur of the world, and check our need to remain humble.

It was during that journey that John came up with the idea to market a brand of wine that has since become one of the best-selling brands in the country. And it was during that epic journey that I started to realize just how fundamentally different I wanted my business life to be going forward. I wouldn't find answers to exactly how I wanted things to change until a year and a half later, but that journey to Kilimanjaro is what kick-started my desire to experience change.

A few years later, I challenged myself again. I decided I wanted to learn how to fly a plane. Only I didn't want to take years to learn, as some pilots do. So I signed up for lessons and flew every single day in the early morning, for three straight months, until I earned my pilot's license. I followed that by getting my instrument rating, so I could be a safer pilot. In a way, learning to fly has been more profoundly freeing than when I bought my first car, the burgundy Pinto, back in Modesto at the age of seventeen.

It's difficult to imagine anything that changes your perspective more than soaring above all of our small problems and imaginary borders that disappear into the tiny landscape down below.

Next? As I'm beginning to bring the writing of this book to a close, I'm making plans to take a journey in the opposite direction—by diving into water. I don't know how to swim! My kids make fun of that fact almost daily. Growing up in Iran, I just never had a chance to learn. And the fact that my grandfather was drowned for his religion caused my mom to create a fear in me and my siblings early on, which meant that we were always afraid of water. I was so busy during my formative years in California that the pools, lakes, and ocean all around me just never had a chance. There was a small pool at the first complex where my brother and I lived, in the one-bedroom apartment with the shag carpet, and I would sit by that pool sometimes, just enjoying the sunshine. But I never dared to get in. I never made the time to learn. To be honest, the idea of going into the water terrifies me! Yet I know that conquering that fear will free me, and I'm pretty certain taking that journey so far out of my comfort zone will lead me to somewhere I cannot yet imagine.

I know it sounds really small to most people, but for me, learning to swim is a major mountain to climb. I think it would be easier for me to build another multimillion-dollar business than it will be to learn how to swim.

Yet I know: With each new challenge, with each new journey, we unlock opportunities for learning; along with new insights and potentials that we may never have seen if we didn't face the challenge before us.

Gouya and I have passed this passion of journeying and challenging ourselves to our daughters as well, drawing from our own international experiences as a means to help them to see the world outside of their own suburban existence.

For example, in 2019, my wife and I decided it was time for our girls to get a more global experience in their daily lives. So we decided to move to the Czech Republic. We made the decision quickly, just before the start of the school year, without hesitation and without looking back. We found a place to rent in a town of about four thousand people, an hour and a half from Prague and two hours from Vienna. And less than ninety days after making the decision, the four of us were on a plane. We enrolled our girls in an international school that had 150 students from thirty countries, and it was an experience of a lifetime. For all of us.

Unfortunately, much like the experience I had when my parents moved us to India forty-some years earlier, our stay in the Czech Republic was cut short. The pandemic hit. With so much uncertainty in the world, we decided to move back to our home in the Bay Area. But it wasn't long before we decided, "You know what? This still isn't doing it for us." We wanted the girls to experience a more global and diverse setting, so we took them to New York City for their final years of high school. We made this decision in the wake of George Floyd's slaying, as the country once again rose up for civil rights and an end to racism in America. We just thought, *Why not give our daughters the opportunity to experience one of the most diverse and most global places in America?* So that's what we did. The girls started going to school in New York, and my wife and I have split our time between the East and West coasts.

I know that I come from a place of privilege that has made many of these decisions easier. However, for all of us, it is always difficult to get out of our comfort zone and trade what's easy for something unknown and new. While our girls would have preferred to stay put and stay close to their friends at the time, without putting words in their mouths, I think I can safely say that these moves have helped both of our daughters to open their horizons and think differently. And I know that will serve them well in whatever they choose to do with their lives in the years ahead.

Yet, I don't think moving to a new city, climbing a mountain, or learning to fly a plane are necessary steps for anyone to take in order to grow.

I think half the battle of awakening our minds and seeing new possibilities is simply a matter of recognizing the journeys we've already taken, of giving ourselves the grace to learn from our mistakes, while also being grateful and thankful for the fact that we're alive—that we've overcome so much and that we've made it this far. It does not matter if you were raised in a country filled with political or religious persecution or if you were raised in a comfortable middle-class suburb in a safe corner of the U.S. Each of us has taken our own journey thus far, and every one of us has had to overcome obstacles of various sorts along the way. What matters is whether or not we've paid attention to the journeys we've taken and been willing to learn from the experiences we've had.

The real question is what's the underlying purpose that animates us? And I'd argue that it needs to be a spiritual one in order for it to touch our core and motivate us for a lifetime of joy and meaning.

I have asked many questions throughout this book aimed at stimulating your thoughts on this matter, and I hope you'll take the time to consider those questions all over again now that you've reached the end of my story. (Or rather, the end of this book: My story, in many ways, is just getting started!)

Every one of us has a place in this world. Every one of us has certain talents and gifts. Every one of us has dreams and desires. And every one of us can play our part in helping to make the world a better place. I know it can be frustrating to look around at the status quo, at everything that's wrong in our world, and to think that it's all too much to fix.

But that's where the optimism comes in. Looking back at our lives, and all of the many obstacles we've overcome—as well as looking back at history, and all of the many obstacles we've overcome as humankind—we should all be full of hope for a better tomorrow. For a better tomorrow always comes.

In the meantime, each one of us can do what we can.

In the daily work of One Planet Group, and in what I hope will become a growing and ongoing series of annual One Planet Summits to discuss and act upon topics of reimagining capitalism, spiritual capitalism, and elevating business to serve humanity, my employees and I, and all those who've started on this journey already, will continue to do our parts. And we hope you will do yours, too.

It all comes back to that Michael Jackson song, doesn't it? "Man in the Mirror."

It goes back to paraphrasing Gandhi: "Be the change you want to see in the world."

It goes back to the core principles found not only in the Baha'i Faith, but in all faiths: Focus on what you can do better. How you can lead. How you can serve as the example that others might follow. How you can help. How you can stand tall and walk in the image of whatever God, prophet, or power you believe in.

Be decisive.

Take action in your life.

And don't be afraid to take the next step on whatever journey lays before you.

Embrace the journeys. Step up to the challenges. Keep looking forward. And let your own spirituality and faith guide you. For life and work are nothing—they are meaningless; they are empty and ultimately destined to fail without faith, and without love.

On the other hand, with faith and love—as I hope you've seen and felt through the pages of this book—anything is possible.

With faith and love at the center of all we do, together we will rise and live our most fulfilling lives.

ACKNOWLEDGMENTS

I know you're finished with the book, but I hope you'll take a moment to read these final pages. These people mean the world to me, and some of them you really should know. I would not have had a reason to write this book—and would not have been able to write this book—if not for the people I have included here.

Thank you, from the bottom of my heart, to:

The Baha'is of Iran, and in fact all Iranians, particularly the youth, and even more so the women of Iran who continue to live in that country, for having endured so many decades of hardship and atrocities. Your resilience and your commitment to service, to Iran and the Iranian people, inspires me.

The U.S. and my fellow Americans. You welcomed me when the country where I was born rejected me. Your love and support of the downtrodden of the world is nothing but a spiritual destiny and a privilege bestowed upon you. You have given hope to the world, and may this country continue to be that shining city on the hill.

My parents, Mahboobeh and Abdul Zamani, for your ceaseless encouragements, love, and dedication to live a life of impact; for your resilience through some of the most challenging situations anyone can ever experience; for your love for me, Gouya, Sophia, and Ella; and for serving as role models for how we should always show love to all those who cross our paths. The life you've led has been nothing short of inspirational and a model to follow.

My dear wife, Gouya. If it weren't for your encouragement, I'd have never written this book. Your partnership in life, your love, your kind and spiritual heart, your entrepreneurial mind, and your dedication to the betterment of the world have allowed me to expect more from life. I love you very much.

My dearest daughters, Sophia and Ella, you give me the courage, the energy, and the enthusiasm to push forward. I learn so much from you, every day.

My siblings, Addy and Farhang, for all your support, particularly in the days after I arrived in Pakistan and my early years in the U.S. Without your help and love it would have been impossible for a sixteen-year-old to endure all that life threw at me.

The One Planet team, you have allowed me and my crazy ideas to have the space to come to life, and through all the failures and success, so many of you have stood by me.

Justin Baldoni, your friendship through so many chapters of my life has meant the world to me. Thank you for always being there.

Ken Bowers, for your guidance and friendship throughout the years.

Miriam Cohen, for helping me better communicate the values and the ideals that are so important to me.

Mark Dagostino, my partner in getting this book written and published. I simply could not have done it without you.

Jamey Heath, for being there when I needed a friend the most. I'm forever grateful for your kindness.

David Langness and David Greene, for so patiently working with me and twice helping me write the early versions of this book. Your encouragement and hard work were the foundation for this final outcome.

Julian MacQueen, my favorite Alabaman. You're a true inspiration as a businessman, as a philanthropist, as one who lives a coherent life, and as a dear friend who also knows how to enjoy life.

Layli Miller-Muro, getting to know you and serving as a board member of the amazing organization you founded, Tahirih Justice Center, has been pivotal in shaping my views on business and capitalism.

Talieh and Mansour Movafagh, my dear in-laws, for constantly showering me and my family with kindness and love. Your constant support has always been a source of inspiration for both Gouya and me, and has empowered us to seek new challenges.

Mark Ross, you were the first person to believe in my brother and me. Your $150,000 of investment in us in 1996 made it all possible.

Steve Sarowitz, few people are as hardworking when it comes to dedicating their life and resources to the betterment of the world. You've been an inspiring role model.

Andre Segovia, you were the first business colleague asking me to write a book. Your friendship and leadership at One Planet has been critical to getting us to where we are today.

Shahin Sobhani, you're a friend that everyone needs to have. Your love and support are endless. Thank you.

Becky Sweren, the best book agent anyone could ask for. Thank you for showing interest in my story.

Shane Tedjarati, I get tired just listening to the number of projects you are involved in. You embody the fact that living a life of impact should not be optional. You're a dear friend and trusted mentor.

John Truchard, my all-American friend, born on Independence Day in Texas. Your raw interest in entrepreneurship and optimistic view combined with a can-do and must-be-a-way attitude have been huge motivators to me.

Leah Wilson, the most loving and kind editor. You helped make this a much better book than it would have been without your involvement.

Rainn Wilson, you've been a true friend through it all. Thank you for inspiring me to want to do more.

APPENDIX A

SOME FURTHER THOUGHTS ON THE BELIEFS OF THE BAHA'I FAITH

I f you've read this far, and you're intrigued by the bits and pieces I've shared in this book, then I encourage you to read more about the Baha'i Faith and to explore it on your own so you can come to your own conclusions about how the Faith may align (or not) with the beliefs you feel in your heart. But I also feel it's important to share just a little more here about why the Baha'is believe as they do, and why a religion founded as recently as the 1800s, which has faced such intense persecution in some parts of the world, has grown to have millions of followers around the world.

Baha'is believe that if there is only one God, then there can only be one truth.

They also believe in the concept of progressive revelation, which basically means that God will never leave us humans alone. Every thousand years or so, religion renews itself and the social teachings are updated. That's why all religions in fact share the same foundation, and their fundamental teachings are almost identical. They only differ in their social teachings, which need to be in line with the needs of the day. To put it another way: Baha'is believe in "and" rather than "or." They believe in the unity of religions and their oneness, as they also believe in the oneness of God and the oneness of humanity.

Interestingly enough, all religions believe in the concept of progressive revelation, but most believe that the revelations end with their religion. This creates many problems, including leaving the updating of the religions to clerics. As we know, clerics rarely agree, which creates many factions within religions that don't agree with each other. That conflict turns many people away, especially young people in this day and age. Who can blame them? They see religion (as practiced) as a source of many of the challenges humanity faces, rather than the solution, even while the original teachings remain the foundation of a virtuous, joyful, and meaningful existence. This leaves people looking for spirituality everywhere but within religions—because they have lost their core.

This is not how religions were designed to operate. Baha'is believe religions will continue to get updated by the Divine Physician, as they have in the past, and not by people. That is one of the reasons why the Baha'i Faith has no clerics, and that is one reason why many people who study the Baha'i Faith today conclude that it "just makes sense." As a religion should.

Religions should make sense and not simply ask people to believe in things contradictory to science, or that serve as a cause of discord. Religion should serve humanity as a source for unity and the betterment of the world. Otherwise, the remedy becomes the cause of illness itself, and—as Baha'u'llah says—it's better not to have religion at all under these circumstances.

To learn more you can visit Bahai.org, or BahaiTeachings.org—the latter being a website my wife and I launched years ago to enable Baha'is from all walks of life to share their own articles, inspired by the teachings of the Baha'i Faith.

APPENDIX B

The following is the complete text of the 2017 letter from the Universal House of Justice, which laid out a series of economic principles for the betterment of humankind—principles that aligned with what we were already attempting to put into place at One Planet Group, and which inspired us to go even further. I believe that the principles outlined in this document could help us change the world, and help to redefine capitalism for the good of all.

THE UNIVERSAL HOUSE OF JUSTICE
1 March 2017

To the Baha'is of the World

Dearly loved Friends,

In an increasingly interconnected world, more light is being cast on the social conditions of every people, giving greater visibility to their circumstances. While there are developments that give hope, there is much that should weigh heavy on the conscience of the human race. Inequity, discrimination, and exploitation blight the life of humanity, seemingly immune to the treatments applied by political schemes of every hue. The economic impact of these afflictions has resulted in the prolonged suffering of so many, as well as in deep-seated, structural defects in society. No one whose heart has been attracted to the teachings of the Blessed Beauty can remain unmoved by these consequences. "The world is in great turmoil," Baha'u'llah observes in the Lawḥ-i-Dunyá, "and the minds of its people are in a state of utter confusion. We entreat the Almighty that He may graciously illuminate them with the glory of His Justice, and enable them to discover that which will be profitable unto them at all times and under all conditions." As the Baha'i community strives to contribute at the level of thought and action to the betterment of the world, the adverse conditions experienced by many populations will more and more demand its attention.

The welfare of any segment of humanity is inextricably bound up with the welfare of the whole. Humanity's collective life suffers when any one group thinks of its own well-being in isolation from that of its neighbours or pursues economic gain without regard for how the natural environment, which provides sustenance for all, is affected. A stubborn obstruction, then, stands in the way of meaningful social progress: time and again, avarice and self-interest prevail at the expense of the common good. Unconscionable quantities of wealth are being amassed, and the instability this creates is made worse by how income and opportunity are spread so unevenly both between nations and within nations. But it need not be so. However much such conditions are the outcome of history, they do not have to define the future, and even if current approaches to economic life satisfied humanity's stage of adolescence, they are certainly inadequate for its dawning age of maturity. There is no justification for continuing to perpetuate structures, rules, and systems that manifestly fail to serve the interests of all peoples. The teachings of the Faith leave no room for doubt: there is an inherent moral dimension to the generation, distribution, and utilization of wealth and resources.

The stresses emerging out of the long-term process of transition from a divided world to a united one are being felt within international relations as much as in the deepening fractures that affect societies large and small. With prevailing modes of thought found to be badly wanting, the world is in desperate need of a shared ethic, a sure framework for addressing the crises that gather like storm clouds. The vision of Baha'u'llah challenges many of the assumptions that are allowed to shape contemporary discourse—for instance, that self-interest, far from needing to be restrained, drives prosperity, and that progress depends upon its expression through relentless competition. To view the worth of an individual chiefly in terms of how much one can accumulate and how many goods one can consume relative to others is wholly alien to Baha'i thought. But neither are the teachings in sympathy with sweeping dismissals of wealth as inherently distasteful or immoral, and asceticism is prohibited. Wealth must serve humanity. Its use must accord with spiritual principles; systems must be created in their light. And, in Baha'u'llah's memorable words, "No light can compare with the light of justice. The establishment of order in the world and the tranquility of the nations depend upon it."

Although Baha'u'llah does not set out in His Revelation a detailed economic system, a constant theme throughout the entire corpus of His teachings is the reorganization of human society. Consideration of this theme inevitably gives rise to questions of economics. Of course, the future order conceived by Baha'u'llah is far beyond anything that can be imagined by the present generation. Nevertheless, its eventual emergence will depend on strenuous effort by His followers to put His teachings into effect today. With this in mind, we hope that the comments below will stimulate thoughtful, ongoing reflection by the friends. The aim is to learn about how to participate in the material affairs of society in a way that is consistent with the divine precepts and how, in practical terms, collective prosperity can be advanced through justice and generosity, collaboration and mutual assistance.

Our call to examine the implications of the Revelation of Baha'u'llah for economic life is intended to reach Baha'i institutions and communities but is directed more especially to the individual believer. If a new model of community life, patterned on the teachings, is to emerge, must not the company of the faithful demonstrate in their own lives the rectitude of conduct that is one of its most distinguishing features? Every choice a Baha'i makes—as employee or employer, producer or consumer, borrower or lender, benefactor, or beneficiary—leaves a trace, and the moral duty to lead a coherent life demands that one's economic decisions be in accordance with lofty ideals, that the purity of one's aims be matched by the purity of one's actions to fulfill those aims. Naturally, the friends habitually look to the teachings to set the standard to which to aspire. But the community's deepening engagement with society means that the economic dimension of social existence must receive ever more concentrated attention. Particularly in clusters where the community-building process is beginning to embrace large numbers, the exhortations contained in the Baha'i Writings should increasingly inform economic relationships within families, neighbourhoods, and peoples. Not content with whatever values prevail in the existing order that surrounds them, the friends everywhere should consider the application of the teachings to their lives and, using the opportunities their circumstances offer them, make their own individual and collective contributions to economic justice and social progress wherever they reside. Such efforts will add to a growing storehouse of knowledge in this regard.

A foundational concept to explore in this context is the spiritual reality of man. In the Revelation of Baha'u'llah, the nobility inherent to every human being is unequivocally asserted; it is a fundamental tenet of Baha'i belief, upon which hope for the future of humankind is built. The soul's capacity to manifest all the names and attributes of God—He Who is the Compassionate, the Bestower, the Bountiful—is repeatedly affirmed in the Writings. Economic life is an arena for the expression of honesty, integrity, trustworthiness, generosity, and other qualities of the spirit. The individual is not merely a self-interested economic unit, striving to claim an ever-greater share of the world's material resources. "Man's merit lieth in service and virtue," Baha'u'llah avers, "and not in the pageantry of wealth and riches." And further: "Dissipate not the wealth of your precious lives in the pursuit of evil and corrupt affection, nor let your endeavours be spent in promoting your personal interest." By consecrating oneself to the service of others, one finds meaning and purpose in life and contributes to the upliftment of society itself. At the outset of His celebrated treatise *The Secret of Divine Civilization*, 'Abdu'l-Bahá states:

> And the honour and distinction of the individual consist in this, that he among all the world's multitudes should become a source of social good. Is any larger bounty conceivable than this, that an individual, looking within himself, should find that by the confirming grace of God he has become the cause of peace and well-being, of happiness and advantage to his fellow men? No, by the one true God, there is no greater bliss, no more complete delight.

Viewed in this light, many seemingly ordinary economic activities gain new significance because of their potential to add to human welfare and prosperity. "Every person must have an occupation, a trade or a craft," explains the Master, "so that he may carry other people's burdens, and not himself be a burden to others." The poor are urged by Baha'u'llah to "exert themselves and strive to earn the means of livelihood," while they who are possessed of riches "must have the utmost regard for the poor." "Wealth," 'Abdu'l-Bahá has affirmed, "is praiseworthy in the highest degree, if it is acquired by an individual's own efforts and the grace of God, in commerce, agriculture, art and industry, and if it be expended for philanthropic purposes." At the same time, the Hidden Words is replete with warnings of its perilous allure, that wealth is a "mighty barrier" between the believer and the proper Object of his adoration. No wonder, then, that Baha'u'llah extols the station of the wealthy one who is not hindered by riches from attaining the eternal kingdom; the splendour of such a soul "shall illuminate the dwellers of heaven even as the sun enlightens the people of the earth!" 'Abdu'l-Bahá declares that "if a judicious and resourceful individual should initiate measures which would universally enrich the masses of the people, there could be no undertaking greater than this, and it would rank in the sight of God as the supreme achievement." For wealth is most commendable "provided the entire population is wealthy." Examining one's life to determine what is a necessity and then discharging with joy one's obligation in relation to the law of Ḥuqúqu'lláh is an indispensable discipline to bring one's priorities into balance, purify whatever wealth one possesses, and ensure that the share which is the Right of God provides for the greater good. At all times, contentment and moderation, benevolence and fellow feeling, sacrifice and reliance on the Almighty are qualities that befit the God-fearing soul.

The forces of materialism promote a quite contrary line of thinking: that happiness comes from constant acquisition, that the more one has the better, that worry for the environment is for another day. These seductive messages fuel an increasingly entrenched sense of personal entitlement, which uses the language of justice and rights to disguise self-interest. Indifference to the hardship experienced by others becomes commonplace while entertainment and distracting amusements are voraciously consumed. The enervating influence of materialism seeps into every culture, and all Baha'is recognize that, unless they strive to remain conscious of its effects, they may to one degree or another unwittingly adopt its ways of seeing the world. Parents must be acutely aware that, even when very young, children absorb the norms of their surroundings. The junior youth spiritual empowerment programme encourages thoughtful discernment at an age when the call of materialism grows more insistent. With the approach of adulthood comes a responsibility, shared by one's generation, not to allow worldly pursuits to blind one's eyes to injustice and privation. Over time, the qualities and attitudes nurtured by the courses of the training institute, through exposure to the Word of God, help individuals to see past the illusions that, at every stage of life, the world uses to pull attention away from service and towards the self. And ultimately, the systematic study of the Word of God and the exploration of its implications raises consciousness of the need to manage one's material affairs in keeping with the divine teachings.

Beloved Friends: The extremes of wealth and poverty in the world are becoming ever more untenable. As inequity persists, so the established order is seen to be unsure of itself, and its values are being questioned. Whatever the tribulations that a conflicted world must confront in the future, we pray that the Almighty will help His loved ones to overcome every obstacle in their path and assist them to serve humanity. The

larger the presence of a Baha'i community in a population, the greater
its responsibility to find ways of addressing the root causes of the poverty in its surroundings. Although the friends are at the early stages of
learning about such work and of contributing to the related discourses,
the community-building process of the Five Year Plan is creating everywhere the ideal environment in which to accrue knowledge and experience, gradually but consistently, about the higher purpose of economic
activity. Against the background of the age-long work of erecting a divine
civilization, may this exploration become a more pronounced feature of
community life, institutional thought, and individual action in the years
ahead.

[signed: The Universal House of Justice]

ABOUT THE AUTHOR

Payam Zamani is an entrepreneur, an investor, and the founder of One Planet Group, a closely held private equity firm that owns a suite of online technology and media businesses. Infused with Zamani's deeply held beliefs from the Baha'i Faith, One Planet's mission is to support strong business ideas while building an ethos that helps improve society and gives back to communities.

Born in Iran, Zamani was forced to flee at the age of sixteen due to his religious beliefs as a Baha'i. He was offered asylum in the United States in 1988. Upon graduation from the University of California, Davis, he and his brother founded AutoWeb, one of the first online car marketplaces, which they took public in 1999.

Over the years, Zamani has built and now owns multiple technology and media businesses, spanning ad tech, publishing, and media. Owned and operated businesses of One Planet Group include Buyerlink, AutoWeb, One Planet VC, One Planet Studios, and others. As part of its nonprofit arm, One Planet Group also operates One Planet – One People and BahaiTeachings.org. In 2023, the company launched the One Planet Summit, an annual conference exploring how we can navigate capitalism with a spiritual compass and elevate business to serve humanity.

In 2020, One Planet Group was named a "Best Place to Work" and received the Better Business Bureau's Torch Award for Ethics. Zamani has won numerous awards for diversity and inclusion and has received the Tahirih Justice Center's "Hope Award" and an Award of Distinction from UC Davis. Zamani and his wife, Gouya, have two daughters, Sophia and Ella.

⬡ @payamzamani